WINNING THE BATTLE
TO LOSE THE WAR

T0347160

WINNING THE BATTLE TO LOSE THE WAR

Brazilian Electronics Policy Under US Threat of Sanctions

Maria-Ines Bastos

FRANK CASS

First jointly published 1994 in Great Britain by
FRANK CASS AND COMPANY LIMITED
Newbury House, 900 Eastern Avenue
Ilford, Essex IG2 7HH England

and in the United States of America by
FRANK CASS
c/o International Specialized Book Services Inc.
5804 N.E. Hassalo Street
Portland, OR 97213-3644

and United Nations University Press
The United Nations University
5-53-70 Jingumae
Shibuya-ku, Tokyo 150
Japan

Transferred to Digital Printing 2004

Copyright © 1994 Frank Cass & Co. Ltd.
and The United Nations University

British Library Cataloguing in Publication Data:

Bastos, Maria-Ines
   Winning the Battle to Lose the War:
   Brazilian Electronics Policy Under US
   Threat of Sanctions
   I. Title
   338.476213810981
   ISBN 0-7146-4111-1

   Library of Congress Cataloging-in-Publication Data:
Bastos, Maria-Ines.
   Winning the battle to lose the war: Brazilian electronics policy
under US threat of sanctions / Maria-Ines Bastos.
      p. cm.
   Includes bibliographical references.
   ISBN 0-7146-4111-1
   1. Electronic industries–Government policy–Brazil. 2. Economic
sanctions, American–Brazil. 3. Computer software–Law and
legislation–Brazil. 4. Intellectual property–Brazil. I. Title.
HD9696.A3B6725 1994
338.4'7621381'0981–dc20   94-338
                                                                 CIP

CONTENTS

CONTENTS (cont.)

LIST OF TABLES

PREFACE

In this study, I analyse the conflict that developed from September 1985 to October 1989 between the United States and Brazil over the Brazilian protectionist policy for the electronics industry. The conflict's development and outcomes are analysed within a descriptive approach to bargaining. The conflict's evolution is described as a process by which a choice among a set of possible outcomes is reached through negotiation between the two players who exchange information, promises, and threats. My main arguments are (i) that the conflict's development led to the definition of a focal point within a feasible set of mutually satisfying outcomes which could be agreed on by interested groups; (ii) that the threat of economic sanctions was the key strategic tool that moved the players to define this focal point; (iii) that the effectiveness of the threat of sanctions was due to the economic losses it could have imposed and to its political effects upon uncommitted interest groups within the target country.

Regulation of intellectual property rights of software in Brazil was the focal point of the conflict. This outcome allowed the suspension of American threats of sanctions and led to the solution of the conflict. This solution was satisfactory to the Americans who had been fighting internationally for trade-related aspects of IPRs and for the adoption of the copyright regime for software. Although they had rejected it since the late 1970s, Brazilian authorities agreed in 1986 to adopt copyright protection for software because it satisfied interested parties and those uncommitted groups who pressed the government for a settlement to the conflict that could prevent economic sanctions. The conflict had a non-zero-sum solution. Brazilian gains were cancelling the threat of economic sanctions, maintaining their protectionist policy for electronics for some more years, and little impact on the domestically controlled electronics industry. American gains were a wider access to the Brazilian IT market, softening of Brazilian opposition in GATT negotiations on new issues, and the international display of what could happen to any other country that tried to emulate the Brazilian policy.

Measures taken by the Brazilian government after the closing of the conflict have been to promote an immediate liberalization of the electronics market and to ensure that the protectionist policy ends in 1992. The suddenness of Brazil's current process of economic liberalization suggests that what Brazil fought to keep during the conflict has, now, a large chance of being lost.

ACKNOWLEDGEMENTS

Much of this book was originally published as a Ph.D. thesis at the Institute of Development Studies, the University of Sussex. This work would not have been possible without the encouragement, guidance, and support of a number of people, to whom I am extremely grateful.

Raphael Kaplinsky, as my thesis supervisor, was an unfailing source of technical support, faith, and tolerance.

Constructive comments and suggestions were given by the participants of the 'Brazil Hi-Tech' study-group, co-ordinated by Hubert Schmitz, including Jose Cassiolato, Tom Hewitt, Fatima Gaio, Ruy Quadros, Helena Lastres, Sergio Banhos, and Ana Paola Teixeira.

My family and friends gave me the inspiration and encouragement to persevere throughout this work. Mariana and Maximo Luciano gave me continuous backing, were patient with my long absence, and were always eager to help. I am particularly grateful to Euclides Migliari for his support and for taking care of our children while I was writing my thesis. Vivaldo Mendes inspired me to view this work as an opportunity for self-improvement.

Ronaldo Archer and Mick Moore made helpful comments on a draft of the main arguments of this work, Mari'Stela Bernardes helped to disentangle my ideas for the introduction, and Nigel Barker copy-edited the original thesis, and Mark Withers edited this version for publication.

Archival research and interviews with Brazilian politicians, members of nongovernmental organizations in the IT area, and people who occupied central positions in the Brazilian state apparatus during the Brazilian 301 case were the source of much of the data analysed in this study. The list of persons interviewed and interview structure are presented in appendices III and IV, respectively.

Finally, I would like to thank CNPq and the Brazilian Senate for funding the research, the Dudley Seers Fund and the Institute of Development Studies for material support during the last stages of the study, and the Institute for New Technologies of the United Nations University, UNU/INTECH, for material support in the preparation of this book for publication.

ABBREVIATIONS

ABES — Associação Brasileira das Empresas de Software (Brazilian Association of Software Vendors)

ABDI — Associação Brasileira de Direito de Informática (Brazilian Association for Informatics Law)

ABCPAI — Associação Brasileira de Controle de Processos e Automação Industrial (Brazilian Association for Process Control and Industrial Automation)

ABICOMP — Associação Brasileira da Indústria de Computadores e Periféricos (Brazilian Association of Computer and Peripheral Industries)

ABINEE — Associação Brasileira da Indústria Eletro-Eletrônica (Brazilian Association for the Electric and Electronic Industries)

ADAPSO — Computer Software and Services Association

AEA — American Electronics Association

AEB — Associação dos Exportadores do Brasil (Association of Brazilian Exporters)

APPD — Associação dos Profissionais de Processamento de Dados (Association of Data-Processing Professionals)

ASIC — Application Specific Integrated Circuit

ASSESPRO — Associação Brasileira de Empresas de Serviços de Informática (Association of Data-Processing Service Enterprises)

BNDE — Banco Nacional de Desenvolvimento Econômico (National Economic Development Bank)

CACEX — Carteira de Comércio Exterior (Foreign Trade Department of Banco do Brasil)

CAPRE — Comissão de Coordenação das Atividades de Processamento Eletrônico (Coordinating Commission for Eletronic Processing Activities)

CBEMA — Computer and Business Equipment Manufactures Association

CCTCI — Comissão de Ciência e Tecnologia, Comunicação e Informática - Câmara dos Deputados (Committee of Science and Technology, Communication and Informatics - House of Representatives)

CDE — Conselho de Desenvolvimento Econômico (Brazilian Council for Economic Development)

CEPAL — Comision Economica para America Latina y el Caribe (Economic Commission for Latin America and the Caribbean)

CNDA	Conselho Nacional de Direito Autoral (Brazilian Council for Authors Rights)
COBRA	Computadores e Sistemas Brasileiros SA (Brazilian Computers and Systems plc)
CNI	Confederação Nacional das Indústrias (National Federation of Industries)
CONCEX	Conselho de Comercio Exterior (Foreign Trade Council)
CONIN	Conselho Nacional de Informática (National Council for Informatics)
CPU	Central Processing Unit
CRUB	Conselho de Reitores das Universidades Brasileiras (Brazilian Council of University Chancellors)
CSN	Conselho de Segurança Nacional (National Security Council)
DEC	Digital Equipment Corporation
DECEX	Departamento de Comércio Exterior, Secretaria Nacional de Economia (Department of Foreign Trade, National Secretariat for the Economy)
DEPIN	Departamento de Política de Informática e Automação - Secretaria de Ciência e Tecnologia (Department for IT Policy and Automation - Secretariat for Science and Technology)
DIGIBRAS	Empresas Digitais Brasileiras S. A. (Brazilian Digital Enterprises plc)
DRAM	Dynamic Random Access Memory
ESNI	Escola Nacional de Informações (National Intelligence School)
EU	European Union
FDI	Foreign Direct Investment
FIESP	Federação das Indústrias do Estado de São Paulo (Federation of São Paulo Industries)
FINEP	Financiadora de Estudos e Projetos (Studies and Projects Financing Agency)
FNE	Federação Nacional de Engenheiros (National Federation of Engineers)
GATS	General Agreement on Trade in Services
GATT	General Agreement on Tariffs and Trade
GDP	Gross Domestic Product
GEICOM	Grupo Interministerial de Componentes e Materiais (Interministerial Group for Electronic Components and Materials)
GES	Grupo de Assessoramento para Exame de Similaridade (Advisory Group for the Assessment of Similarity of Software)
GNP	Gross National Product
GSP	Generalized System of Preferences
GTE	Grupo de Trabalho Especial (Special Working Group)

IBM	International Business Machines Corporation
IMF	International Monetary Fund
INPI	Instituto Nacional de Propriedade Industrial (National Institute for Industrial Property)
IPR	Intellectual Property Rights
IT	Information technology
ITAMARATY	Brazilian Ministry of Foreign Relations
LAN	Local Area Network
LSI	Large System Integration
MBI	Movimento Brasil Informática (The Brazilian Movement for Informatics)
MCT	Ministério de Ciência e Tecnologia (Ministry of Science and Technology)
MIC	Ministério de Indústria e Comércio (Ministry for Industry and Commerce)
MINICOM	Ministério das Comunicações (Ministry of Communication)
MINIFAZ	Ministério da Fazenda (Finance Ministry)
MITI	Japan's Ministry of International Trade and Industry
MNC	Multinational Corporations
NBM	Nomenclatura Brasileira de Mercadorias (Brazilian Nomenclature for Commodities)
NCR	National Cash Register Corporation
NGO	Nongovernmental Organisation
NICs	Newly Industrializing Countries
OECD	Organisation for Economic Cooperation and Development
OSI	Open Systems Interconnection
PBX	Private Branch Exchange
PLANIN	Plano Nacional de Informática e Automação (Plan for Informatics and Automation)
PMDB	Partido do Movimento Democrático Brasileiro (Brazilian Party for Democratization)
PSDB	Partido da Social Democracia Brasileira (Brazilian Social Democratic Party)
R&D	Research and Development
SBC	Sociedade Brasileira de Computação (Brazilian Computing Society)
SBPC	Sociedade Brasileira para o Progresso da Ciência (Brazilian Society for the Progress of Science)
SCSS	Special Commission on Software and Services
SCT	Secretaria de Ciência e Tecnologia (Secretariat for Science and Technology)

SECOMU	Seminario de Computação na Universidade (Seminar of Computation at the University)
SECT	Secretaria Especial de Ciência e Tecnologia (Special Secretariat for Science and Technology)
SEI	Secretaria Especial de Informática (Special Secretariat for Informatics)
SEPROESP	Sociedade dos Empregados em Processamento de Dados do Estado de São Paulo (Society of Workers in Data Processing in the State of São Paulo)
SERPRO	Serviço Federal de Processamento de Dados (Federal Data-Processing Service)
SNI	Serviço Nacional de Informações (National Intelligence Service)
SPA	Software Publishers Association
SUCESU	Sociedade de Usuários de Computadores e Equipamentos Subsidiários (Society of Computer and Subsidiary Equipment Users)
SUFRAMA	Superintendência da Zona Franca de Manaus (Manaus Free Zone Administration)
TELEBRAS	Telecomunicações Brasileiras (Brazilian Telecommunication Holding Company)
TNC	Trans National Corporation
TRIM	Trade-Related Investment Measures
UCC	Universal Copyright Convention
UNCTAD	United Nations Commission for Trade and Development
UNCTC	United Nations Centre for Transnational Corporations
UNESCO	United Nations Educational, Scientific, and Cultural Organization
US	United States of America
USTR	United States Trade Representative
VLSI	Very Large System Integration
WIPO	World Intellectual Property Organization

INTRODUCTION

From September 1985 to October 1989, the governments of the United States and Brazil were involved in a trade conflict over Brazil's information technology (IT) policy. Brazil's IT policy had evolved - like industrial development policies in many developing countries - to promote the development of a domestic electronics production capability. The two central elements of Brazil's IT policy - also called the 'informatics' policy - were the control of imports and of foreign direct investment. In September 1985, the US government initiated the conflict in accordance with Section 301 of the American Trade Act, which authorizes the executive branch to act bilaterally to combat other countries' policies considered harmful to American interests. The conflict thus became known as the 'Brazilian 301 Case'. This case is a noteworthy example of the complex interplay of domestic and international political constraints on economic and technological development policies in developing countries. It also serves to illustrate the current toughness of international relations in high-technology issues.

In this study, I examine how this conflict evolved, what were its immediate outcomes, and why these outcomes came about.

My argument centres on three main points.

1. Evolution of the Brazilian 301 Case is understood most clearly as a bargaining process to define a *feasible set* of mutually satisfying outcomes that could orient the negotiations, a *focal point* to which the expectations of an outcome for both players could converge, and a *win set* that could contain the outcome that might be agreed upon by the interested groups. Protection of intellectual property rights of software in Brazil was such a focal point in this conflict.

2. The American threat of economic sanctions was the central strategic tool that moved the players to define this focal point. In this case, sanctions were effective in both their *instrumental* and *expressive* components.

3. The effectiveness of the threat of trade sanctions in pressing Brazil to accept a solution was due not only to the potential economic losses that sanctions could have imposed, but also to the impact of these anticipated costs on the domestic balance of forces in support of the policy. I will argue that the effectiveness of sanctions was due to their effect on previously uncommitted interests groups, who thus 'tipped the balance' toward opposition to the policy.

Brazil's 'market reserve' policy limited the importation of IT goods and restricted market access for foreign investment in the production of some electronics goods and the rendering of IT services. The foreign trade side of the Brazilian IT policy complemented its regulation of investment. The trade restrictions were, nevertheless, in accordance with the General Agreement on Tariffs and Trade (GATT), which allows exceptions to the most-favoured-nation clause for balance of payment, infant industry, and national security objectives. The policy aimed not only to establish a local electronics industry, but, primarily, to foster domestic technological capability in electronics. Local control of this dynamic industry was deemed to be the only effective way to internalize technological knowledge that would be increasingly costly if obtained from abroad.

The relatively free availability of technology for the production of microcomputers in the late 1970s and early 1980s, and the significant number of engineers and other university-trained researchers produced by Brazil's science and technology policy, facilitated the launching of Brazil's IT policy. Problems in the balance of payments lended support to the ideal of controlling importation of data-processing equipment.

Notwithstanding these technological and economic factors, political conditions were central to the establishment of the policy. Strong backing by a variety of domestic social groups united by the nationalist ideal of overcoming technological dependence legitimized such measures despite their high social costs. Insulation from direct social pressures in the executive branch of an authoritarian state helped to shield the policy from its major opponents, especially those of foreign origin. But the most effective protection against the policy's opposition was the fact that before the early 1980s the policy's successes, although impressive on a Brazilian scale, were very modest in international terms. Only after the 'boom' of microcomputer production in the Brazilian market in the early-1980s did access to that market become sufficiently attractive to induce potential exporters of products and capital to oppose the policy.

The policy produced a number of successful results. Production in Brazil's electronics industry grew rapidly during the 1980s, despite general economic stagnation. Overall production in the electronics industry, comprising 'professional' electronics, electronics components, telecommunications equipment, consumer or 'entertainment' electronics, and software reached US$ 8 billion[1] in 1986, when the conflict was at its height. Production of computers and other data-processing equipment in Brazil rose from US$ 860 million in 1980 to US$ 2 billion in 1985 and US$ 4 billion in 1989. Locally owned companies' share

---

1.   In this book I use the North American definition of *billion* (i.e., a thousand million).

jumped from one-third of the whole Brazilian electronics industry in 1980 to 52 per cent in 1985 and 58 per cent in 1989. Employment of university-trained personnel reached 23,894 in 1989, representing an average annual growth rate of more than 22 per cent in the period 1981-89.[2] This has made the electronics industry the sector with the highest level of formal education in industrial employment in Brazil. The majority of this highly qualified staff has been absorbed by locally owned companies, which employed 75 per cent of them in 1989.

Despite these successes, many of the conditions that had favoured the establishment of the IT policy and the development of an electronics industry in Brazil changed in the late 1980s. The relatively free availability of information technology of the mid-1970s and early 1980s soon disappeared. Growing knowledge-intensity in production during the 1980s prompted technology-leading countries to battle to defend their proprietary rights over advances in knowledge in science and technology in order to guarantee the return of investment in research and development. They have fought for the establishment of legal mechanisms to protect industrial and intellectual property rights in technology-follower countries with dispositions that could facilitate subsequent adoption of an internationally agreed global regime. This has been the case in electronics-based technology, particularly for semiconductor design and software. For software, copyright has been the preferred regime for the protection of intellectual property rights. United States government actions in this direction have also been linked to the large American trade deficit. Market access for American products and proprietary technology were at the centre of many cases of trade conflict between the United States and its trade partners during the 1980s.

At a domestic level, the economic and political situation also changed and affected the IT policy's development. Deficits in the Brazilian balance of payments, which had favoured the import control policy, were aggravated by the two oil crises and by the increase in international interest rates. These factors contributed to a huge foreign debt, whose negotiation has been made conditional on, among other requirements, liberalization of the electronics market. Economic crisis and the policies designed to overcome it were accompanied by a reduction in the availability of financial resources for investment in the electronics industry. Modernization of industrial production came to a standstill. And the users of electronics-based products, particularly in industry, felt the costs they had been bearing for the establishment of a domestically controlled electronics production capability were too high.

---

2.   SEI *1991*.

All of these factors combined to erode domestic social support of the policy from within and without the state apparatus. Negotiation of the foreign debt, and the needs to attract foreign investment and to accelerate the modernization of Brazilian industrial production were one factor. A second factor was the precarious political coalition of liberals and interventionists who formed the first civilian government in Brazil in more than two decades, and who pushed various segments of the administration to criticize the strictness of the IT policy. The restoration of democracy pushed the military and intelligence sectors to the back stage of the IT policy. The reduction of public resources for investment in science and technology in general, and particularly in electronics research and development, aggravated the disillusionment of Brazilian researchers with the IT policy.

It was in this environment of economic crisis, political instability, and erosion of public support for the IT policy in Brazil that the United States initiated the Brazilian 301 Case. American IT industrialists had opposed the Brazilian IT policy since it was established in the early 1970s. Initially, the policy's reserve of the domestic market for locally owned companies was limited to the production of mini- and microcomputers and their peripherals. In the early 1980s, however, protection was extended to a wider variety of IT goods and services. In launching their case, the Americans demanded withdrawal of Brazil's protectionist policy in the name of restoring most-favoured-nation treatment and fairness in international trade. The Brazilians fought, on the other hand, to maintain their policy, which was designed to develop domestic technological capability in electronics.

Various rounds of bilateral negotiations were needed before the nations reached agreement on the many contentious issues. The United States failed to achieve immediate deregulation of foreign direct investment and IT goods importation in Brazil. However, legal protection of intellectual property rights of software and more liberal administrative treatment in the electronics industry were finally accepted by the Brazilians after the United States threatened to impose sanctions against Brazilian exports to the US market. Surprisingly, then, despite the asymmetry in structural power of the two governments, this case ended with an outcome that was far below the initial demands of the stronger player.

This clash with the United States was the most severe conflict the Brazilian government and society have ever confronted to maintain policies to protect local industry. The conflict sharpened the arguments of the IT policy's enlarged opposition; it also blocked the search within Brazilian society for ways to correct the policy's acknowledged imperfections and mistakes without dismantling it and risking the loss of its achievements.

After the case was closed in late 1989, Brazil's economic crisis deepened and the first democratically elected President took office, in March 1990, pledging to stabilize the economy and liberalize Brazilian markets. His initial measures related to the IT policy were to promote immediate liberalization of the electronics market and to ensure that the protectionist policy would end in 1992. At the end of June 1991, the IT policy's alternations proposed by the Brazilian government were being discussed in the House of Representatives, where some representatives of opposition political parties were fighting to improve the policy without dismantling it. Brazil had won a battle when some concessions made in the negotiations of the Brazilian 301 case prevented the collapse of the whole IT policy. There is, now, a large chance that it will lose the war.

PART I

SETTING THE CONTEXT:
THEORY AND PROPERTY RIGHTS

1

A BARGAINING APPROACH TO THE US/BRAZIL CONFLICT OVER THE BRAZILIAN 'INFORMATICS' POLICY

In this study I analyse a conflict between two countries over trade and investment issues. In this chapter I will define the basis of a descriptive bargaining approach to this conflict. This approach allows an analysis of the conflict as a two-player game in which the governments of the two countries involved have the central role of negotiating an agreed solution at the international level which can also be accepted by their constituencies. The bargaining is played with an agenda for negotiations, the scope of which is itself the first agreement the players have to reach. They have to define a 'feasible set' of outcomes within which their coordinated action will find a 'focal point' to which their expectations converge. As the negotiation is a two-level game, played simultaneously at the international and domestic levels, the convergence of both parties' expectations which makes room for a solution to the conflict results in an outcome that has to be ratified domestically.

I believe the US threat to impose economic sanctions was an effective weapon to convince Brazil to agree on a focal point. In this clearly asymmetric game, the United States - the structurally stronger party - also had larger relative power to influence the Brazilian government's action in its favour. Nevertheless, and despite its structural weakness, the Brazilian negotiators were not in a completely weak relative position. The Brazilian authorities had some control over an outcome highly desired by the Americans (i.e., compliance with new rules for trade and opening the Brazilian market to American products and capital). These circumstances gave Brazil some relative bargaining power. That is why the final outcome of the conflict, when it was closed in October 1989, was non-zero-sum, despite the flagrant structural asymmetry in this two-player game.

In this chapter I define the central issues and concepts addressed in this book. To this end, I define the basic concepts of *players, agenda, preference ordering, outcomes, strategy, sanctions,* and *bargaining power,* and discuss their implications for a bargaining approach to analysing international conflict. Special attention is given to the strategic use of threats of economic sanctions.

CONCEPT OF TRADE WAR

According to Mitchell [*1989: 17, 29*], conflict situations [i.e., those in which 'two or more social entities or "parties" (however defined or structured) perceive that they possess mutually incompatible goals'] lead to conflict behaviour (i.e., 'actions undertaken by one party in any situation of conflict aimed at the opposing party with the intention of making that opponent abandon or modify its goals').

In this study I analyse a conflict between the governments of two countries over the mutually incompatible goals of protectionism and market access. The conflict's stylised structure involved actions taken by both governments aimed to persuade the opposing government either to withdraw the protectionist policy, to 'flexibilize' its implementation, or to respect national sovereignty decisions based in GATT and withdraw from the dispute. A key 'weapon' used by one of the government-players was the threatened imposition of trade sanctions upon the other country's exports to its market. Central weapons used by the other player were threats to extend the IT protectionist measures in time or to other high-technology industries, and to impose more rigorous controls on foreign direct investment in the country.

This general description fits well into Conybear's [*1987: 3*] concept of *trade war*. 'Trade wars are a category of intense international conflict where states interact, bargain, and retaliate primarily over economic objectives directly related to the traded goods or service sectors of their economies, and where the means used are restrictions on the free flow of goods and services'.

Two features of the conflict shall be discussed at length to justify its treatment as a case of trade war: one relates to the intensity of the conflict, the other to the conflict's scope. Conybeare conceives of trade conflict as a continuum measured by a combination of intensity and duration. Trade conflicts of high intensity and long duration are considered 'trade wars'. *Intensity*, roughly meaning 'politicisation', refers to 'the extent to which the conflict reaches the highest, or executive, levels of state'. *Duration* refers to the extent to which retaliatory measures are taken by each party: 'at a minimum, there should be at least one round of retaliation by the actor that does not initiate the conflict'. The Brazilian 301 case could be considered a trade war because it displayed the characteristics of 'politicisation' of an economic conflict as it reached the highest levels of both governments. But, at the same time, it lacked the necessary duration, because it lacked at least one round of retaliation by the actor that had not initiated the conflict. However, despite the Brazilian 301 case not enduring long enough in Conybeare's definition to be considered a trade war, it nevertheless developed throughout four years, during which belligerent acts - although not actual retaliation - were exchanged by the two countries. Therefore, in relation to the intensity of the conflict, the Brazilian 301 case can be treated as a mild trade war, or perhaps more appropriately, as a case of severe trade friction.

Treating the Brazilian 301 case as a trade conflict (trade war or trade friction) as I do here does not mean to disregard its investment dimension. Although the case did have a trade dimension (because one of the Brazilian protectionist policy's instruments is import restriction), the Americans' central goal was to obtain access to Brazilian markets for goods, services, and capital. Trade and investment issues were thus united in the Brazilian policy. Therefore, despite not being limited to the single issue of trade, the case was predominantly a conflict over trade and the central weapon used by the government that initiated it was the threat of trade sanctions.

BARGAINING

Herein, I approach the conflict between the two governments as a bargaining process: 'A process of exchange of information, proposals, promises, threats by which a choice among a set of possible outcomes is reached in a situation where this choice involves an element of conflict between the interests of players or groups' [*Johansen, 1987: 691*].

Bargaining belongs, then, to the sphere of cooperative games in which the players can communicate and make agreements before decisions are made and actions are taken [*Johansen, 1987: 690*]. In a bargaining process, players are, by definition, opponents (they are in a conflict situation), but each determines his/her moves taking into account information obtained from the opponent's preferences or moves.

In this study I use what Johansen [*1987: 699*] called a 'descriptive approach' to bargaining and Raiffa [*1982: 11*] names 'strategic analysis'. I describe and explain how the bargaining process in the Brazilian 301 case developed and why the immediate outcomes were reached. Information is conceived to be incomplete, the range of possible offers and threats, and the timing of the moves themselves are difficult to reconstruct empirically. Thus, approaching the 301 case as a bargaining game does not imply the use of a formal model leading to an elegant solution.

PLAYERS

International conflicts are processes that involve states. It is thus important to discuss the implications of states as players or actors in international bargaining. I start this discussion with a brief comment on the concept of *state*.

Much of the research on international relations is build upon a concept of state as a national-territorial totality [*Northedge, 1976: 15*] or as a unity of territory, people, and government [*James, 1986: 13*]. Although this concept is useful for studies of relations among states, its 'legalistic' bias gives no indication of the political or social content of the state, It gives only a construct of a legally equal member of the system of states. Different concepts are given by sociological approaches of Weberian or Marxian inspiration. These focus not on territoriality but on the set of coercive and administrative institutions that distinguish state from society. The relationship between these two domains of social life has involved an unresolved debate among political scientists of both traditions. Both traditions dwell, however, on the 'autonomy' or 'relative autonomy' of the state in relation to society. In relation to this subject, Halliday [*1989: 44*] pointed out that the central issue is to conceptualise the 'degree to which [the state] can act autonomously and represent values separate from that society, even if it is ultimately constrained by it'. As Skocpol concludes in her review of recent studies on the state, the perspectives for the analysis of the state, rather than being 'embroiled in a series of abstruse and abstract conceptual debates', or looking for a 'new or refurbished grand theory of "The State"', point instead to 'solidly grounded and analytically sharp understandings of the casual regularities that underlie the histories of states, social structures, and transnational relations in the modern world' [*Skocpol, 1985: 28*].

To analyse bargaining toward a mutually satisfactory solution of bilateral international conflicts, I adopt Rueschmeyer and Evans definition of the state as a set 'of organisations invested with the authority to make binding decision for people and organisations juridically located in a particular territory and to implement these decisions using, if necessary, force' [*Rueschemeyer and Evans, 1985: 46-7*].

The state cannot escape being used as an instrument of domination by the most powerful classes or class fractions, but this particular set of organisations, being as it is a network of people, 'exists in its own right and possesses interests of its own' [*Cardoso, 1979: 51*]. This aspect of corporate unity of the state does not eliminate the divisions within it in relation to substantive goals. These divisions are captured and deepened by various social groups in their attempts at using the state to benefit their particular interests. However, despite being an arena of social conflict, the state, at the same time, claims to represent the interests of society as a whole. This claim is not ideological or fictitious because 'it is the need for organised collective action which transcends individual capabilities and yet is necessary for individual interests that lies at the core of such a state mission in the general interest' [*Rueschemeyer and Evans, 1985: 47-8*].

This approach to the state, despite the controversies still present in the literature, offers a rich analytical tool for understanding international bargaining. This is because it calls attention to an aspect of the state that the 'legalistic' approach disregards. That is, representatives of any state in a situation of international bargaining act simultaneously in two dimensions, the domestic and the international [*Raiffa, 1982; Putnam, 1988*]. As an international player, any

6

state cannot be relieved of its commitments to domestic goals and to manage domestic conflicts among interests possibly affected by its international moves. To dismiss social and political reality or to place undue pressure on its society due to its international moves may put at risk the existence of state institutions and governments. Alternatively, pursuit of domestically advantageous policies or the commitment to safeguard particular domestic interests may limit the state's range of possible moves in international bargaining.

A final point about states as players in international bargaining is necessary to avoid the pitfalls of considering states as monolithic or unitary actors. Much of the analytical inaccuracy of treating states as unitary agents results from reducing the whole administrative apparatus (the state, which is itself a relatively stable ensemble of institutions with diversified attributes and authority) to the executive personnel formally occupying for some time top positions in this apparatus (i.e., the government). This mistake is explained easily as arising from the attempt to avoid the greater methodological error of personifying institutions, such as an administrative apparatus, so that they may be said to 'behave', 'act', or 'bargain'.

The state-government distinction, then, is fundamentally relevant to analysis of international bargaining, in which the firmness of players may be affected not only by skirmishes within the government but also by resistance or active opposition from within the state apparatus.

Using the bargaining approach, I describe the Brazilian 301 case as a two-player game in which the two governments have the central role of negotiating an agreed solution for the international conflict while simultaneously having to deal with pro- and anti-protectionist domestic forces, including their expression within the state apparatus and the government itself. Nongovernmental organisations, such as the associations representing interested parties, also have a role in bargaining for a solution to the conflict, but theirs, despite sometimes being decisive, is a kind of 'supporting' role, as these organisations have no authority to make any agreement.

AGENDA

Bargaining can only be played when an agenda is defined for negotiations. These negotiations aim to define the outcomes among which the players must choose to be mutually satisfied. Satisfaction with an outcome (payoff) is a concept that refers to the *utility function* of each player and has usually been defined in the literature as maximisation of income or profits when companies are players, or of the nation's income or welfare when governments are players. Applying bargaining to conflicts that involve not only economic considerations, as in the Brazilian 301 case, requires a broader view of the utility function of the players. At least two other utilities, not measurable in commensurate terms, have to be satisfied with the outcomes of such bargaining between countries: maximisation of each government's conflict management within its domestic constituencies and maintenance of its international image.

The agenda's scope is itself the first agreement the players have to reach for negotiations to proceed. The two players' sets of negotiable outcomes at the onset of the process frequently have a small intersection than is necessary for negotiations to proceed. In fact, what the negotiators tend to find soon is a 'feasible set' of outcomes (payoffs) so that 'any point that belongs to this set can be reached by coordinated actions by the two parties; if they fail to reach an agreement to coordinate their actions, then they receive nothing' [*Johansen, 1987: 701*].

As bargaining is an iterated game (i.e., is not resolved in one step but involves many rounds of negotiations),

> if the first claims prove to fall outside the feasible region, then a second round of revised claims will usually come forth, and if these do not yet succeed, then there will possibly be more rounds, perhaps finally ending up in a feasible position which gives some gain to both parties [*Johansen, 1987: 703*].

Johansen's concept of 'feasible position' is similar to Schelling's 'focal point', which defines the convergence of bargainers' expectations, or the mutually consistent perceptions about what outcomes to which the other will agree. According to Schelling [*1960: 70*], a focal point emerges if bargaining leads to a situation beyond which each player expects the other 'not to expect to be expected to retreat'. The particular characteristic of a focal point is the intrinsic quality of its outcome that differentiates it from any other possible outcomes. This point that brings the negotiations to a close is one that probably involves concession by at least one of the players. In this case, for the one who is about to make a concession, it is necessary 'to control his adversary's expectations; he needs a recognisable limit to his own retreat' [*Schelling, 1960: 71*].

Although useful in studying bargaining, the concepts of 'feasible set' and 'focal points' may be misleading when applied to international bargaining. Both concepts imply that the only expectations the players have to consider are each other's. However, as I have discussed above, government-players in international bargaining are not monolithic and also have to take into account expectations of their constituencies. As Putnam [*1988*] pointed out, international negotiations are two-level games. At the national level, domestic groups pursue their interests by pressuring the government for some particular outcome and politicians seek power by gaining the support of these groups. At the international level, national governments seek outcomes that maximise their ability to manage conflict's among their constituencies while simultaneously minimizing adverse domestic consequences of foreign developments. In two-level international bargaining, the outcome that leads to conflict solution belongs not only to a 'feasible set' or a 'focal point', but also to a 'win-set', which is the set of all possible agreements at the international level that would also be accepted by domestic constituencies [*Putnam, 1988: 437*].

PREFERENCE ORDERING

During bargaining, each player uses a 'set of preferences or a scale of value underlying the range of potential outcomes, at least *ordering* the latter from most to least desirable' [*Mitchell, 1989: 220*]. Specifying this set of preferences is difficult since the players are governments, which, by definition, are not homogeneous and represent diverse domestic interests. Reducing this complexity somewhat without accepting governments as monolithic players, I assume that the preference ordering at the onset of bargaining is defined by a governmental scale of value in which intragovernmental disagreement is minimised and the interests of domestic groups are already expressed. It is only with the development of the bargaining process that such disagreement and the preferences of domestic groups enter the negotiator's ordering of outcomes. Alteration of this scale of values may have a positive effect upon bargaining when it allows a quicker achievement of an agreed outcome. However, a significant change in the preference ordering of one player may also signal to the other a lack of firmness and provoke an exploitative move that leads to an outcome with a lower payoff for the 'flexible' player.

It is hard to establish empirically each party's preference ordering. As they are never disclosed explicitly, the observer has to infer them from each move in the bargaining process with the help of some assumptions. This difficulty is aggravated by the fact already mentioned that, in international bargaining, the utility of each government-player is not just a function of economic values but also of political and ideological ones. In addition, the ordering of possible outcomes is subject to change during the bargaining process [*Snyder and Diesing, 1977: 488*]. This happens, as argued in the preceding paragraph, because the negotiators may be led to reconsider their preference ordering by their opponent's moves or by interference of preferences coming from the domestic-level game.

OUTCOMES

There are two important points to be made in relation to the final outcome of bargaining (i.e., the resolution of a conflict). Firstly, it is necessary to consider the balance of gains and losses for each player. Secondly, it would be useful to assess the significance of a particular outcome in relation to other possible solutions.

The balance of gains and losses of a conflict's specific outcome has been treated in the game-theory literature either as a zero-sum or a non-zero-sum solution. Zero-sum outcomes in a two-player conflict are those in which the gains of one player are equal to the losses of the other player; the sum of their payoffs is, therefore, equal to zero. In simple words, a zero-sum outcome is one in which the winner takes all. Non-zero-sum outcomes are those in which each player gains something, although the gains are distributed unevenly. In other words, a non-zero-sum outcome is one in which there is no absolute winner or total loser: each player has some gain, but one may reap greater benefit than the other.

In a real-world bargaining process, it is not easy to assess the balance of an outcome. This is because, as I have already pointed out, the 'utility function' of each player is not stated explicitly. The utility function is complex, as it involves preferences of both the government and relevant domestic social groups, as well as a different ordering process by the different groups. Moreover, these preferences are generally not quantifiable. Unless the analyst can measure the extent of pay-off to each player on a quantitative scale - as the axiomatic approach to bargaining does - assessment of an outcome as a zero-sum or a non-zero-sum solution must be taken as approximate or even metaphorical. With these cautionary remarks, I will argue in Chapter 8 that the final outcome of the conflict, at least at the moment of its formal closure in October 1989, was a non-zero-sum solution.

The significance of a particular outcome in relation to other possible solutions has been assessed in the game-theory literature in terms of its efficiency in maximizing the players' utility function. Much of this literature assumes that cooperative games have an outcome that is Pareto efficient. This means that the players, making binding agreements, reach an outcome that maximises both players' utility functions such that there is no other outcome that could make one better off without the other being made worse off. An outcome is not Pareto efficient when an alternative set of actions exists that would make all the players better off, but when it is in no player's interest unilaterally to act differently. Johansen claims that bargaining is often likely to lead to outcomes that are not Pareto efficient due to (i) the lack of convincing balanced solutions, as strategies are not chosen on the basis of pure rationality and the moves do not necessarily give 'sincere' information; and (ii) the exploitation of relative power positions that restrict the choices for the weaker player [*Johansen, 1987: 705*].

In this study, I do not assess the efficiency of the final bargaining outcome in relation to other possible outcomes. I take instead the final solution not as a deterministic outcome of bargaining, but as one possible solution among a feasible set of outcomes that resulted from the bargaining process as it unfolded under conditions of imperfect information and the exploitation of power positions. In this sense, it is pointless to discuss this solution in relation to other

10

possible outcomes that could have improved both players' pay-offs if the evolution of bargaining had been different.

STRATEGIES

In order to set the general framework for the analysis of bargaining strategies, it is useful to point out that 'all negotiations are alike in one fundamental fact: that the process takes place within an environment of implicit threat, the ultimate sanction on the other negotiating party for not conceding a vital point being an end to negotiations and a return to some status quo from which negotiation was designed to provide an escape' [*Mitchell, 1989: 218*].

According to Mitchell, there are two broad strategies for negotiating an agreement to a conflict: (i) to reach accord by 'fractionating' the conflict, or (ii) to arrange several issues in a 'package deal'. Splitting the agenda into a number of issues is used to separate agreeable subjects from contentious ones so that agreement is facilitated either because this strategy develops trust and a spirit of compromise between the players, or because an easier agreement on some issues may have spillover effects upon negotiation of the more contentious subjects. If, however, fractionating the conflict involves avoidance of its central issues with the risk of no later settlement on them, if their isolation implies a loss of significant leverage by one opponent, or if their isolation creates a zero-sum situation, in which a gain by one player represents a loss to the other, then this strategy is likely to produce undesirable and unintended outcomes [*Mitchell, 1989: 219*]. Package deals involve simultaneously settling a number of issues that are part of the conflict. The strategy is to include as many issues as possible in a single agreement so that, for both parties, losses in some of them may be offset by gains in others.

The fact that bargaining is an iterative game has interesting implications for the strategy of each player. Awareness that the game involves more than one round influences each party to put forward greater demands than if the negotiations were limited to one round and greater than what each party expects to gain in the end. To start with 'excessive' claims and to move, subsequently, to a smaller feasible set is a strategic approach that shows willingness to cooperate. Another strategic move is to put forward a claim which can give a small gain to the other party and to convince him/her that this is a final claim, not to be modified. In this circumstance, the small gain and the possible breakdown of negotiations that would leave no gain at all may lead to acquiescence and to a solution to the conflict [*Putnam, 1988*].

Bargaining processes are, in the real world, a multiple game in which any single dispute may be used as a strategic tool. This is particularly the case in international bargaining when bilateral conflicts are being negotiated simultaneously among many pairs of government-players who also confront each other in multilateral negotiations. Mitchell's discussion of negotiating tactics [*1989: 223*] suggests that negotiations for conflict settlement between two countries may be used to provoke side-effects in third parties, as is the case of disputes used as exemplary cases to show to other countries in similar situations what could happen to them, or when bilateral compromises are used to 'soften' the opposition in multilateral negotiations. Bilateral disputes and their concluding agreements may also be used by one player to establish a reputation of toughness in anticipation of additional conflicts with the same or other countries.

SANCTIONS

In international trade conflicts, threats of sanctions are a powerful strategic bargaining tool. Threatening the imposition of economic sanctions (especially, but not only, trade sanctions) is used to give credibility to the seriousness of the claims and is a way to signal strategically that, in the absence of agreement, they may simply play noncooperatively. Threats of sanctions can influence outcomes by either preventing an opponent from beginning a course of action, or by stopping a course of action already underway. The basic assumption in threatening economic sanctions in international bargaining is that this threat may coerce the target country to change its policies or any single behaviour in order to avoid or reduce the costs imposed by the sanctions.

A long time ago, Hirschmann, who was already trespassing from economics to politics, pointed out:

> For the political or power implications of trade to exist and to make themselves felt, it is not essential that the state should exercise positive action, i.e., organise and direct trade centrally; the negative right of veto on trade with which every sovereign state is invested is quite sufficient [*Hirschmann, 1945: 16-17*].

The discussion of the effectiveness of using this veto on trade as a strategic tool in international conflicts has not been conclusive in the economic and political literature. The pervasive view, however, is that their use in the twentieth century has shown that they do not 'work', that they are ineffective [*Knorr, 1975; Douidi and Dajani, 1983; Hufbauer and Schott, 1985; Deardorff and Stern. 1987; Srinivasan, 1987*]. This conclusion about the ineffectiveness of economic sanctions is based on their inability to change policies of the target country against which the sanctions were imposed [*Hufbauer and Schott, 1985: 32*]. On the other hand, some analysts dispute the conventional wisdom of the ineffectiveness of sanctions [*Baldwin, 1985; Kaempfer ad Lowenberg, 1988; Nossal, 1989*].

Johan Galtung, in the late 1960s, introduced the ideas now used by political scientists and economists to assess better the effectiveness of economic sanctions. Galtung explored the 'expressive' function of sanctions (i.e., their use 'to send a clear signal to everyone that what the receiving nation has done is disapproved of' [*Galtung, 1967: 412*]). In contrast to the possible ineffectiveness of economic sanctions in their 'instrumental' function, that is, as a tool to produce a change in the target country's policy, sanctions may be much more effective in their 'expressive' functions, either in sending a message to other countries not involved in the conflict or to the constituency of the sanctioning government. When economic sanctions are used not with the intention of changing other country's policies but to punish the country in retribution for its 'wrongdoing', they are always effective, for their effectiveness lies in their capacity to impose some harm on the target [*Nossal, 1989*].

Baldwin, while emphasizing the 'instrumental' function of economic sanctions, argued that they are effective tools for influencing others in the international system. In his words 'changing the behaviour of the embargoed state may indeed be - and often is - more important than influencing the perceptions and attitudes of onlookers; but sometimes the reverse in true' [*Baldwin, 1985: 17*]. In fact, Baldwin's central point is that the assessment of the ineffectiveness of economic sanctions presented in much of the literature that has dealt with empirical cases cannot be taken as conclusive due to the inadequacy of the evidence and arguments adduced in support of the contention that sanctions were, in those cases, an indisputable failure [*Baldwin, 1985: 204-05*].

Hirschmann's [*1945*] discussion of the conditions that may make effective the power to interrupt trade is of great interest here. According to his reasoning, international trade sanctions may be an effective weapon in international conflicts when it is difficult and onerous for the target country either to dispense entirely with the trade it has with the sanctioning country, or to replace that country as a market or supplier. The target country's decision to forgo the trade with the sanctioning country depends on (i) the economic significance of its trade with the sanctioning country; (ii) the length and painfulness of the adjustment to the interruption of trade; and (iii) the strength of the vested interests within the target country which are linked to its trade with the sanctioning country. The alternative of diverting the trade to a third country depends not only on the absolute amount of trade between the two countries but also on its relative share of the target country's total trade [*Hirschmann, 1945: 17-18*]. In line with this reasoning, Hufbauer and Schott [*1985*] have found that effective sanctions are generally those that impose heavy costs on target nations.

In this study, I explore the idea that, although costs imposed by economic sanctions may help to explain their effectiveness, it is the effect of these costs upon the domestic balance of forces in support of the policies which motivated retaliation that moved the Brazilian government to change them.

The role interest groups play in the definition of international economic sanctions and in making them effective has been dealt with by Kaempfer and Lowenberg [*1988*]. Elaborating Galtung's distinction of instrumental and expressive functions of sanctions, they suggest a formalised model to show (i) that sanctions may have an altogether different goal, namely, to serve the interests of pressure groups within the sanctioning country, and that these interests are not only pecuniary but also of an intangible nature as 'taking a moral stance against some other nation's objectionable behaviour'; and (ii) that sanctions' apparent ineffectuality might be illusory because even when their economic impacts are small, they can still generate political change if they are designed selectively to affect the appropriate interest groups [*Kaempfer and Lowenberg, 1988: 786*]. They conclude that sanctions are most likely to be effective in changing the target country's policy when they (i) concentrate economic losses on groups benefiting from the target policy; (ii) give support to the policy's opposition; and (iii) persuade individual supporters of the policy to 'free ride' on the political activities of their group with the effect of reducing that active support of the policy.

In this study, I argue that the threat of trade sanctions against Brazilian exports to the US market was effective not because losses were concentrated on groups benefiting from the IT policy, as expected in Kaempfer and Lowenberg's framework, but because the sanctions were directed to uncommitted interest groups. I agree with Putnam's reasoning about strategies in international and domestic bargaining: 'an across-the-board trade concession is less effective than a concession that tips the balance with a swing voter' [*Putnam, 1988: 450*].

Conversely, sanctions are more effective when they 'tip the balance' bringing in uncommitted groups. In this way, the threat of sanctions not only provides arguments for the policy's opposition, but, more significantly, sways new interest groups to join the opposing team.

BARGAINING POWER

The concepts of *asymmetric bargaining* and *bargaining power* complete the analytical framework of this chapter.

In a game-theory view of international trade negotiations, McMillan [*1990*] refers to the 'asymmetry' of a bargaining situation when the issue being negotiated is worth much more to one player than to the other. In controlled situations, such as the laboratory experiment McMillan commented on in which some external parameter might have been used to compare the individual's scale of values, this view of the symmetry between two players can be accepted. In complex situations, such as the conflict analysed in this study, it would be difficult to decide to which player the issue under negotiation was more important: Both players displayed their commitment to solve the conflict, which, for different reasons however, was important to both of them. If, from the Brazilian standpoint, to keep its domestic policy was a highly relevant point, to obtain a change in the Brazilian domestic policy was also a very important point from the US standpoint. In this case, there is no way for the analyst to compare the two countries' assessments of the subject being negotiated in order to find out to whom it was worthier.

Asymmetry in international relations has also been studied in relation to differences in power among states. In this context, asymmetric negotiations refer to bargaining between a markedly weaker and a markedly stronger party. The international strength of a state has, however, been defined in the literature only tautologically: States are strong because they have international power, which is itself a measure of a state's strength.

Without aiming to overcome this definitional gap in the literature, I will say that, for the purposes of this analysis, asymmetry in bargaining between two players arises from differences in each one's ability to influence the other's decisions in their favour at a bilateral as well as multilateral level. This concept is very close to that of relational power (i.e., the ability to get others to do something they would not do otherwise).

In any relationship involving states, the relative power of each party depends on its structural power. That is, the ability to influence another's actions in one's favour is a function of one's control over structural components relevant to the world system. The received wisdom in political science has stressed either the security structure or the production structure as the central sources of state's power. I accept Strange's [*1988*] formulation which adds control over international credit and generation/diffusion of knowledge as two central sources of structural power. This 'realist' conception of international relations is, in this study, altered with the use of the concept of 'bargaining power'. In a two-player game, A's bargaining power is greater the more A has to offer that B wants (via reciprocal bargaining) and, conversely, the more B would be harmed if A withheld what A has (in retaliation for violation of the agreement) [*McMillan, 1990: 38*]. Therefore, even structurally weaker states may have their positions strengthened in particular circumstances of international conflict by their 'bargaining power'.

The concept of bargaining power in this analysis contrasts with Snyder and Diesing's [*1977: 190-93*] 'actual bargaining power', which refers to each party's perception of the credibility of the other's threat to stand firm compared to its own risk. Snyder and Diesing's concept of bargaining power is related to the perception of the maximum risk of bargaining breakdown that the party is willing to accept in standing firm. This perception either is a function entirely of each party's own values (inherent bargaining power) or involves comparison with the opponent's values (actual bargaining power). The perceived risk of bargaining breakdown seems better to express the *limit* of the bargaining process rather than bargaining *power* (i.e., the parties' real capacities to influence each other). In this study, I do not emphasise the subjective dimension of the decision-making process in negotiation stressed in Snyder and Diesing's concept of bargaining power. Instead, I focus on the features of each party's structural position of relational situation that can be used to influence the other party's moves in the desired direction.

The conflict analysed in this study involved two states in nearly opposite positions of structural power: one that had occupied a hegemonic position - despite declining - in the global political economy since World War II; the other, a dependent developing country with a large foreign debt and some regional leadership. Despite the differences in structural power that could give the stronger party leverage to increase its relational power and influence the outcome of the negotiation, the two players were, in the conflict analysed in this study, paradoxically in less disparate terms - although still asymmetric - in relation to their 'bargaining power'. The possibility of opening the Brazilian IT market for American goods and capital, and Brazil's compliance with the new international trade rules that the United States sought, gave the Brazilian government a stronger bargaining position than might have been expected from the balance of structural power, despite the country's foreign indebtedness and technological dependence.

2

INTELLECTUAL PROPERTY RIGHTS
IN INTERSTATE CONFLICT

According to the framework set out in Chapter 1, I contend that negotiations between the United States and Brazil defined a feasible set of possible outcomes and the conflict came to an end when a focal point within this feasible set was found which was also a win set (i.e., a solution that satisfied domestic constituencies in both countries). In this chapter I argue that regulation of intellectual property rights (IPRs) of software was such a focal point. From each player's standpoint, regulation of IPRs of software in Brazil became, with the evolution of bilateral negotiations, a solution of the conflict that was satisfactory to both parties. This outcome allowed the suspension of American threats of economic sanctions against Brazilian exports and led to a solution of the conflict.

This chapter is divided into two sections, each dedicated to discussion of the relevance of the regulation of IPRs in general, and for software in particular, in relation to each player's interests. Section 2.1 discusses American interest in Brazilian regulation of IPRs of software. This issue is presented in two parts. Subsection 2.1.1 deals with the issue at a multilateral level. It describes US involvement in negotiations on new areas for multilateral trade agreements in the current Uruguay Round, where Brazil, among other developing countries, has opposed developed countries' propositions, including those on trade-related IPRs. Subsection 2.1.2 identifies US interest in international adoption of copyright protection for IPRs of software. Section 2.2 discusses the Brazilian perspective on why establishment of copyright protection for IPRs of software was an agreeable solution.

THE US INTERNATIONAL CAMPAIGN FOR
REGULATION OF IPRS

While the deficit in the American trade account was already of domestic concern in the early 1980s, not all social actors were equally aware of its long-term causes. The effects of macroeconomic policies on the US deficit soon became clear to analysts of the American economy and were certainly known within the Reagan Administration. But these effects were persistently ignored in Congress, where the unpopularity of more efficient and thorough measures necessary to correct the undesired deficits was circumvented by making 'unfairness' of trade partners the American public enemy. Protectionism in trade policy and sub-mission of other countries' policies to the American concept of fair trade became more palatable than domestic efforts to improve competitiveness. It became politically easier not only to accuse importers of dumping, but also to blame sectoral policies of other countries for the disappointing achievements of American exports.

The United States accordingly focused an international offensive against foreign countries' initiatives in three policy areas: (i) targeting by governments of particular industries for development; (ii) restrictions on access of foreign producers to domestic markets; and (iii) failure to protect IPRs [*US Congress, Congressional Budget Office, 1987: 47*]. Such American offensives included actions in both multilateral forums and bilateral negotiations.

American actions at the multilateral level have been centred on the Uruguay Round of the GATT negotiations, where the United States has initiated trade discussions with a view to the establishment of internationally agreed rules in three new areas: (i) trade-related IPRs, (ii) trade in services, and (iii) trade-related investment measures (TRIM).

In bilateral negotiations, the US has scrutinised closely the industrial policies of Japan, the Southeast Asian newly industrialising countries (NICs), and Brazil. Although Japanese policies triggered the US attack on targeting, Brazil's IT policy was the only other 'clear example of coordination of government policies for the benefit of a chosen industry' cited by the US Congress [*US Congress, Congressional Budget Office, 1987: 53*].

From an American point of view, the Brazilian IT policy was paradigmatic. To begin with, this policy was directed toward a high-technology industrial segment in which the United States had been losing international competitiveness. In addition, American access to Brazilian markets became important in the United States due to the negative American trade balance. The IT policy was also a case of targeting against a whole industrial segment and, while this targeting cannot be blamed for threatening American producers in the US market (as has been the accusation against Japan), it was viewed as restricting American exports to Brazil and American companies' manufacturing activities in Brazil. The latter is another important reason why the Brazilian IT policy became an exemplary case for American action: The policy defined strict limits to foreign investment, including local content, export, and local research and development (R&D) requirements. The policy's goal of developing local high-technology capabilities without a mechanism to protect IPRs was believed to encourage domestic infringement on IPRs. Therefore, the United States could further its interests in concurrent multilateral negotiations by simultaneously pursuing bilateral negotiations with Brazil.

US Initiatives in the Uruguay Round

The new issues brought to GATT by the United States, despite warranting separate treatment, are nevertheless intermingled: The rights of establishment for companies that provide services in another country involve changes in domestic regulations towards foreign investment, and much of the service to be provided (computer and data-processing services and telecommunications, for instance) also depends on some standardisation of protection to intellectual property. Conflation of the three new issues of great interest to the United States has been resisted by GATT contracting parties since the launching of the Uruguay Round of negotiations [*Kaplinsky, 1988a*]. Developed and developing countries are on opposing sides in relation to these new issues and an agreement on each of them will not only imply some agreement in the others, but also will depend on concessions involving familiar areas of negotiation like agriculture and textile-clothing. Industrial countries are much more united in respect to these new areas of negotiation than are developing countries. Those less developed countries who actively aim to promote industrialisation, especially the NICs, take a firmer stand in relation to these issues. But among the more combative developing countries, those more heavily indebted are showing signs of changing towards a more favourable treatment of foreign capital and, therefore, they may be persuaded to agree to some liberalisation in the new areas. In any case, at least Brazil and India have been 'persuaded' since the mid-1980s, through strenuous cases of trade frictions, to conform to these points which are of such vital interest to the United States and which are now being negotiated in multilateral terms.

The ministerial declaration that launched the Uruguay Round defined the following guiding principles for the negotiations: an increase in trade liberalisation, inclusion of new issues within GATT jurisdiction, and differential treatment for developing countries based on nonreciprocity. At the same time, however, the developing countries were called on to improve their contribution to the multilateral trade system, depending on their rates of growth, and to accept the principle of graduation. Member countries were also asked to negotiate mutual concessions within each sector or area.[1]

Trade in services

Multilateral negotiations on trade are required in this sector because, except for services provided from a long distance across a border, international transactions in services require international movement of production actors implying establishment of operations by the service provider in the country of the receiver. In this case, regulations that each country establishes for its own service sector constitute a restriction for international transactions. A central issue in the present round of multilateral negotiations is, then, whether a General Agreement on Trade in Services (GATS) will apply only to cross-border services[2] or also to transactions that involve movement of production factors. If services implying movement of factors are included, it will have to be negotiated whether GATS will extend only to the right of companies to establish in foreign countries or whether it should also apply to movement of persons involved in production of services. As regulations on establishment of foreign companies differ among countries, an agreement of international transactions in services will require some harmonisation of regulatory frameworks across countries. This general point is also approached in another negotiating group which discusses TRIMs. This group seeks reductions in restrictions to foreign capital.

Right of establishment and domestic regulation are approached in diverging ways by developed and developing countries in their respective versions of draft framework agreements.[3] The US draft proposes the right of establishment and national treatment for foreign capital in the service sector and recognises the right of each country to regulate its sector on the condition that such regulation is not prepared, adopted, or applied in order to nullify the obligations of the agreement. It recognises a safeguard for balance of payment purposes, does not make any provision for movement of labour or for special treatment of developing countries, but opens the possibility of 'reservations' on the application of the agreement to specific services or specific aspects of existing legislation [*Hindley, 1990: 137-138*]. On the other hand, the two draft versions by developing countries reject the right of establishment and require that labour and capital be treated equally. They also propose (i) that policy objectives of national laws and regulations applying to trade shall be respected; (ii) that parties, especially developing countries, shall be allowed to grant exclusive rights in certain sectors in order to implement national policy objectives; and (iii) that parties shall be allowed to adopt and enforce regulations necessary to control suppliers. The developing countries' drafts also provide safeguard (i) for balance of payments reasons; (ii) to avoid or alleviate unforeseen economic damage related to the process of liberalisation; and (iii) to promote the creation of certain services and correct structural problems such as those related to technological change and capital formation [*Hindley, 1990: 139-40*]. Controversy on such essential provisions suggests that agreement will require concessions by the developed countries to developing countries in other areas under negotiation. It is probable that the final agreement will be a modified version of the US draft. In that case, another issue will be how many signatories the GATS will initially have [*Hindley, 1990: 143*].

Trade-related intellectual property rights

'Intellectual property is an asset generated by the creation of new information with commercial or artistic usefulness' [*Maskus, 1990: 164*]. It has been put on the agenda of multilateral negotiations because technology-exporting countries, especially the United States, but also some EEC countries and Japan, cannot tolerate erosion in the return of investment in R&D due to inconsistent and deficient regulation of intellectual property. Establishment of an international standard or harmonisation of domestic regulations became imperative as the growing knowledge intensity in production demanded larger investments in R&D. Industrial countries argue that deficient regulation of intellectual property stimulates counterfeiting, unauthorized duplication of copyrighted material, and unauthorized use of patented products and processes. Current guidelines provided by the World Intellectual Property Organisation (WIPO) have been considered insufficient as standards, and the institution is alleged to be incapable of disciplining cases of copyright and trademark infringements even less complicated than those related to the new technologies.

Developing countries have been notorious transgressors of IPRs for some time - but so were the United States and Japan in their industrial 'infancy'. Most of them are and will continue to be technology-importers for a long time ahead. For them, protection of intellectual property means creation of monopoly rights, the exploitation of which results in high, monopoly prices, increased costs of licenses, limited and expensive technology transfer, and consequently, slower growth [*Maskus, 1990: 165*]. They reject the idea that protecting IPRs would increase their own potential for creative activity because they are aware that these types of regulations are inadequate to overcome structural limits to innovation.

Technology-exporting and technology-importing countries, therefore, have clearly diverging interests in the current negotiation of protection of intellectual property. Each category of countries is not, however, uniform in its views on the subject. The United States and the EEC agree on two core provisions of an agreement: (i) that no products or processes should be excluded from patentability; and (ii) that compulsory licenses should be given only under very special circumstances and with a payment of approximately the economic value of the asset to the intellectual property owner. Technology-exporting countries disagree, however, on significant points, such as copyright protection for software in contrast to *su generis* protection for chip topographies and biotechnology products, and whether patents should be granted on a first-to-invent or a first-to-file basis. Many developing countries take no position for one of three reasons: (i) they are not aware of the relevance of the subject; (ii) they foresee little prospect of developing their own domestic software industry; and/or (iii) they cannot afford to pay for IPR rights for the software they use. The NICs and those who aim actively to promote industrialisation, however, have strong positions on the matter. They require no changes in standards of intellectual property protection beyond ensuring that each country provides national treatment. They would also favour exclusion of various products from patentability, make compulsory licensing less restricted, and leave levels of compensation to be decided by the government that requires the license [*Maskus, 1990: 171*].

With such deep differences of opinion, its seems that negotiations can result in an agreement either with weak standards but wide membership or one with stronger standards and limited membership. If it depended only on the significance of the subject for industrial countries, the most likely outcome would be an agreement with strong protection. Nevertheless, many other aspects will have to be considered, including those emanating from the form the agreement will assume. If it is an amendment to GATT, it will require approval of two-thirds of the contracting parties, which is approximately 64 votes. In this case, concessions will have to be offered to developing countries to gain the necessary votes. One such concessions could be a balance between rights and obligations of intellectual property owners, which would make possible the initiation of GATT actions against private companies for abuses of these rights and restrictive business practices. Another possibility is for the agreement to be negotiated as a special code establishing standards, enforcement obligations, and a mechanism for dispute settlement. The code would be open to adherence but would not ensure the extension of nondiscrimination to nonmembers. In this case, a smaller number of countries would initially be signatories. In practical terms, the United States, a necessary participant on any agreement on the subject,

> might exempt code members from action under its Special 301 provisions but redouble its efforts to pursue perceived infringement elsewhere. Each country would need to calculate whether its interests lie in joining the code and upgrading its intellectual property systems at the expense of its perceived development interests (and at the risk of absorbing GATT-sanctioned retaliation for failure to enforce its high standards) or in remaining outside the code and risking retribution outside the confines of the GATT [*Maskus, 1990: 175*].

Trade-related investment measures

Protection of foreign investment under GATT had been unsuccessfully attempted by the United States since the early 1980s until a compromise granted the necessary support to include the subject on the agenda of the Uruguay Round, under the restrictive title of 'trade related investment measures'. What have been negotiated in this area are means to reduce trade effects of restrictions to foreign direct investment. One of the most common TRIMs is the requirement of national content, which is deemed to discriminate against imported goods relative to domestically produced substitutes. The United States, Japan, and the EEC advocate an agreement forbidding the following TRIMs: local-content requirement, export-performance requirement, local-manufacturing requirement, trade balance targets, production mandates, and foreign-exchange restrictions. The United States and Japan would add prohibition of mandatory technology transfer and the United States would stand alone in asking for prohibition of limits on equity participation and on remittances [*Graham and Krugman, 1990: 152*]. Developing countries see TRIMs as a necessary tool to contain the perceived excessive power of foreign companies. Divergence among developing countries in this respect is, however, likely to deepen as some of those most heavily indebted revise their attitudes towards foreign capital. In this case, some developing countries might support the industrial countries' draft agreement. This has not yet happened, however. Therefore, approval of a strong agreement on TRIMs containing the list of prohibited measures, a 'standstill' clause banning the imposition of new TRIMs, a 'rollback' mechanism by which existing TRIMs would be phased out, and a 'grandfather' clause allowing certain existing TRIMs covered by the prohibition to remain in effect is very unlikely without concessions to developing countries. Such concessions might include a credible scheme for liberalising trade in textiles and clothing, substantial liberalising measures on trade in agriculture, and 'reform of the GATT dispute settlement mechanism, accompanied by revision of Section 301 to bring its procedures more closely into line with GATT discipline' [*Graham and Krugman, 1990: 157*].

Copyright Protection for IPRs of Software

The 1980s were market by a sudden international awareness of the importance of establishing legal protection for IPRs of software. Two factors explain this phenomenon. Firstly, the growth of software production and the need to ensure the returns on investment in its development were economic forces pushing for such legislation. Secondly, the proactive role of the United States - the major world producer of software - in defining an international regime of IPRs for software based on copyright was an additional political component to explain the dominance of this legal regime in the 1980s wave of software legislation.[4]

As a product of human inventiveness with commercial use, software, as much as all other useful outcomes of human creativity, could be argued to give its author the right to be rewarded by his/her ingenuity. In the case of software (and all other knowledge-intensive products), this right is even more acutely claimed in light of the large amount of resources invested in its production, either directly by individual authors or mostly by collective organisations such as companies which hire engineers and other personnel to develop software. Within the IT area, it was only after software became a segment in its own right, superseding its previous conception as a subsidiary part of the computer systems' trade - which happened in the 1970s[5] - that how to guarantee the reward of the inventiveness of software authors came to be a major issue.

Authors' rights on their inventions have so far been granted by three legal systems: patents, trade secrets, and copyright [*Ploman and Hamilton, 1980: 168*]. Patents are awarded to an invention that can be proved to be novel, original, and capable of industrial application. This means that patents protect technical ideas behind the industrial product or process. The patent owner has exclusive rights over the economic use of the invention for a time period limited to less than 20 years. Trade secret protection is based upon restrictions on the flow of information related to the invention; the details of such protection are defined in accordance with contract law. Copyright is provided for all written works that are original, not copies. It does not require the work to be novel (i.e., to express a new idea), only original (i.e., authentic). Thus copyright protects the expression of ideas but not the underlying idea nor the use of the work. The copyright owner has exclusive rights over the distribution of his/her written work among the public for a specific time period that varies in different national regulations, but is generally significantly larger than that pertaining to patents.

In the early 1970s, legal specialists suggested extending patent protection to software. The patent system was viewed as an adequate mechanism to protect the IPRs of software, especially from software manufacturers' point of view. By protecting the idea, and not only its expression, patents seemed to afford an unequivocal remedy against unauthorised imitation, copy, and use of software. However, only a few programs meet the 'novelty' requirement for being patented. When a given software is patentable, this legal protection leads to a virtual monopolisation of ideas as all independent development of a similar program would be an infringement of its patent. This is why patents for software are of limited interest to technology-following countries and companies that are entering software production.

Ploman and Hamilton commented that 'in the past the computer industry has relied heavily upon trade secret protection and contract law for the protection of computer programmes against piracy' [*1980: 169*]. However, as they have pointed out, trade secret protection, based as it is upon restrictions on the flow of information, is rather limited when applied to software. In fact, it seems difficult for a product such as software to maintain some of its main features in secret without their disclosure to outsiders. Protection of software through trade secret and contract law would seem inconsistent, as the scope and conditions of such protection vary from case to case and between countries. It is also difficult to prevent disclosure by former employees.

Copyright has been considered, then, the least limiting form of legal protection to cover author's rights over software. In contrast with patents, copyright may be granted to all software that is original, even when it is not novel. Consequently, independent development of the same or a similar program would not be an infringement of copyright. Compared with trade secret protection, copyright is predictable and has been subject to some attempts at establishing international regulations. The latter is one aspect of the copyright system that has favoured its extension to the protection of IPRs of software.

As a legal regime to safeguard the rights of authors (whose concept has been extended to companies under the dominant situation in which the author is an employee), copyright is undoubtedly a form of protection that benefits software producers. Its main positive features from the point of view of software producers include the long term of protection conferred; the long acquaintance with the rules of protection; the commencement of protection mostly on the date of the software's creation; and, finally - a crucial point for the international operation of the software industry - the existence of international copyright conventions which facilitate cross-border protection.

International copyright conventions resulted from dissatisfaction among publishing nations with the quality and extent of protection afforded to their products outside their territory. In 1886, the Berne Convention established the basic principles of national treatment, minimum standard's of protection, and automatic protection to be followed by the signatory countries which comprised the major publishing countries at the time. After World War II, a substantial number of states had adhered to the Berne Convention, with the notable exceptions of the United States and the Soviet Union. In 1952, the Universal Copyright Convention (UCC), under the auspices of UNESCO, defined lower standards of reciprocal protection in the hope of inducing the United States to adhere to the convention. It was only in 1955 that the United States became a signatory of the UCC. In relation to software, international copyright conventions provide a general framework for cross-border protection. However, from the point of view of the United States and other major software exporters, the developing countries' push for relaxation of these conventions[6] has made them unsatisfactory for protecting IPRs of software.

Notwithstanding its advantages for the software producer, the copyright regime has a major limitation, which is becoming more evident with its adoption by software legislation in various countries. As copyright protects the expression of the idea, not the underlying idea itself, it has shown limited power to deter unauthorized use and, most of all, it cannot prevent third parties from basing the development of similar software on an existing idea whose previous expression is copyrighted.[7] Contradictorily, in the latter situation, this disadvantage of the copyright regime for established software producers is a major advantage for those who are entering this industry.

Copyright protection for software, favourable as it may be for producers, is not, however, a satisfactory legal regime to protect users' rights. Biased as it is in favour of authors' rights, it minimises their obligations. Unlike patents, copyright generally does not establish any working obligation and protection may be granted even without disclosure of the work that is being protected. As a consequence, there is no protection for the user against defects or lack of assistance. In addition, the long terms of protection far beyond the software's 'productive life' do not allow society to benefit from the free use of the work within a reasonable period of time. Finally, the 'moral rights' granted to authors by copyright - particularly the right to claim integrity of the work - are considered inadequate to a work such as software that is constantly being adapted and improved [*Correa, 1989a: 26-27*]

Copyright, compared with other legal regimes, has been taken as the least limiting among the available means to protect intellectual rights of software. However, given the specificities of software and, most of all, the diversity of interests involved in its production and diffusion, protection for its IPRs is still controversial. Despite its limitations and the ongoing controversy over its adequacy and effectiveness, copyright protection for software is now the dominant regime in countries which have so far legislated on this matter.

To date, Bulgaria and South Korea are the only countries where software is subject to a special regulatory regime. The Bulgarian case is explained by the particular legal system of a socialist country. There is no proper protection of software authorship in Bulgaria, but a regulation of its production and use. Institutions that produce software are entitled to a payment from the user equivalent to 10 per cent of the total amount spent in salaries and social security during the development of the software. This payment is shared among those who worked to develop the software in proportion to each one's contribution. The user cannot transfer the software to someone else, even if payment is made to the developer. The producer must correct any errors found during one year's use of the program. Foreign software - imported, developed in Bulgaria in a joint-venture, or in international cooperation between foreign and Bulgarian companies - is entitled to the same remuneration as local products. South Korea's software law of 1986 established that copyright law shall be applied only in cases not specified in that 1986 law. Foreign software is protected when it is first published in South Korea, or by international convention.[8] Protection begins upon creation of the software and is guaranteed for 50 years. Modification of the software is allowed when necessary for its use in specific computers, to make it more efficient, or when the user's operations demand such alterations. Backup copies and other copies to be used privately in a specific place, such as the home, are legitimate. There is a registry for software but it is not compulsory [*Correa, 1989b: 211-12*].

All of the other fifteen countries that approved software legislation up to 1989 have accepted the copyright regime, with some of these countries substantially altering copyright provisions to adapt them to the specificities of software.

Table 2.1 presents the main modifications of copyright law in national legislation that established such protection for IPRs of software.

TABLE 2.1
ALTERATION OF COPYRIGHT LAW IN COPYRIGHT PROTECTION
FOR SOFTWARE

	Copyright Law	Copyright for software
Term of protection	Life of the author + 25 or 50 years	25 or 50 years
Authorship	Author	Author; employer
Copies	Only with authorisation	Backup and others allowed for private use without authorisation
Author's moral rights	No change or adaptation without authorisation	Some adaptation allowed without authorisation
Rights of foreign authors	Same as national's	Same as national's on condition of reciprocity

Source: Correa *[1989b]*.

French and Japanese legislation on software are among those which incorporate significant changes in their nations' copyright laws. They are of particular interest here because they were defined before the Brazilian 301 case started and, therefore, constituted examples, among the few at hand, for the Brazilian government to consider when the time came to propose legislation on the matter. In the French legislation, rights on software developed by an employee belong to the employer; all copying, except the backup, and unauthorized use are infringements of the law; protection is provided for 25 years; there is an established procedure for apprehension of unauthorised copies; and the rights of foreign authors are protected under the condition of reciprocity [*Correa, 1989b: 209*]. The Japanese software law enacted in 1985 was much more moderate than that proposed by the Ministry of International Trade and Industry (MITI) in 1983, which suggested a special regime for software. The main provisions of the MITI proposal were extension of protection to the source code and the object code;[9] exclusion of author's moral rights; the right to modify or up-date the software by its legitimate user; limitation of the term of protection to 15 years; creation of a system of registration and deposit that would determine the date protection would begin; publication of a general description of the functions of the software; transfer to the employer of the rights over software developed by an employee; institution of 'rent rights', by which previous authorisation of the author would be required to lease the software; and establishment of compulsory licensing of software [*Correa, 1989b: 209*]. The existing Japanese software law makes the following changes in the copyright law: Rights over software developed by an employee belong to the employer; the user is authorised to make two copies and two adaptations for private use without

27

previous consent by the author; the date of registration is considered to be the date of the creation of the software; the commercial use of a copy is considered an infringement if this copy is unauthorised and the user is aware of its fraudulent origin.

REGULATION OF IPRS OF SOFTWARE IN BRAZIL

Like some other developing countries, the Brazilian government has dealt with the issue of protection for IPRs with the general intent of subordinating proprie- tary rights over knowledge and technology to the collective goal of the country's development. For some specific kinds of invention proprietary rights are not acknowledged in Brazil - as occurred in the developed world during the initial stages of industrialisation - and for others Brazilian legislation limits these rights for economic and ethical reasons. The Brazilian Industrial Property Code, Law No. 5772, of 1971, grants protection for industrial property rights, except for inventions such as pharmaceutical products,[10] food, and newly discovered use of species of microorganisms (Article 9). The Industrial Property Code estab- lishes the same privileges for both foreign and domestic patent-owners in Brazil, in accordance with international conventions and treaties ratified by Brazil, on the condition that the invention is deposited in the country (Article 3). Patents for inventions are granted for fifteen years, and for models and industrial design for ten years, starting with the date of deposit. Compulsory licensing will occur if the patent-owner does not use his/her invention productively within three years following its granting, when its use stops for more than one year, and for reasons of public interest (Article 33). The Brazilian Copyright Law No. 5988, of 1973, follows the principles established by the Berne Convention, of which Brazil is among the original signatories. The term of protection is the life of the author plus 60 years; registration is not compulsory; authors have the right to claim authorship, to keep the work unpublished, to claim the integrity of the work, to modify it before or after its use, to take it out of circulation, or to suspend the authorisation of its use; rights of foreign authors are granted in accordance with conventions and treaties ratified by Brazil.

Up to 1986 the Brazilian government had considered all available regimes for legal protection for IPRs of software to be detrimental to the development of the local IT sector, including a potential domestic software industry. To protect software either as an industrial property or as a literary work was seen as equally unacceptable to Brazil. Terms of protection, which in the copyright regime are almost unlimited, and the payment of royalties were argued to make any legal protection of software more of a hindrance than a help in efforts to curb deficits in the balance of payments and to promote development. Brazilian authorities were convinced that instead of fostering a Brazilian software indus- try, patents and copyright would jeopardise its growth [*Secretaria Especial de*

Informática (SEI), 1981: 48]. The dominant view was that existing legal provisions in Brazil could be invoked to protect investments made in software development. Provisions of Brazilian contract law prohibited the disclosure or unauthorised use by an employee of secrets of production and business [*SEI, 1981: 49*]. The evolution of the Brazilian IT market and international commitments of the country soon changed this position. In 1984, the Brazilian government attempted to prepare a Software Bill to be debated at the same time that the Brazilian Informatics Bill was being discussed in the Brazilian Congress.[11] A draft software bill was prepared in the executive branch but never introduced into the Brazilian Congress. Bill No. 260/84, introduced into the Brazilian Senate two months after the approval of the Informatics Law, proposed a regime of protection for software very close to the conventional patent law, but without the requirement of originality.

The Brazilian government's inclination to adopt a *sui generis* regime was emphasised by the Brazilian delegation to the meeting of the group of specialists held in Geneva, in 1985, where they maintained that copyright was not an adequate regime for protection for IPRs of software. In accordance with this disposition, the Conselho Nacional de Direito Autoral (CNDA, the government agency in charge of coordinating and implementing Brazilian copyright law and other international conventions ratified by the country) made various decisions against the classification of software as literary work, thus denying software copyright protection [*Pereira dos Santos, 1987*]. The first precedent in the Brazilian judicial system against this government orientation occurred in May 1986, when the São Paulo Court of Justice concluded that the Brazilian company Microdigital Electrônica had infringed the copyright of software owned by Sinclair Research Limited. With this issue at the focal point of negotiations between Brazil and the United States, in the same year CONIN approved the adoption of a copyright regime for software. A software bill establishing this regime was introduced in the Brazilian Congress and passed into law in 1987.[12]

In the late 1970s and early 1980s, Brazilian authorities justified their rejection of any legal regime of protection for IPRs of software as a way to alleviate economic obstacles facing the locally owned hardware industry in its initial stages of development. Any legal protection that could have been given to IPRs of software would also have meant additional cost to hardware producers and computer users. Considering the already high operating costs in this infant industry - due to both high expenditures for imported components and the small scale of production - and the almost nonexistent local production of software, payment of royalties for such programs would have jeopardised the policy of a reserved market for hardware.

As Farias [*1986*] argued, local production of software would not have been sufficient to meet the demand created by the expansion of local mini- and microcomputer production. In fact, before the diffusion of microcomputer production - which happened in Brazil during the 1980s - opportunities for local companies dedicated to development and trade of software had been small and limited to administrative applications. Up to that time, computer services had been provided either in-house or by data-processing bureaux. The software used was mainly of foreign origin [*Gaio, 1990: 199*]. The boom of microcomputer manufacture in Brazil in the 1980s was not met by a significant local production of basic or applications software, to say nothing of operating systems, without which the diffusion of such equipment would have been totally undermined. It was only in 1983 that local development of operating systems was made the object of policy measures and their results appeared only some years later.[13] On the other hand, locally developed and manufactured microcomputers have been, since the very beginning of their production in Brazil, entirely compatible with equipment produced in the international market, a fact that has facilitated the immediate use of software developed for the world market. Therefore, a liberal orientation towards the importation of software and lack of legal protection of IPRs aided the launching of local microcomputer production in Brazil.

These conditions, which helped the establishment of the microcomputer industry, were, however, incompatible with sustained development of the whole IT sector, which included a newly born software industry, and, therefore, could not persist as justification for a long-term policy orientation. A re-orientation towards software by the Brazilian government resulted from two basic factors. Firstly, the lack of protection of IPRs of software implied tolerance of piracy and unauthorised copies, which jeopardised the local development of software. Secondly, the lack of a legal regime of protection for IPRs of software would provoke, sooner or later, a reaction from software producers who had had their product copied without authorisation.

While the Brazilian market for smaller computers was still very small, unauthorised copying of software did not draw the attention of foreign producers, nor affect the interests of eventual local producers. Acceleration of domestic microcomputer production in the early 1980s, however, reminded Brazilian authorities of the need to legislate property rights for software by foreign and domestic software producers. On the other hand, the international debate on legal protection for software and a domestic drive towards a more integrated IT policy, which occurred simultaneously with the Brazilian microcomputer production 'boom' were additional forces pressing for a definition of legal protection of software in Brazil.

We can see now that conditions in Brazil were ripe for legislation to protect IPRs of software when the conflict with the United States started. At that time, it was unnecessary to convince the Brazilian government of the need to make such legislation. Rather, the central point was the kind of protection to be established in Brazilian law. The *sui generis* approach - a combination of a copyright regime with elements of patent legislation - expressed in Bill No.

260/84 was for many reasons unacceptable to the Americans, who then pressed for adoption of a copyright regime. With the Americans demanding changes in the central components of its IT policy, Brazil's compliance with the US call for a copyright regime for software was an agreeable compromise not only in relation to maintenance of those central elements of the IT policy, but also in terms of the affected domestic interests. It was easier for Brazil to make new legislation adapting copyright protection for software that, at least in principle, could benefit the small and weaker group of domestic software producers, than to accept changes in the rules that could affect the stronger group of hardware industrialists, especially the microcomputer producers.

SUMMARY

Summing up the argument presented in this chapter, I contend that the definition of legal protection for IPRs of software in Brazil came to be a focal point in the negotiations between the two countries because this issue satisfied both parties and an agreement on it resulted in the solution of the conflict. Making such legislation in Brazil was satisfactory from an American point of view for both economic and political reasons. Economically, American software producers would benefit from such legislation, which would grant them legal basis for action against any infractor. Politically, Brazilian copyright legislation for software would contribute to the international dissemination of such a regime and might influence other developing countries to emulate the Brazilian experience. Softening Brazil's positions on regulation of IPRs was equally relevant for American interests in the Uruguay Round of multilateral trade negotiations, where Brazil had been in the forefront of developing countries opposed to the developed countries' propositions for regulation of new issues, including IPRs.

On the Brazilian side, the need to adopt legal protection for software had already been acknowledged before the opening of the conflict with the United States. Brazilian authorities did, nevertheless, yield to American pressure to adopt the copyright regime, which they had previously considered undesirable under Brazil's particular circumstances. A compromise on this issue was, however, satisfactory to some Brazilian interests. Firstly, the adoption of such a regime could deter the use of economic sanctions and, therefore, please Brazilian domestic groups threatened by the American retaliation. Secondly, Brazilian acceptance of a copyright regime for software could be taken as a major and significant concession to American pressure and might allow solution of the conflict without other substantial changes in the central components of the IT policy, which could have affected the interests of the stronger group of domestic hardware producers.

In a nutshell, the policy of market reserve could be kept almost untouched in exchange for the adoption of a copyright regime for software. Therefore,

Brazilian regulation of IPRs of software became a focal point in the negotiation between the two countries because, under the economic and political conditions at the time, it could satisfy domestic constituencies in both countries and bring about a solution to the conflict.

PART II:

THE DISPUTE

3

POLICIES FOR THE FORMATION OF THE BRAZILIAN IT INDUSTRY

Chapters 3 and 4 are dedicated to analysis of one side of the dispute's foundation - the Brazilian IT policy - emphasizing the features subjected to American criticism and Brazilian praise. In this chapter I present a detailed account of the Brazilian government's actions to build up a local electronics industry. Four major policy issues are analysed: determination of the market to be reserved for nationally owned companies, the instruments for state intervention, the strategy towards foreign capital, and the software policy. These issues were the main topics challenged by the US government in this conflict.

As the analysis in this chapter shows, evolution of the Brazilian IT policy narrowed the conditions for foreign direct investment in the local market. Restrictions on foreign capital in the booming microcomputer market and the limitation on international trade of IT goods created an arena of international friction with market-seeking countries, especially the United States, which was concerned that a successful Brazilian experience might become an inspiration to other developing countries. Thus both economic and political factors had to be considered during bargaining for a mutually satisfactory solution to the conflict. Disarticulation of sectoral policies for the electronics industry in Brazil also had political implications for the definition of a satisfactory solution to the conflict.

THE CONCEPT OF NATIONAL COMPANY

Apart from consumer electronics, state actions towards the other sectors were aimed at establishing a local electronics industry with national control over the companies' capital and technology.[14] One of the principal instruments used for this purpose was to reserve part of the domestic market for national companies. The concept of 'national company', however, differed in regulations governing the telecommunications and other sectors. In the telecommunications sector, a national company is one in which Brazilian citizens or foreigners resident in the country hold the majority of voting shares.[15] Transfer of the majority of the voting shares of the telecommunications foreign subsidiaries within the Brazilian market did not affect their ties with the parent companies, which maintained control over the majority of the total shares. In the computer sector, however, the concept of national company has, since 1981, been much more restrictive. As defined in SEI's Normative Act 16, of that year, effective control of the capital should lie permanently and exclusively in the hands of individuals born, residing, and domiciled in Brazil. The two different conceptions coexisted until Article 12 of the Informatics Law defined *national company* as those corporations constituted and with headquarters in Brazil, whose control upon decision-making, capital, and technology are permanently, exclusively, and unconditionally in the hands of individuals resident and domiciled in Brazil, or in the hands of domestic public law entities. *Decision-making control* is the power to elect corporate administrators and to direct the operations of the corporate organization. *Technological control* is the power to develop, generate, purchase and transfer, and vary the technology of the product and the production process, *Capital control* means to hold directly or indirectly the whole capital, with effective or potential voting power, and at least 70 per cent of the equity or share capital. For *open capital corporations*, the voting stock and the fixed or minimum dividend stock shall correspond to a minimum of two-thirds of the equity capital and may be owned, subscribed, or purchased only by individuals resident and domiciled in Brazil, by domestic public law entities, and by national business.[16]

The concept of national company defined in Article 12, of the Informatics Law should have been the only one used in relation to Brazil's electronics industry from 1984 onwards. However, the preceding situation was not altered by the Law; nor did it supersede existing legislation affecting the telecommunications and consumer electronics sectors. Thus, some firms that do not meet the conditions established by Article 12 continue to operate within the reserved area of the electronics industry. They are, predominantly, in the sectors of telecommunications and consumer electronics. Since 1988, based on the new Brazilian Constitution, these companies are defined as 'Brazilian corporations' and are distinguished from the 'Brazilian national corporations' [*Brazilian Constitution, Article 171*].

SCOPE OF THE IT POLICY

Until the late 1970s, the various state regulations towards each of the sectors of the electronics industry had not only been institutionally separated, but also unrelated. There had been no integrated set of principles, political guidelines, or instruments that could be referred to as an 'IT policy'. Nevertheless, beginning in the area of data-processing equipment, awareness of the need for such an integrated policy can be traced back to the mid-1970s, when the restructuring of CAPRE, the institution in charge of allocating computer access by state agencies, gave this agency the new responsibility of proposing a national IT policy and an integrated IT development plan.[17] This new task seems to have

36

been outweighed by its other responsibility of building the foundation for a domestic computer industry: There is no sign of an integrated plan and the majority of CAPRE's decisions until its dissolution in 1979 were restricted to the area of data processing.[18]

The first formally expressed attempt at a comprehensive approach to the electronics industry by the Brazilian state is found in the National Security Council's *Guidelines for a National Informatics Policy*,[19] which will be analysed later in this section. The scope of an integrated policy sketched in the guidelines was subsequently built up through various regulations, which were finally merged into the Informatics Law, particulary in Article 3. As noted above, formalization of a more comprehensive policy for the electronics industry had been insufficient to guarantee the integration of governmental activities in the area. Despite the articulated goals set out in the First Plan for Informatics and Automation (I PLANIN), conflicting regulations and institutional friction remained that prevented combined action in the area.[20]

The *Guidelines for a National Informatics Policy [1979]* extended the scope of governmental action in the field from controlling the use of data-processing equipment and stimulating nationally owned production of mini- and micro-computers and their peripherals to:

(i) the development and utilization of the technologies involved in the inputs, components, equipment, software, and services;
(ii) national production of linear and digital electronic components and their basic inputs;
(iii) extension of market reserve and import control[21] to the production by national companies of small- and medium-sized equipment, other than data-processing or peripherals;
(iv) development of software and services by national industry.

Beyond the ambitious technological goals, the *Guidelines* set up a basis for including electronic components and their inputs, small- and medium-sized electronic equipment, software, and services in the market reserve. These policy orientations were implemented by the Special Secretariat for Informatics (SEI), which after 1979 superseded CAPRE as the central entity in charge of the IT policy.[22] In relation to the scope of the policy, special commissions were set up by SEI to study the areas of software, services, and process-control equipment, with a view of definition of a development strategy for each of them.[23]

The most relevant decision affecting the scope of the policy was formalized in SEI's Normative Act 016/81, which defined the goods whose local production would only be authorized to national companies.[24] The majority of the listed goods lie in the professional electronics and the telecommunications sectors. This list was subsequently enlarged to include services (Normative Act 023/83), digital technical instruments (Normative Act 024/83), operating systems for microcomputers (Normative Act 026/83), and digital equipment for use in motor vehicles (Normative Act 001/84). State regulations towards software will be discussed later in this chapter.

Import control over certain goods was another component of the IT policy that widened its scope gradually during the 1980s to cover most of the electronics industry. As shown in the previous section, import control has been extended to a larger and more diversified set of products than computers and their peripherals. SEI controlled importation of some electronics components, such as doped crystals, nonlinear semiconductor resistors, transistors, and printed circuit boards, from 1983 until very recently. This alteration, indicated the state's response to demands for changing the wide scope of the policy.

The regulations mentioned so far in relation to the scope of the policy were finally integrated in Article 3 of the Informatics Bill introduced by the Brazilian Executive into the Brazilian Congress in June 1984. The Bill defined IT activities as follows:

(i)   research, development, production, importation, exportation, and marketing of semiconductor electronic components, optical-electronic, and like components, as well as their inputs;

(ii) importation, exportation, manufacturing, marketing, and operation of machines, equipment, instruments, and devices based on digital techniques destined to collecting, treating, structuring, storing, switching, retrieving, displaying, and transferring information, its respective inputs, elements, parts, and physical operation bases for the registry of information;

(iii) importation, exportation, production, operation, and marketing of programs for computers and automatic information treatment machines;

(iv) structuring and exploiting data bases;

(v)   rendering technical information services (Law No. 7232, Article 3).

The scope of the IT policy defined in the above terms received great attention within the Brazilian Congress. The most controversial aspects were the wide range of activities (from R&D to manufacturing and marketing) and subjects (from semiconductors to telecommunications equipment). The substitute bill prepared by the House-Senate Committee deleted *marketing* of semiconductor components and added *electronic* to qualify their inputs; included *research* on data-processing equipment and deleted *machines* with the *function of transferring information* as well as this equipment's electronic inputs, elements, parts, and physical operation bases; and changed the scope of the item related to software, making *automatic information treatment machines* synonymous with *computers*. The amendments presented in this substitute bill restored almost entirely the terms used in the Executive's Bill to define *informatics activities*, except for marketing of electronic components, which was excluded from the

Informatics Law. Thus, the definition of *informatics activities* in the Law is broad enough to cover most of the present activities of the electronics industry and, phrased as it is, to include many other future activities.

This extension of the policy's scope was accompanied by some difficulties in its enforcement, a matter not only of institutional friction but also of divergent political goals. Institutional conflicts arose due to the powers SEI had acquired in areas of the Ministry of Communication (MINICOM) and the Ministry of Interior, to which the Manaus Free Zone Administration (SUFRAMA) is subordinated.[25] Conflicts with MINICOM were dealt with by SEI's participation in GEICOM, an interministerial group created to discuss the subject of components and materials for the telecommunications sector. In June 1988, the Brazilian government, based on advice from the President's Office legal department,[26] restricted SEI control over projects for the manufacture of IT goods in the Free Zone of Manaus. SEI's analysis of such projects was to be limited to the items listed in Normative Act 016/81, not to the ones that would fit the broad definition of the Informatics Law. Thus, SEI lost control over various IT goods that would have been under its power if the Informatics Law were followed strictly. Among these were new products based on digital technology, as in the case of those used in motor vehicles.

In concluding this section, I suggest that evolution of Brazil's comprehensive IT policy, which was extended gradually in scope to cover most of the electronics industry, showed a clear governmental perception of the linkages between different elements of this industry. However, Brazilian policy-makers did not recognize the technological convergence of this industry's various sectors, nor the implications of this convergence for effective governmental intervention, until after policies towards these sectors had already been launched. Thus, the different objectives and strategies became obstacles to a fully integrated policy and a hindrance to the development of the electronics industry.

IT POLICY INSTRUMENTS

Import control, market reserve for national companies, state procurement, and financial incentives were the major instruments of Brazilian IT policy.

The trade deficit in the early 1970s was one of the main justifications for creating CAPRE to control the use of computers, an important Brazilian import at the time. *Import control*, of finished products at the beginning of state intervention and of an expanding list of goods afterwards, became an essential instrument for the policy to attain its goals of reducing the trade deficit and promoting local technological development, inducing local firms to manufacture the products and to design them in Brazil.

Import control operated in a rather simple way. Firstly, the Brazilian Council for Economic Development (CDE) established annual quotas for importation of IT goods depending on the country's availability of hard currency. Secondly, SEI examined the import requests presented by state agencies or private companies, a task it performed until 1992 (Informatics Law, Article 8). Finally, CACEX, the Foreign Trade Department of the Banco do Brasil, issued an import licence for requests approved by SEI. Import control of computers and their peripherals was exercised initially by CAPRE,[27] and since 1980 by SEI,[28] which followed published criteria for evaluating import applications. The basic criteria for import approval involved consideration of both the availability of national alternatives and the convenience of changing to a locally manufactured machine considering the existing assets in imported equipment and software.[29] Actual imports of IT goods have always exceeded the quotas defined for each year, growing from US\$ 108 million in 1976 to US\$ 800 million in 1987 [*Paiva, 1989: 118*].

CACEX Communication 41, of 1983, defined a list of fifty-two goods whose importation would require SEI's prior approval. This list was in force until 1986, when American pressure induced the publishing of a narrower list of twenty-five items in CACEX Communication 171. Import control on analogue instruments and printed circuit boards was taken out of SEI's power, but two other items - computer tomography and optical fibre - were included. The most significant change, however, was reduction of SEI's power over the import of numerical control components of whole systems.[30]

The *reserved market* for national companies was implemented by SEI's authorization to companies for the local manufacture of IT goods. This authorization was a necessary condition for SEI's consideration of import requests. Market reserve started with CAPRE Resolution 01 [*of 15 July 1976*], which defined the strategy for fostering the local manufacture of smaller data-processing equipment. SEI Normative Act 016/81 defined the conditions a company should comply with in order to be allowed to manufacture a list of IT products in the Brazilian market. The purpose of this instrument was to control the entry and expansion of IT companies in the local market. Also, since it was a condition for the concession of an import licence, it was used to stimulate the use of locally made inputs and to prevent Brazilian manufacturers from being dependent on a single foreign supplier. The approval of projects for local manufacture did not take into consideration market size and potential demand, or the management and financial situation of the company, but simply the perspective of local capability in product technology [*Paiva, 1989: 122-3*]. This orientation was justified by SEI as composing a liberal strategy of leaving the selection of the best or stronger companies to the market. This strategy was not seen by analysts and some state officials as a positive one because it led to fragmentation of some parts of the IT market, with consequent reduction in economies of scale.[31]

The *procurement power of the state*, despite being the principal focus in the creation of CAPRE, a major target of many SEI regulations,[32] and formalized in Article 11 of the Informatics Law, was used effectively as a policy instrument only in the telecommunications sector. In fact, it was only in the market for electronic-based telecommunications equipment and for process control equipment that the state companies' demands were dominant. In the telecommunications sector, Telebras has been the only customer for electronic-based telephone exchanges and transmission materials. In the area of industrial automation, Petrobras - in oil production - and Siderbras - in steel production - have been the major buyers of electronic process-control equipment. The Brazilian federal administration's share of the domestic demand for computers, however, has not followed this pattern. In fact, data-processing equipment for the state administration and state financial institutions has been supplied mostly by importation or local production by foreign companies. In 1987, almost half of the production of foreign subsidiaries in the segment of data-processing equipment destined for the Brazilian market was absorbed by the Brazilian state. In contrast, just 24 per cent of the national companies' production of such equipment was acquired by state institutions in the same year [*SEI, 1989: 23*]. In relation to software, the federal administration's needs are met by in-house development. Only a small proportion of the federal administration's total spending in IT goods is in the acquisition of software, and the major share of this is of foreign origin [*SEI, 1986*]. This limited use of procurement power of the state to stimulate the national manufacture of data-processing equipment and software may be explained by centralization of the state administration which has carried out the policy of modernization of the state apparatus since the early 1960s [*Paiva, 1989*]. Centralization has required central agencies to process a large volume of information, thus pressing for data-processing equipment more powerful than those manufactured by national companies. This has created a feedback effect by which outdated equipment in the central administration is not replaced by national substitutes because of the existing software and processing 'culture' which has grown up within the state agencies. Prospects for a more effective use of government procurement power depend on decentralization of public administration, which would result in a larger demand for medium- to small-sized computers by lower-level state administration, and the establishment of standards and technical specifications that could stimulate local development of software.[33]

Financial incentives were created by the Informatics Law, Articles 13 to 15, and are regulated by Decree 92187, of 20 December 1985.[34] They are directed towards R&D, development of human resources, production and export of IT goods and services, development of software, and establishment of a domestic microelectronics sector.[35] Granting of these incentives started in 1986, after I PLANIN had defined the policy's goals for the period 1986-88. National IT companies in the microelectronics sector were the only ones eligible for the whole set of incentives defined in the Informatics Law. National companies acting in other IT areas could apply for some specific incentives. In fact, only 50 national companies out of the 300 registered at SEI applied for the incentives during that period [*Paiva, 1989: 157*]. Reporting their activities to SEI, 34 national companies that had taken advantage of the incentives appropriated just US$ 32 million in the period, complementing their own investments of around US$ 250 million. Thus, the incentives represented a much smaller proportion of the resources effectively spent - 13 per cent - than the limit defined by the Informatics Law - 30 per cent [*Paiva, 1989: 160*]. Small as these incentives might be, they nevertheless seem to have been significant for the development of a domestic microelectronics sector.

IT POLICY STRATEGY TOWARDS FOREIGN CAPITAL

Participation of foreign capital in the Brazilian electronics industry has been much less restricted than some liberal critics of the IT policy believe. Most of the telecommunications equipment sector is controlled by foreign capital; the same occurs in the production of consumer electronics.[36] Foreign capital dominates the Brazilian market for large computers, and this market has also benefited from the procurement power of the state. Foreign capital is also allowed to participate in the capital of national companies and, thus, indirectly to enter the reserved area. In this case, however, its participation can be only as a minority shareholder and may not lead to decision-making control on technological matters.[37] Furthermore, foreign capital is ineligible for fiscal incentives and can benefit from them only through participation in the composition of the capital of national companies. In fact, provisions of the Informatics Law link participation of foreign capital in the Brazilian market to high complexity technology (Article 22). Minority participation in the reserved portion of the market, increasing national content, and export performance are the IT policy's major limits on foreign capital.

However minor these restrictions may be, especially when contrasted with the overall benefits foreign companies have reaped from the strategy of market segmentation and state procurement, the IT policy's limitation on their participation in the profitable segment of smaller computers has provoked active antagonism. This has taken the form either of open confrontation, as was the case when IBM's subsidiary defied CAPRE Resolution 01,[38] or their refusal to transfer technology that national companies were willing to purchase, as was the case of minicomputers in the mid-1970s and UNIX some ten years later. This animosity has, nevertheless, changed with the implementation of the IT policy. Foreign subsidiaries have adapted well to the market reserve policy. Very few of them decided to withdraw and those that remained in the market have developed flexible strategies to cope with the IT policy. These strategies include bargaining from a position of strength without exchanging technology with national firms (IBM and Burroughs); bargaining from a position of weakness, agreeing to share technology with national partners (Sperry Rand, CII Honeywell Bull); and adapting to government restrictions by innovative marketing strategies without investing in manufacturing activities (Control Data, DEC, NCR) [*Katz, 1981: 140*]. The strategy of adaptation and closer collaboration with national hardware manufacturers and software companies seems to have become more widespread throughout the 1980s. This change is likely to be oriented by the desire of foreign subsidiaries to preserve their direct or indirect presence in all sectors of the Brazilian electronics industry.[39]

I have shown in this chapter how the Brazilian IT policy evolved from its first measures to allocate state agencies' use of data-processing equipment to the establishment of a comprehensive set of regulations institutionalized in Law 7232, the Informatics Law, in 1984. Extension of the policy's scope to cover most of the electronics industry reflected the government's perception of the linkages between different sectors of this industry. However, state actions towards the introduction of a more integrated IT policy happened some time after the launching of policies directed to the sectors of consumer electronics and telecommunications. The former is only partially covered by the present IT policy. These different objectives and strategies governing state actions towards sections of the electronics industry constituted a hindrance to the industry's development, as will be argued in Chapter 4. Market reserve for locally owned firms and import control were the two central instruments for the implementation of the policy. According to the Informatics Law, only the latter was due to end in 1992. The protectionist policy was less restrictive to foreign capital than would have been expected: Foreign subsidiaries dominate the sectors of consumer electronics and telecommunications, and are banned as independent producers only from domestic manufacture of smaller computers and other professional electronics equipment; foreign capital is allowed to enter the reserved market in association with local capital and in minority share. Foreign subsidiaries have not only benefited from state procurement, but the two biggest (IBM and Burroughs) have been protected from competition with other would-be entrants into the professional electronics sector of the market.

BRAZILIAN SOFTWARE POLICY BEFORE THE CONFLICT

Up to 1980, government action towards fostering the software industry in Brazil was almost nonexistent. Financial support for companies willing to develop software had been discussed by the Financiadora de Estudos e Projectos (FINEP) and by CAPRE, but without any concrete outcome. The Banco Nacional de Desenvolvimento Econômico (BNDE) had also made specific recommendations for its financing of projects in this sector, but these never became effective. Import control and authorization for local manufacture, which had been used successfully for hardware, were almost absent in governmental actions towards software. Beyond the practical difficulties in controlling the importation of goods such as software, import control was limited to those cases in which the remittance of foreign currency was involved. For those cases, contracts to purchase software should have been approved by INPI (Instituto Nacional de Propriedade Industrial), which would treat it either as specialized technical services or as a technology transfer agreement.[40] However, since foreign subsidiaries were not allowed to remit foreign currency as payment for imports from its parent company - a mechanism responsible for the majority of software imports up to 1980 - the bulk of software imports were out of the control of the Brazilian government. Authorization of local production was an efficient instrument to control development of the local hardware segment because it was required to obtain authorization to import parts and components. As software production relies heavily on the technological capability of engineers and technicians, and because software 'parts and components' are of an intangible nature, authorization of local production would be meaningless for the software sector.

The lack of explicit and clear governmental action towards the software sector (and also towards microelectronics) was one of the major criticisms that came out of the study made by the commission set up to analyse CAPRE's activities at the beginning of the Figueiredo administration, and which led to CAPRE's demise and the creation of SEI in 1979. The *Guidelines for National Informatics Policy* (discussed earlier in this chapter) prescribed governmental incentives for the local development of a software industry as one of its objectives. The directive was 'to stimulate, encourage and guide the development of software and services by national companies: to further the development of operating systems, support and application software, systems for distributed processing and communication network, software for data banks, and software that makes different equipment compatible'. In accordance with this general orientation, two actions were taken by SEI soon after its establishment: (i) setting up of a joint commission (SEI/INPI) to analyse the process of software imports and (ii) creation of a special commission for software and services to analyse the local market and recommend specific policy measures to foster this sector.

The report of the Special Commission for Software and Services, published in 1981, made recommendations for the protection of locally owned industry and for the control of software imports. These became the central core of the policy. Protection for the locally owned software industry was to be granted by a 'buy-Brazilian' policy and by actions to defend the property rights of software producers. In the first case, government procurement was the stronger recommendation coupled with a drive for software import substitution. In relation to property rights for software, as the adoption of any legal regime was rejected, the report recommended that (i) professionals and entrepreneurs in the IT area themselves identify any infringements to property rights and present them to their associations; (ii) SEI, INPI, and associations study and publish guidelines for protection of software; and (iii) the associations elaborate, publish, and enforce a code of ethics [*SEI, 1981: 95*].

The Commission made a real effort to strengthen the mechanism for the import control of software. They concluded that only control of commercialization could prevent indiscriminate entry of foreign software into the country, and that, in this way, it would be possible to reserve the local market for locally owned companies [*Costabile, 1982: 22*]. To control commercialization of software, the Commission advocated (i) creation of a registry for all software commercialized in the country; (ii) separation of the prices of hardware and software; (iii) participation of SEI and representatives of the associations of software companies in the approval of software import contracts; and (iv) inclusion of basic software in the list of products requiring INPI approval for importation [*SEI, 1981: 99-111*].

The recommendation for a software registry deserves closer examination. The suggestion was not merely to create such a registry, but to make registration a precondition for purchase of the software by state agencies, for the importation of equipment to which the software was linked, and for concession of fiscal incentives and financial support. It also recommended that INPI approve registration of software not developed locally; that SEI and INPI study the legal definition of software (technology transfer, copyright, or industrial property) in relation to payment for imports; and that SEI get from the Central Bank the agreement not to allow the remittance of foreign currency for payments of royalties for copyright on software, including its manuals and necessary documentation [*SEI, 1981: 99*].

Some of the Commission's recommendations were subsequently implemented by SEI. During the first years of its existence, SEI issued various normative acts to regulate the commercialization of foreign software in the country and to stimulate the local software industry. SEI's Normative Act 016/81, of July 1981, made incorporation of locally developed software a factor to be considered in the examination of projects for the local manufacture of hardware. SEI's Normative Act 022/81 created a registry to classify software: category A, locally developed by national individuals or companies; category B, foreign developed, without local equivalent, transferred to national companies by contract approved by INPI; category C, all other cases. Article 4 of SEI's Normative Act 022/81 declared that registration of software in category C (in which much of the imported software would fit) would not be accepted whenever there was a locally developed alternative, and/or if there was the possibility for local development of an equivalent. Registration, valid for a two-year period, was made a condition for government procurement of software. SEI's Normative Act 023/83 directed government procurement of software and services to locally owned companies. SEI's Normative Act 026/83 defined adoption of locally developed operating systems as a condition for approval of projects for local manufacture of microcomputers.

The Brazilian software policy, which had been launched in 1981 with the publishing of the report of the Special Commission for Software and Services, was still in its infancy when the Informatics Bill was sent to Congress in June 1984. As there had not been enough time since the recent measures had been issued for them to produce noticeable effects, there was no way to ascertain their usefulness before institutionalizing them, or any substitute, into law. In addition, views on the best way to protect IPRs of software were, in the early 1980s, highly controversial at both the domestic and international levels. These facts help to explain why the Informatics Law left open the regulation of software.

In December of that same year, a few months after the approval of the Informatics Law, Bill No. 260/84 defining principles for regulation of IPRs for software was introduced into the Brazilian Congress. This bill defined a *sui generis* regime of protection for the IPRs of software according to the following principles. (i) In addition to granting rights to the software producer, the law would grant rights to software users to high technical quality and good product performance. (ii) The rights of the software producer would have limited duration so that at the end of the term of protection there would remain technological content and economic interest in the software. (iii) Rules of protection for software would be compatible with those applied to the commerce of any other kind of technology. The rights granted to software producers by this bill were to use or authorize use of the program, including its various versions and derivations; to reproduce or authorize reproduction of the program by any physical means; to display, store, and commercialize programs and their versions; and to authorize third parties to display, store, and commercialize them. There would be no infringement of these rights when (i) reproduction of backup copies or adaptation was needed for adequate use of a legally acquired program; (ii) a program was similar to an existing program if the similarity was due exclusively to technical constraints, legal rules, technical specifications, use of algorithms, mathematical models, or formal procedures of public domain. Registration would be a condition of granting the rights and would require presentation of the source-code, internal specifications, program description, user's manual, and code language adopted when it was not of public knowledge. Protection would be granted for 15 years starting on the application date for registration. Software whose term of protection had expired or whose registration application was rejected would enter the public domain. A compulsory licence (i.e., compulsory granting of permission to use registered software) would be granted for (i) revision of alteration of registered software for specific applications in activities of relevant economic and social interest; (ii) the use, reproduction, or commercialization of software that had not been used, reproduced, or commercialized during the previous two years; (iii) making domestically manufactured machines compatible with foreign equipment currently used in Brazil. A fair price for the compulsory licence would be defined by a commission to be created by CONIN. The central government would also be able to expropriate software when required by public interest.

Bill No. 260/84 was read in the Senate floor and distributed to the Senate Committees of Constitution and Justice, Economy, and National Security, on 3 December 1984, immediately before legislative activities ended that year. On 16 May 1985, the Committee of Constitution and Justice delegated a Senator to study the matter and give an opinion on it. Almost three months later, the Brazilian 301 case was opened. Then, on 25 September 1985, Bill No. 260/84 was approved by the Senate Committee of Constitution and Justice. During October and November 1985, the Committee of Economy delegated in turn three different Senators to discuss the bill, which was finally approved by the Committee by the end of November. In April 1986, the bill was passed to the Committee of National Security. By this time, negotiations between the two countries had already reached a focal point. Another software bill was prepared and soon approved by both houses.[41] In December 1987, Bill No. 260/84 was shelved.

Concluding this section, I would say that until the Brazilian 301 case was opened, the Brazilian software policy had been in its infancy. There was a clear awareness of the limitations of transposing to the software sector the mechanism of import control that had been used effectively in fostering a locally owned hardware industry. Control of the commercialization of software within the Brazilian market became the central point of the policy. Toward this goal, a registry of software was created and used to prevent the commercialization of foreign products that had a 'local similar'. Notwithstanding the goal of attaining local capacity for the development of a variety of types of software by the mid-1980s, in 1986 the Brazilian software market, especially the segment of products for microcomputers, was dominated by software of foreign origin, an unknown amount being provided by piracy. Despite this, since CAPRE's time the Brazilian government had rejected copyright protection for IPRs of software, which had been already adopted in the developed countries (although not without considerable controversy, especially in France and Japan). The need by the rapidly growing microcomputer industry for liberal trade of foreign software, the short time period since the government's first fostering measures, and difficulties in approving a *sui generis* regime for software resulted in the software segment being among the few areas left open by the Informatics Law for future regulation.

CONCLUSIONS

The purpose of this chapter was to analyse one side of the foundation of the US/Brazil dispute - the Brazilian government's actions towards building a local electronics industry - which set the basis for the definition of an agenda for negotiation. I chose to approach this subject from the standpoint of the major policy issues that were the main topics in the conflict: the definition of the area reserved for nationally owned companies, including the measures for fostering domestic software production; the instruments for state intervention in the area; and the policy's strategy towards foreign capital.

Evolving from regulations to allocate the state agencies's use of data-processing equipment, the policy followed what I call a 'sideways and backward building strategy', in which the incentive to produce small computers and peripherals was enlarged sideways to cover other professional electronics goods and services and backward to include electronics parts and components. Thus, restrictions to market access and foreign direct investment in the Brazilian electronics industry were extended far beyond the initial measures taken in the late 1970s to restrict local manufacture of mini- and microcomputers and their peripherals to Brazilian-owned companies. Despite these restrictions, controlled importation of electronics components and local manufacture of electronics equipment by foreign subsidiaries in the nonreserved part of the Brazilian market were a means of access for foreign products and capital to that market left open by the protectionist policy. In contrast to the protective measures towards hardware, the Brazilian software policy was much less strict. During the mid-1980s, the Brazilian software market was dominated by foreign products, some of which were provided by illegal means. Protection for IPRs of software had, however, been rejected by the Brazilian government. Therefore, the Brazilian government's actions to foster a local electronics industry, besides being an experience that some other developing countries might want to emulate, had also created various contentious issues for international trade, despite being, as some of them were, in accordance to GATT.

4

ACHIEVEMENTS OF THE BRAZILIAN IT POLICY

In this chapter I discuss how domestic interests were affected by the IT policy's implementation and achievements, how they influenced the composition of the agenda, and how they helped define possible outcomes of the conflict. As discussed in Chapter 1, states as players in international games maintain their commitments to domestic goals and must consider domestic interests possibly affected by their international moves. In addition, states as players are not monolithic entities, and their negotiators must represent various interests - including state agencies and corporate interests - in negotiating a solution that can also satisfy domestic constituencies. Here, I show the achievements of the Brazilian IT policy and the challenges facing it, which come not from foreign sources but from the policy's implementation and the development of the domestic electronics industry itself. The discussion focuses on how the achievements and challenges of the IT policy impacted various domestic interest groups. A wide array of these groups had vested interests in the content of the IT policy and its implementation. These interests influenced the powers of negotiation as the relevant constituencies who would have to ratify any agreed solution to the conflict.

The discussion is presented in three main parts. The first summarizes the general achievements of the policy in terms of an overall appraisal of the evolution of the Brazilian IT market, the national corporations' market share, imports and exports, and employment I also compare Brazil's situation to that of other developing countries. In the second section I analyse the challenges still facing the policy in relation to costs of production and prices, capitalization of national corporations, forward and backward industrial linkages, and human resources. The third section presents the conclusions of the chapter. The analysis is based on published data and recent literature.[42]

IT POLICY ACHIEVEMENTS

Production in the Brazilian electronics industry has been growing rapidly since establishment of the IT policy in the mid-1970s. The latest available data show combined IT industry production to have reached US$ 6.8 billion in 1986, a figure almost twice as great as at the beginning of the decade. If the services and software sector is included, the Brazilian electronics industry in that year was worth more than US$ 8 billion. As can be seen in Table 4.1, the consumer electronics sector has had the greatest share of the industry's output, a position that does not, *prima facie*, suggest the efficacy of the IT policy, as this sector has not been subject to the policy's regulation. Nevertheless, the achievements of the professional electronics sector, which has had the second largest share of the industry's output and has been growing at the highest rate, provide a hint of the policy's effectiveness. In fact, production of the professional electronics sector is estimated to have been worth US$ 2.8 billion in 1988, of which manufacture of microcomputers by national firms was worth US$ 1 billion. These figures put the Brazilian market among the world's major IT markets, especially in relation to production of microcomputers.[43]

TABLE 4.1
THE BRAZILIAN INDUSTRIAL ELECTRONICS INDUSTRY, 1980-1988
(US$ MILLION CURRENT)

Sector	1980	1981	1982	1983	1984	1985	1986	1987	1988
Telecommunications	712	718	776	697	674	842	1050	na	na
Professional	860	1040	1508	1487	1833	2241	2380	2949	2848
Consumer	2174	1845	2101	1930	1914	2259	3137	na	na
Components	176	153	177	180	192	220	280	400	na
Software	na	na	na	na	na	914	1186	1346	1415
Electronics industry*	3922	3756	4562	4294	4613	5562	6847		

Source: GEICOM, for the sector of telecommunications, extracted from Tigre 1988:110; SEI 1989, for the sectors of professional electronics and software/services; Baptista [*1987*], for consumer electronics and components
Na (not available)
Data for 1988 are estimates
*Excluding the sector of software/services for which the data available are from 1985 onwards.

This performance of the Brazilian electronics industry is particularly significant when contrasted with overall industrial production under the instability that has characterized the Brazilian economy since the second oil crisis and the rise of international interest rates. The growing deficit in the Brazilian balance of payments and rising domestic inflation triggered the adoption of a recessionary monetary policy, which resulted in strict credit limits on public spending, and cuts in direct investments by the state, in governmental agencies' spending, and in imports by state companies. During this period, economic output fell: Between 1980 and 1983, the average annual growth rate of industrial production was minus six per cent and that of industrial employment was minus seven-point-three per cent [*Carneiro, 1986: 170*].

Foreign direct investment began a sharp decline in 1982. Worth US$ 2.8 billion in that year, the net direct foreign investment (total foreign investment minus reinvestment and repatriations) fell to US$ 1.1 billion in 1983 and US$ 850 million in 1984 [*Serra, 1988: 126*].[44] In contrast with these figures, foreign direct investment in the industrial branch of electrical goods, electronics, and communication grew throughout this period (Banco Central do Brasil 1990).

Despite its generally good achievements in the 1980s, especially relative to other industries, the electronics industry was affected by the economic instability reflected in different intensity in its various sectors (Table 4.2). The electronics industry showed a general trend of continuous growth in the 1980s which was, however, disturbed by fluctuations during the first three years of the decade.

TABLE 4.2
EVOLUTION OF BRAZILIAN INDUSTRIAL PRODUCTION, THE ELECTRONICS
INDUSTRY, AND THE PROFESSIONAL ELECTRONICS SECTOR, 1980-1988 (1981 = 100)

Year	Total industry	Electronics industry*	Professional electronics	Consumer	Telecommunications
1980	111.34	104.42	82.69	117.83	99.16
1981	100.00	100.00	100.00	100.00	100.00
1982	100.03	121.46	145.00	113.87	108.08
1983	94.86	114.32	142.98	104.61	97.08
1984	97.42	122.82	176.25	103.74	93.87
1985	108.93	148.08	215.48	122.44	117.27
1986	116.54	182.29	228.84	170.03	146.24
1987	126.68		283.55		
1988	119.26		273.84**		

Source: Fundação Getulio Vargas [*1990*]; SEI [*1989*].
* Excluding the sector of software/services.
** Estimate

These fluctuations in relation to the general trend were due mostly to the effects of economic instability, and the policies tailored to overcome it, especially in the consumer electronics and telecommunications sectors. And, as a consequence of decreases in the production of consumer electronics, the small domestic production of components, which is mostly directed to that segment, fluctuated accordingly.[45] Production of telecommunications equipment, highly dependent on Brazilian state investment, was directly affected by the measures taken to reduce government expenditures. Therefore, the significant achievements of the electronics industry in the economically unstable 1980s were due predominantly to the performance of the professional electronics sector, whose high growth rates were catalysed especially by the demand for banking automation. The significant role of banking automation in the growth of production of data-processing equipment is shown by the large share of domestic production destined for private or state-owned financial institutions. Their share of domestic data-processing equipment was around 30 per cent of the national companies' production until 1984, dropping to an average of 20 per cent afterwards, and around 30 per cent of the foreign subsidiaries' production in 1986-87 [*SEI, 1989: 23*].

One might be tempted to interpret the performance of the electronics industry in the 1980s not as a consequence of the IT policy but as a result (i) of a general modernization trend in the Brazilian economy and (ii) of the strategy of industrial companies acting in the domestic IT market. According to this alternative explanation, the growth of the Brazilian electronics industry would have occurred with or without any specific policy. This seems valid for the sector of consumer electronics, but definitely does not apply to the sector of professional electronics, particularly the manufacture of data-processing equipment. Here, the IT policy, with its instruments of market reserve and import control, was probably decisive in the establishment of a domestic production capability oriented to supply some of the goods the Brazilian economy needed. Domestic control of manufacturing decisions and a capability in production technology were built up as a direct consequence of the implementation of the policy. Technological capability and control over manufacturing decisions allowed the Brazilian financial institutions, for example, to satisfy their needs for banking-automation equipment within the domestic market. If it were not for the IT policy, banking automation would have relied on importation of equipment adapted to the particular Brazilian accounting procedures or would have been delayed until the unknown time when foreign subsidiaries in the local market became interested in designing a product specific to Brazilian conditions.

The national companies' share of production in the professional electronics sector is further evidence of the efficacy of the IT policy. As Table 4.3 shows, the national companies' share increased consistently throughout the 1980s, surpassing the foreign subsidiaries' share in 1984, eight years after the IT policy's first definition of a reserved market for nationally owned firms. The four foreign subsidiaries that had been operating in the Brazilian market since 1980 were four years later accompanied by another 23, reaching a total of 27 subsidiaries in 1984. On the other hand, the 37 national companies in 1980 had multiplied sixfold to become 230 national firms in 1984.

The significance of this accomplishment is understood better in historical perspective. The Brazilian industrial sector of electrical goods that became dedicated to the production of professional electronics equipment had been internationalized before the diffusion of digital electronics. IBM installed a subsidiary in Brazil in 1939 and Burroughs did so in 1953. This early participation in the Brazilian market gave these foreign subsidiaries two important advantages when they moved into the market of digital professional electronics: a close relationship with the user and a large marketing and maintenance base. These advantages reduced their costs of entering the new market [*Piragibe, 1988: 23*]. In 1961, the first IBM computer was assembled in Brazil and Burroughs started manufacturing peripheral equipment for computers in the Brazilian market in 1967. Foreign subsidiaries dominated the whole Brazilian market for professional electronics equipment until 1983. In fact, as recent analysis points out, the market reserve policy had the dual effect of freezing some of these historical relationships, giving the two previously established firms, IBM and Burroughs, substantial advantages over would-be entrants [*Evans and Tigre, 1989: 29*]. Since 1984, production by national companies has exceeded that of foreign subsidiaries, reaching an estimated value of US$ 2.9 billion in 1988 (Table 4.4). In computers excluded from the booming micro-computer market, the growth of production by foreign subsidiaries has fluctuated during the 1980s, slowing in 1983 and 1986. Production of smaller computers by national companies has grown continuously during the same period.

TABLE 4.3
NATIONAL COMPANIES' AND FOREIGN SUBSIDIARIES' PRODUCTION IN THE
BRAZILIAN PROFESSIONAL ELECTRONICS MARKET, 1980-1988
(US$ MILLION CURRENT)

Year	National	Foreign	Total	National %	Foreign %
1980	280	580	860	33	67
1981	370	670	1040	36	64
1982	558	950	1508	37	63
1983	687	800	1487	46	54
1984	952	881	1833	51	49
1985	1400	1278	2678	52	48
1986	2081	1311	3392	61	39
1987	2378	1638	4016	59	41
1988*	2948	1480	4428	66	33

Source: SEI [*1989*].
* Estimate

Thus, an important effect of the IT policy's implementation was development of a significant group of Brazilian industrialists in this high-technology area, particularly in the sector of professional electronics. Brazilian microcomputer producers were among the major beneficiaries of the protectionist policy. In contrast with other industrialists hurt by the economic instability of the 1980s, they expanded their activities in that period, increased their share of Brazilian industrial production, and, consequently, augmented their ability to influence political decisions related to the electronics industry.

TABLE 4.4
EVOLUTION OF BRAZILIAN PRODUCTION OF DATA-PROCESSING EQUIPMENT,
1980-1988 (1981 = 100)

Year	Total	National	Foreign
1980	82.69	75.68	86.57
1981	100.00	100.00	100.00
1982	145.00	150.81	141.79
1983	142.98	185.68	119.40
1984	166.15	228.92	131.49
1985	203.36	292.93	154.18
1986	204.42	335.68	131.94
1987	247.88	371.62	179.55
1988*	237.02	407.84	142.69

Source: SEI [*1989*].
* Estimate

It is noteworthy, however, that achievement of the national share of the data-processing market in Brazil resulted from the activity of a plurality of small companies, and that concentration of production in conglomerates began only recently. IBM billings in 1988 were three and a half times larger than those of the biggest national company, SERPRO, a state-owned company in the segment of services, and almost five times the aggregate billings of four companies (Itautec, Itaucom, Itaucam, and Rima) belonging to the biggest Brazilian conglomerate, Itau, which has activities in each sector of the electronics industry [*Dados e Idéias, 1989*]. Despite this fragmentation, the burgeoning national share of the domestic data-processing industry is an undeniable result of the Brazilian IT policy. The implications of this plurality of small companies for the development of the domestic electronics industry will be explored later in this chapter.

The Brazilian IT policy affected the domestic software sector very differently than it did the professional electronics sector. Besides the difficulties in applying to software the same policy instruments used to foster domestic hardware production (import control and authorization for production in the local market), governmental actions came later and were less consistent. Until 1980, there was almost no policy for fostering domestic software production.[46] Import control was limited to cases involving remittance of foreign currency, which excluded intrafirm operations and, therefore, affected only a small part of total software imports. The issue of regulation of IPRs for software had not been tackled by

54

Brazilian authorities until the mid-1980s. As discussed in Chapter 3, this liberal approach to software at that time facilitated growth in domestic hardware production, especially microcomputers. Thus, the software policy seems to have been subordinated to the interests of Brazilian microcomputer producers and the growth of the Brazilian software market has probably been linked only indirectly to the IT policy. The domestic software market followed the growth of domestic hardware production.

Considering the rapid growth of the Brazilian electronics industry in the last decade, it is not surprising that the Brazilian software market has been ranked among the world's fastest growing during the 1980s. According to the Organisation for Economic Cooperation and Development [*OECD 1988: Table 2*], this market was worth US$ 363.5 million in 1984, which put it among the ten largest in the world. The figures for 1987 (US$ 2,186.2 million) placed the Brazilian software market in sixth position in the international ranking.

According to Engel [*1986*], during the mid-1980s, the market comprised three major layers. The largest consisted of software for mainframes and medium-sized computers and was dominated by products of foreign origin. Basic software was distributed by manufacturers -mainly foreign subsidiaries - who also supplied some of the support software. Software houses supplied support software and some applications software. This latter type of software, when not supplied by the hardware manufacturer, was developed in-house or by locally owned companies. There were no noticeably significant cases of piracy. The second layer was made of software for minicomputers. This equipment was manufactured mainly by locally owned companies, and the great majority was incompatible with those in foreign markets. Basic and support software were developed and distributed by the hardware manufacturer. Applications software was developed in-house or supplied by locally owned software houses. There was a small occurrence of piracy, and this layer had a small share of the Brazilian software market. The third layer comprised software for microcomputers. Hardware was entirely compatible with its foreign equivalent and packaged software developed abroad ran on almost all microcomputers made locally. Basic software was distributed by the hardware manufacturer and, as a result of SEI's Normative Act 027/83, some operating systems had been developed locally. Support software was hardly developed in the country. They were supplied from abroad by representatives, smugglers, or the user him/herself. Applications software was either imported, developed in-house, or developed and distributed by locally owned software houses. This was the largest growing segment of the market. Because the equipment is compatible with foreign products and in the absence of efficient import control mechanisms, foreign software for microcomputers was made freely available (the only possible restriction coming from SEI's Normative Act 022/82) through representatives of foreign software houses, the users themselves, or piracy.

The software segment represented a small share of the Brazilian software and services market in the late 1980s. As Table 4.5 shows, data-processing services followed by technical assistance were the largest segments of domestic software and services production.

TABLE 4.5
BILLINGS OF THE BRAZILIAN SOFTWARE AND SERVICES SECTOR, 1986-88
(US$ MILLION CURRENT)

Segments	1986	1987	1988
Category I			
Programming and related services	87.6	98.7	104.9
Category II			
Data-processing services	551.8	560.2	525.9
Computer facilities management	62.9	95.5	97.5
Category III			
Technical assistance	254.3	270.3	351.1
Data-bank information services	54.3	122.7	110.8
Consultancy in IT	47.9	56.7	54.7
Training	17.9	25.6	25.5
Planning	10.5	13.6	20.9
Engineering	13.9	12.8	15.4
Auditing	35.1	36.8	44.2
*TOTAL**	1,186.3	1,346.3	1,415.4

Source: SEI [*1988d*].
* Including unclassified services.

Software - category I - was responsible for only 7 per cent of each year's total production of the sector.

Import control was one of the main justifications for launching the IT policy in the late 1970s and, as I have already pointed out in this chapter, one of the strongest policy instruments. In 1975, Brazilian imports of electronics goods were valued at US$ 574 million, of which half was telecommunications and broadcasting equipment, 26 per cent computers, and 16 per cent electronic components. In the same year, Brazilian electronics exports were worth US$ 135 million, of which 44 per cent were computers and 37 per cent products of mass communication and entertainment [*Piragibe, 1988: 92, Table 2*]. Import controls began in 1976 and electronics imports fell from US$ 574 million in the preceding year to less than US$ 150 million in each of the subsequent four years. The 1975 level of IT imports was restored only in 1984, when the domestic market had already reached a considerable size. As can be seen in Table 4.6,

56

while the Brazilian non-oil imports have fluctuated due to the restrictive policies already mentioned, importation of electronics, despite being controlled, has grown throughout the 1980s due to development of the domestic electronics industry. Electronics goods' share of total non-oil imports has increased from less than two per cent in the period 1977-80, to around nine per cent since 1984.

TABLE 4.6
BRAZILIAN NON-OIL IMPORTS AND IT IMPORTS, 1977-88
(US$ MILLION CURRENT)

Year	Total non-oil imports	IT goods imports	% IT imports/total non-oil
1977	7,209	102	1.4
1978	9,517	144	1.5
1979	11,681	147	1.2
1980	13,550	259	1.9
1981	11,491	304	2.6
1982	9,828	505	5.1
1983	6,821	440	6.8
1984	6,418	605	9.4
1985	7,735	713	9.2
1986	11,195	729	6.5
1987	9,199	841	9.1
1988	5,786	636*	10.9

Source: Fundação Getulio Vargas [*1990*]; SEI, extracted from Paiva [*1989: 118*].
* Through 30 September

No organized information is available on software imports in Brazil, despite the general acknowledgement of its large share of the market. However, software imports can be estimated from the fragmentary data available. Taking OECD figures for the Brazilian software market in 1984 (US$ 363.5 million)[47] and SEI's data on imported products' share of all software registered at that agency in 1984 (80 per cent),[48] one can estimate software imports to have been around US$ 290 million in 1984. The increase in software imports from the early to the late 1980s in Brazil can be illustrated by contrasting this estimation of 1984 imports with Gaio's estimation of software imports in 1987 at US$ 1,087 million (90.6 per cent of US$ 1.2 billion of software traded in that year).[49] Gaio's estimation of software imports is almost equivalent to the billings of the entire Brazilian software and services sector in that year, and more than ten times the billings of the domestic programming and related services segment. These comparisons must be taken as very crude approximations, but they serve to illustrate the jump in software imports from the early to the late 1980s and the relative significance of imports versus domestic production. While there is wide recognition that some of the imported software was smuggled into the country, there is no way to estimate the share of imports provided by illegal means.

The origin of Brazilian IT imports has predominantly been the US market. Nevertheless, the US share of total Brazilian electronics imports has declined in recent years, falling from 54 per cent in 1984-85, to 50 per cent 1986, and 48 per cent in 1987 [*Paiva, 1989: 119*]. Exports by the Brazilian electronics complex have been very small. Total Brazilian IT exports were worth US$ 267 million in 1986, which represents four per cent of the electronics industry's total production. In 1988, total exports are estimated to have reached the same amount. Data-processing equipment has been the largest share of these exports. The two biggest foreign subsidiaries in the domestic market, IBM and Unisys, have been responsible for almost all exports of this kind of equipment. The leading destination of these products has been the United States, which received 24 per cent of Brazilian data-processing exports in 1987, followed by Japan with 21 per cent, and Canada with 12 per cent. The small volume of Brazilian IT exports may suggest that local market potential has not yet been completely exploited, but it may also suggest lack of export orientation of domestic firms or, as some critics of the policy point out, lack of international competitiveness of Brazilian-made IT products. All three factors may contribute to the poor export performance, especially for the national companies, whose share of total Brazilian IT exports has been very small. In contrast, the parent company's trade strategy seems to be an important factor contributing to foreign subsidiaries' small export volume.

Thus import control has been an effective instrument used by the Brazilian government to foster a domestic electronics industry, excluding the software sector. Control of software imports, as discussed in Chapter 3, was limited to transactions paid in foreign currency, which represented a small share of the total. The major consequence of this control was that 'in practice, this instrument has only hindered the initiative of local firms attempting to import through legal channels, whereas it has little influence on intra-firm operations of local subsidiaries of MNCs [multinational corporations] with their parent company' [*Gaio, 1991: 160*].

Domestic software producers have not reaped significant benefits from the IT policy not only because of the loose implementation of import control, but also due to the lack of protection for IPRs of software. For the producers in other sectors of the electronics industry covered by the IT policy, particularly the telecommunications equipment and professional electronics sectors, import control produced economic opportunities that induced foreign subsidiaries and affiliates to manufacture within the Brazilian market and stimulated nationally owned companies to find their place in it by supplying electronics goods that otherwise would have been imported.

The other side of the coin is that international trade of IT goods, especially the inward flow of electronics products, has been significantly affected by the policy. While this result was exactly what the IT policy was designed to achieve, and despite IT goods' growing share of Brazilian non-oil imports, it has created an area of international friction involving market-seeking countries, especially the United States. Brazil/US trade relations in IT goods during the 1980s have shown a deficit on the Brazilian side and a slight trend toward diversification of foreign suppliers to the Brazilian market. The growth in software imports in Brazil without protection for IPRs has made the country a target for the attacks of software exporters.

This overview of the Brazilian electronics industry would be incomplete without a word about the IT policy's achievements in relation to employment and skill generation. National companies have employed the majority of workers in the domestic IT sector since 1982. These companies' share of total employment in the electronics industry was 78 per cent in 1987 and an estimated 80 per cent in 1988 [*SEI, 1989: 15*]. The majority of highly skilled employees (those with a university degree) have also been with national companies since the beginning of the 1980s. The national firms' share of these highly skilled workers was estimated at 73 per cent in 1987, and slightly higher in 1988. More significantly, while engineers in foreign subsidiaries are mostly employed in non-technical activities such as marketing, management, and administration, national companies employ them in R&D activities [*Piragibe et al., 1983; Hewitt, 1988*]. Analysts of employment patterns in other sectors of the Brazilian electronics industry or in the IT industry of other developing countries agree on the special features of the Brazilian experience. The employment model of the Brazilian sector of professional electronics has shown 'that it is possible to do more than simply assemble goods designed elsewhere and that this can provide jobs within the industry and, indirectly, in other parts of the economy' [*Hewitt, 1988: 167*]. The IT policy has allowed the social benefits of job creation and skill generation to be internalized in Brazil.

Finally, it is useful to assess Brazil's IT policy relative to the development of domestic electronics industries in other developing countries. Brazil's IT policy has been compared to that of the Asian NICs, for example, and was considered less successful due to its domestic orientation [*Cline, 1987*]. Recent analysis has shown that this stereotypical appraisal only partially reflects the Brazilian experience [*Piragibe, 1988; Evans and Tigre, 1989*]. Brazil's electronics market in the late 1980s was about one and a half times greater than that of South Korea, three times greater than that of India, and about eight times greater than that of Argentina [*Piragibe, 1988: 86-7*]. Brazil is the largest and most diversified producer of professional electronics equipment among those countries, having surpassed South Korea in the local production of non-commodity computers, for example. Participation of foreign subsidiaries has been more important in Brazil than in other developing countries. Foreign subsidiaries have a much more important role as producers for both export and domestic markets in Brazil than in Korea' [*Evans and Tigre, 1989: 29*]. Evans and Tigre [*1989*] point out that Brazilian computer firms are still no match for the Koreans in their experience in electronics manufacturing, financial resources, or international market expertise. But they also show that computer sales of the chaebol (the large and diversified IT industrial groups in Korea) are in general smaller - not larger - than those of the firms acting in the Brazilian market and that some national companies in Brazil have begun to acquire experience in multiple sectors of the electronics industry. However, South Korean companies are now the world's third largest producers of VLSI (very large systems integration) memories and India has established a complete technological cycle in the production of LSI (large system integration) and VLSI chips [*Piragibe, 1988; Evans and Tigre, 1989*]. Brazil has yet to produce significant results in these strategic areas.

CHALLENGES FACING THE IT POLICY

Like any other development policy, the Brazilian IT policy had weaknesses that constituted major challenges to be faced by the government and society. These weaknesses nurtured domestic criticism of the policy and generated pressure to change it from within Brazilian society. On the other hand, vested interests that grew with the implementation of the policy, including corporate interests within state agencies, became a prime source of resistance to change. In this section, I explore the linkages between the implementation of the Brazilian IT policy and these domestic pressures that supported and opposed efforts to change it.

Several challenges facing the IT policy stem from the structure of the electronics industry and its history of development. Principal among these are (i) disarticulation among its various segments with consequently poor interindustrial links; (ii) fragmentation in the professional electronics sector; which affects the scale of production; and (iii) weak backward and forward linkages with the rest of the industrial sector. These problems, together with the scarcity of financial resources and the need to keep up with the frantic pace of technological change, constitute the key challenges to be faced by the industrialist and dealt with by the policy.

The electronics industry's various sectors have been subjected to policies implemented in different and sometimes conflicting ways by independent state agencies. The policies' disarticulation has aggravated the poor intersectoral links within the electronics industry, especially links between the components sector and the rest of the industry. Liberal policies towards the consumer electronics sector, which has been purchasing IT components on the international market, have been particularly damaging to the development of local microelectronics production. Components account for more than half of the total production cost of IT goods. They are either imported or supplied by local subsidiaries of transnational corporations. Brazilian-made components supplied by foreign subsidiaries are sold in the Brazilian market for prices two to five times higher than in the international market [*Tigre, 1988: 119-20*], due partly to the small size of the domestic market. This is a serious challenge to the policy: Domestic production of microelectronics components at reasonable prices is necessary to reduce production costs in the electronics industry. However, easy access to foreign products by the major user of these components - the sector of consumer electronics - has restricted development of the strategic microelectronics sector. Consequently, IT industrialists - particularly those in the professional electronics sector - compelled by the IT policy to buy Brazilian-made components at higher prices than in the international market, would probably welcome changes in the policy in the direction of diminishing control on importation of components. On the other hand, the same group of industrialists would probably oppose general liberalization of IT import control. Resistance to change in the policy would come not only from those industrialists directly affected by the reduction of protection but also from within the state agencies in charge of implementing these policies. The policy's disarticulation had originally been an expression of a lack of consensus among state organisations in relation to substantive goals. These different goals crystallized into corporate interests and became a hindrance to attempts at overcoming the problems they created.

Fragmentation in the professional electronics sector has resulted in small-scale production, which, combined with the absence of a strong research base and an inefficient upstream supply industry, has led to high unit costs [*Tigre, 1988: 117*]. Brazilian firms would have to triple their monthly output of some 1,000 professional microcomputers in 1987 to improve their economies of scale and justify more efficient production methods, such as the introduction of automated assembly. Considering the current market size and assuming no exports, this would allow for a single professional microcomputer firm in Brazil where there are today more than thirty [*idem: 118*]. Small-scale production does not stimulate independent design in local firms that have no established research tradition. The most successful cases of local design have occurred in the automation segment, especially with programmable controls, supervision systems for petrochemical and steel-making plants, and numerical control for locally designed tools. For the more sophisticated and standardized numerical control or other industrial automation systems such as robots and CAD/CAM, there is no satisfactory local design and local production is done only under licensing agreements. For small processing systems, technology is acquired via reverse engineering, although in some cases there has been indigenous innovations. However, firms in consumer electronics and many locally owned ones in professional electronics make no effort to improve their products technologically [*idem: 135*].

Although national products are sold at higher prices than their equivalents in the international market, it is worth noting that the price gap has been declining rapidly and that prices are higher in both the reserved and the unreserved portions of the Brazilian market.[50] Price reduction of electronics goods, which has occurred in almost every country, has also been observed in Brazil. The average price of Brazilian-made computers and peripherals, between August 1986 and August 1989, decreased 42 per cent for PC-XT twin disk drive, 52 per cent for PC-XT with 20/30MB hard disk, 18 per cent for monochrome monitors, 44 per cent for printers, and 30 per cent for five-and-a-quarter-inch floppy drives. In a shorter period, from December 1986 to March 1989, price decreases in consumer electronics were less significant: five per cent for a 14-inch colour television and 37 per cent for video-cassette recorders, the latter being similar to the price reduction for computers. PC-XT microcomputers made in Brazil cost, on average, only 22 per cent more than technically similar products available in the English and French markets [*Tigre, 1989*].[51] Related to peripherals, Brazilian prices in 1989 were 11 per cent higher for monitors, 14 per cent higher for printers, and 60 per cent higher for floppy drives.[52] Consumer electronics prices in Brazil exceeded prices in the United States by 38 per cent for television sets, 200 per cent for video-cassette recorders, and 57 per cent for compact-disc players. This suggests that a more liberal import policy for consumer electronics has not resulted in greater production efficiency, measured by price and price reduction, than the protectionist policy for professional electronics. While these data help to put criticism of the IT policy into perspective, reduction of the price gap remains a challenge for industrialists and the state. This price gap is at the root of the increase in illegal imports. It is also an important component of the dissatisfaction of some groups of consumers who have been prevented from buying more advanced and cheaper IT goods.

Brazil's lack of a comprehensive industrial policy has hindered the development of the domestic electronics industry because of the concomitant absence of conditions needed for strong forward and backward linkages. The lack of strong backward linkages may help to explain the high production costs of Brazilian IT products: Prices of nonelectronic inputs are significantly higher in Brazil than in the international market [*Erber, 1989*]. Lack of a comprehensive industrial policy also restricts development of forward linkages between the electronics industry and other industrial activities. For example, introduction of IT into the capital-goods industry was delayed during the 1980s not by technical factors, but by instability in the Brazilian economy and by the policies designed to overcome it. The slowing rate of investment, which was a consequence of a policy of nonselective economic adjustments, paralysed the process of diffusion of IT into the capital-goods industry. Modernization of these industries, being highly expensive, was virtually halted, and the demand for domestic electronics production equipment decreased. This decreased demand provoked an increase in unit production costs and thus higher prices, which further aggravated the trend for decreasing demand. Capital goods industrialists are among those who have pressed the state for some liberalization of import control upon electronics production equipment. One of the strategic challenges still to be faced by the Brazilian state is integration of the IT policy within an overall industrial policy that recognizes modernization of the capital-goods industry as a central goal.

During the rapid growth in the electronics market, national industrialists had no great difficulty in obtaining financial resources for investment in capital and technology. Recently, however, high inflation and high interest rates have made it risky to rely on credit as a source of financing. The alternative of selling shares to the public has produced positive results for a few firms, but the recent failure of three microelectronics companies to sell their shares demonstrates the current difficulties in attracting new investment. Locally owned firms have been encouraged to merge in order to achieve economies of scale and scope, and to strengthen their financial positions. Despite the negative reactions among local industrialists, difficulties in obtaining sufficient investment capital have been pushing medium-sized and smaller firms to merge with local conglomerates. There are five electronic conglomerates in Brazil operating in various sectors of the electronics industry. Itau and Machline (SID) are the two biggest, with significant participation in the sectors of professional and consumer electronics, components, and telecommunications and billings of US$ 424 million and US$ 430 million, respectively, in 1987 [*Tigre, 1988: 125*].[53] For hundreds of other small companies, however, merger has not been the solution to their financing problems. For them, either the Brazilian state must provide the financial support they need or they will have to look elsewhere for the necessary resources. Relaxation of the policy's controls on foreign direct investment, especially facilitating association of locally owned companies with foreign investors, would be welcomed by many Brazilian IT industrialists.

Finally, providing enough properly trained personnel needed for the electronics industry is also a challenge for the IT policy. This includes not only production personnel, but also the highly skilled people needed for research and development. Improving the conditions for research in universities and research centres is also crucial, as conditions of research facilities have been far below acceptable levels [*Toni, 1989: 70*].

CONCLUSION

In this chapter, the achievements and weaknesses of Brazil's IT policy were discussed to show the wide range of domestic interests the Brazilian authorities had to consider in defining an agenda for international negotiations. This policy was responsible for fostering a domestic electronics industry with significant participation by national companies, either in the specific sense of capital and technology control being in Brazilian hands or in the less restrictive sense of Brazilians holding a majority of voting shares. In the professional electronics sector, implementation of this policy has resulted in the development of politically influential group of domestic industrialists. These industrialists comprise a plurality of small producers and a few entrepreneurs of large conglomerates that have achieved diversified production and high growth rates even in a situation of economic instability and recession. This group was among the major beneficiaries of the policy, especially when contrasted with domestic software producers, but also saw its growth prospects limited by the policy's weaknesses.

Brazil's IT policy has also fostered a number of weaknesses in the Brazilian IT industry: poor interindustrial links; fragmentation of the professional electronics sector, producing problems in economies of scale; price gap; weak backward and forward linkages; insufficient financial resources for investment in capital and technology; and poor research facilities. Import control and restrictions to foreign direct investment, which had been responsible for the formation of many groups of Brazilian IT industrialists, also limited the prospects for future development of some of these groups and of various other groups of Brazilian industrialists.

Compared with the IT industries in other developing countries, the weaknesses engendered by Brazil's IT policy are poor development of the microelectronics sector, small company size, limited financial resources, and limited expertise in international markets. Despite its weaknesses, the Brazilian model has become a source of inspiration for other developing countries in the formulation of industrial policies as they attempt to compensate for technological dependence in high-technology areas.

The analysis in this chapter and the preceding one shows the complexity of interests that the Brazilian authorities had to consider in defining the agenda for negotiations. Some interested parties among the IT industrialists would have been receptive to relaxation of the central instruments of the protectionist policy, but others would have opposed it. Nevertheless, all of them would probably fear that any changes, even those they could approve, might signal a general liberalization of the IT sector and, consequently, oppose them. Relaxation of import control on some IT goods might be welcomed by some IT industrialists but considered a threat by others. Loosening of restrictions on foreign direct investment in the Brazilian IT sector would be feared more than loosening of the conditions for association with foreign investors. On the other hand, interested industrialists within other sectors and many groups of IT users would be receptive to a general liberalization of the IT policy. Thus, considering the interests of domestic groups of producers - including many in the IT sector - and users, the agenda for negotiation could have included some points in the policy whose change would be ratified by relevant interested groups.

From the standpoint of the Brazilian state apparatus, definition of the agenda for negotiations was equally complex. Evolution of the IT policy until the passing of the Informatics Law and the opening of the Brazilian 301 case shows that keeping the policy with its wide scope intact was probably high on Brazil's preference ordering of potential outcomes. However, Brazilian negotiators had to anticipate resistance or even active opposition from diverging corporate interests within the state apparatus in setting priorities for negotiating the IT policy.

5

THE US FIGHT FOR MARKET ACCESS AND INTELLECTUAL PROPERTY RIGHTS

The Brazilian 301 case was not the only trade conflict opened by the US government in accordance with the US Trade Act in 1985. Nor was this kind of initiative the only action US trade authorities have taken to change alleged unfair trade practices. The Brazilian 301 case was part of an American offensive against several of its trade partners, including the developed economies of Japan and the EU and the newly industrializing South Korea. This offensive has been motivated, as I will show in the present chapter, by changes in the US position in the world economy and by changes in American trade policy, which, since the Second World War, has been marked by the contradictory trends of protectionism and liberalism. This contradiction in American trade policy has been made exceptionally clear since the 1980s. It is in this context that the US/Brazil conflict shall be analysed.

While in Chapters 3 and 4 I discussed one side of the dispute's foundation - the Brazilian IT policy - this chapter is dedicated to discussion of the other side of the dispute base: the American fight for market access and regulation of IPRs. The purpose here is to discuss the factors that made US economic and political goals incompatible with the Brazilian IT policy. This analysis shows the factors that led not only to the opening of the Brazilian 301 case, but also to the Americans' preference ordering of possible satisfactory outcomes of the dispute related to their goals in bilateral as well as in multilateral games.

The deceleration in global economic growth and international trade, the decline in competitiveness of US exports in relation to those of other developed and developing countries, and the growing knowledge-intensity in production have been cited to justify protectionist trade policies in industrial countries, especially the United States. These protectionist policies in turn have led to a growing number and increased intensity of cases of interstate trade friction. Changes in the world economy during the 1980s have also made the regulation of new issues emerge as an issue in negotiations on world trade liberalization. Bilateral trade conflicts have been exploited as a way to show the need for new international regulations, as a means to ensure third-party compliance with future deals, and to force trade liberalization agreements beneficial to the stronger parties.

MAJOR ECONOMIC TRENDS OF THE WORLD ECONOMY IN THE 1980s

The aim of this section is to depict the most salient changes in the world economy in the 1980s that have triggered initiatives by developed countries to increase the competitiveness of their exports, and to open up foreign markets.

For the purpose of understanding the external environment in which the Brazilian 301 case transpired, the most striking changes in the world economy in the 1980s were (i) accentuation of the slow-down in world economic growth; (ii) declining competitiveness of US exports and increased American comparative advantages in the production and trade of services; (iii) the export performance of newly industrializing countries (NICs),[54] which greatly increased their share of world exports of manufactured goods; and (iv) the growing knowledge-intensity in production and, especially, increased application of information technologies in the production of goods and services. These general trends of the world economy in the 1980s have had three major implications for the Brazilian 301 case: (i) they provided justification for protectionist trade policies in the developed economies; (ii) they led to the emergence of new issues for multilateral trade agreements in the name of which bilateral negotiations have become even tougher; and (iii) they placed a focus on a legal protection system for IPRs to allow producers of knowledge-intensive technologies to enjoy the fruits of their investment in know-how.

Deceleration in Economic Growth

During the post-war period until the early 1970s, world economic growth was made possible by stable currency exchange rates and liberalization of international trade promoted by successive rounds of multilateral negotiations. In the 1980s, growing protectionism among industrial countries and instability in the international economy resulted in a deceleration of world trade that exceeded the decline in the growth of world output. The average annual rate of growth of world production in agriculture, mining, and manufacturing in the period 1980-87 was consistently lower than in the two previous decades. This well-documented tendency can be illustrated by the average annual change in the world production of all merchandise, which fell from six per cent in the 1960s, to four per cent in the 1970s, and to two-and-a-half per cent in 1980-87 [*Sassoon, 1990: 16*]. The decline in growth of world output was sharper in the early 1980s. This decrease affected the rate of growth in production of manufactured goods acutely; only in 1987 did the growth rate reach the average rates of the preceding decade. The positive link between world output and trade was also made clear

68

in the 1980s, when high rates of production growth coincided with higher rates of trade growth. However, the deceleration of international trade growth was steeper than the deceleration in the growth of world output: The average annual growth rate of all merchandise exports fell from eight-and-a-half per cent in the 1960s, to five per cent in the 1970s, and to three per cent in 1980-87. Exports of manufactured goods were affected most: The average annual growth rate fell from 10.5 per cent in the 1960s, to seven per cent in the 1970s, and to four-and-half per cent in the 1980s [*Sassoon, 1990: 16*].

The slowdown in world economic growth impacted developed and developing economies differently. For most of the developed economies, the 1980s was a period of deep economic restructuring and fast technological change, but also of slow recovery in domestic production with its resulting increase in unemployment figures. This was particularly the case for the European countries and the United States. For the developing countries, the 1980s was a period of great differentiation. While the Asian NICs achieved significant rates of growth in production and exports, other developing countries, especially those hit hard by the debt crisis, suffered through drastic downward adjustments, including a reduction of real domestic consumption and sometimes unsuccessful attempts to expand exports. While the Asian NICs' share of world trade increased from 7.8 per cent in 1980 to 9.8 per cent in 1985, the share of Latin America (including the two NICs Brazil and Mexico) fell slightly from 5.7 per cent in 1980 to five per cent in 1985, and Africa's declined from 4.8 per cent in 1980 to 3.6 per cent in 1985 [*SELA, 1988: 83*]. Asian NICs have succeeded in diversifying their exports, but African countries continue to rely on commodities for their export earnings.

Declining Competitiveness of American Exports

Unlike Japan and West Germany, the United States experienced a growing trade deficit during the 1980s. With domestic demand growing at higher rates than in other industrial countries, a collapse of imports by the debt-burdened countries, and its exports being negatively affected by the dollar's 50 per cent appreciation and the more rapid rates of innovation in competitor countries, American exports lost competitiveness and huge deficits accumulated in the current account. As Table 5.1 shows, growing trade deficits in merchandising were not alleviated by the positive (but declining) surplus in trade in services.This, combined with growing unilateral transfers, resulted in large current account deficits which started in 1982 at US$ 8.5 billion and peaked at US$ 154.7 billion in 1987.

The policies developed to overcome the slowdown in growth had a significant effect. The combination of fiscal stimulus and monetary restraint succeeded in pulling the economy out of the 1982 recession, helped to create millions of jobs during the decade, and, with the fall of oil prices, allowed a reduction of the US inflation rate from its peak of 14 per cent in 1980 to around four per cent by 1988. These positive results were counterbalanced, however, by a rising internal fiscal deficit and an external trade deficit. Private saving did not rise to compensate for the public-sector savings and the gap was filled by foreign resources. Significantly, however, the inflow of foreign capital was not directed to investment but to finance private and government consumption [*Cline, 1989*]. Net national investment as a function of net national savings in the period 1962-85 was lowest in the United States compared with some other European countries and Japan [*Hatsopoulos et al., 1990: 125*]. In short, macroeconomic policies and lack of innovation at the micro level in the United States during the 1980s combined to create a large and growing current account deficit.

TABLE 5.1
BALANCE OF US CURRENT ACCOUNT, 1980-1988
(US$ BILLION CURRENT)

Year	Merchandise balance	Service balance	Unilateral transfers	C/account balance
1980	-25.5	34.9	-7.6	1.8
1981	-28.8	42.3	-7.5	6.8
1982	-36.4	36.8	-8.9	-8.5
1983	-67.1	30.3	-9.5	-46.3
1984	-112.5	17.6	-12.1	-107.0
1985	-122.2	22.0	-15.0	-115.2
1986	-144.6	21.0	-15.3	-138.9
1987	-160.3	19.0	-13.4	-154.7
1988	-127.9	2.7	-13.0	-138.2

Source: Cline [*1989: 72-3*].

The decline in competitiveness of US exports also was due to an inadequate level of investment in both visible and intangible capital. This was expressed as a low rate of investment in R&D and in manufacturing, an ensuing lower rate of growth in productivity,[55] and thus a decline in the American managerial edge [*Sassoon, 1990: 18; Hatsopoulos et al., 1990: 109*]. Although American expenditures on R&D were much higher than its competitors' in absolute figures, the US spending as a percentage of its gross national product (GNP) declined constantly from 2.8 per cent in 1964 to 2.1 per cent in 1977-78. Beginning in the late 1970s it recovered, but reached its level of the early 1960s only in the mid-1980s. Meanwhile, in West Germany and Japan, which had spent around one-and-a-half per cent of their GNP in R&D in the early 1960s, these ratios grew steadily throughout the whole period during which US ratios were declining and matched the US figures by the beginning of the 1980s. This investment is reflected in patent registration: by 1970 Japanese patent applications in the

United States already outnumbered those of American residents [*Kaplinsky, 1988a: 68-9*]. More significant, though, than the relative decline in American R&D expenditures is the fact that most of the US resources were directed to defence R&D, while West Germany and Japan invested mostly and increasingly in non-defence research [*National Science Foundation, 1987*]. The spillover of military technology on which much of the technological hegemony of the United States was built until the 1960s has been reduced because military priorities have differed from civilian needs [*Mowery and Rosenberg, 1989: 148-9*].

The result of declining competitiveness of American exports has also been expressed in its share of the world market for high-technology industries. This is the case of electronics based products. A recent study showed that American companies' share of the IT products market in 1984 and 1987 decreased for components [all semiconductors, central processing units (CPUs), dynamic random access memories (DRAMs), and application-specific integrated circuits (ASICs)] personal computers, floppy drives, hard drives, displays, dot matrix printers, and private branch exchanges (PBXs). During those years, American companies improved their share of the world market only in software, local area networks (LANs), and laser printers [*US Commerce Department, 1990*].

Export Performance of Newly Industrialized Countries

Since the 1970s, and especially during the 1980s, some of the NICs emerged as significant players in the world economy. Compared with the industrial coun-tries, which had shown large decreases in growth rates since the 1970s, the performance of the NICs was remarkable. They grew consistently from 1960 to 1981 and survived two major oil crises, while maintaining an average annual growth rate greater than eight per cent. During the 1980s they too suffered an economic crisis, which was reflected in growth rates lower than in the previous two decades. But even so, their average annual growth rate in the first half of the 1980s, 4.8 per cent, was much higher than the 2.3 per cent rate in the industrial market economies [*Moon, 1990: 160*]. Among them, however, the Asian countries performed better than Brazil and Mexico. The Asian NICs grew at average annual rates of 6.8 per cent in 1980-85 while Brazil and Mexico stagnated at 1.3 and 0.8 per cent, respectively [*Moon, 1990: 162*]. At the beginning of the decade the NICs surpassed the industrial economies in manu-facturing share of gross domestic product (GDP), with the Asian countries showing more significant changes in industrial structure than Brazil and Mex-ico.

The most striking feature of the NICs' performance in the 1980s was their achievements in exports of manufactured goods. Their average annual growth rate of exports were very high, with South Korea's being the most impressive at 22 per cent in the 1970s. This export achievement of South Korea was

71

followed by Taiwan and Hong Kong. Mexico, Brazil, and Singapore had slightly lower rates of export growth in the 1970s [*Moon, 1990: 161*]. The structure of the exports by the NICs have undergone a drastic change since the 1960s, and this change was responsible for their performance during the 1980s. For all of them, manufactured goods increased greatly their share of total exports. By the mid-1980s, manufactured goods' share of total exports was over 90 per cent for the Asian NICs [*Naya, 1990: 162*], while their share was only 62 per cent in Brazil and 60 per cent in Mexico [*Urrutia, 1990: 201*]. At the same time, manufactured goods' share of total exports was 98 per cent in Japan and 77 per cent in the United States [*Naya, 1990: 162*].

Growing Knowledge Intensity in Production

Technological changes that had already been acknowledged during the 1970s have greatly developed in the 1980s, being characterized by the growing knowledge intensity in production. The most impressive trend has been the speed with which technologies based on microelectronics have been introduced into the production of goods and services. The increasing information component in production achieved during the 1980s has been interpreted as an indication of a new technological revolution [*Perez, 1985*]. This technological revolution has been fuelled by greatly decreasing costs of microelectronic components, the pervasive applications of IT, and IT's capacity to improve the quality of capital goods, labour, and products. In fact, at least within the developed market economies, the pervasiveness of information technology has made it the central component of the whole economic system. Together with advances in biotechnology and new materials, the rapid diffusion of IT and the great increase in efficiency it brings are shaping a new technological era. The potential world economic growth these new technologies are going to yield and the extent to which their benefits will be shared worldwide are, nevertheless, far from being evident. A crucial point in this respect is the possibility of the new technological 'revolution' spreading to developing countries. The success of the new technologies, especially microelectronics, in increasing the competitiveness of their industries will depend on developing countries' capacity to capture the strategic advantages of unbundling this new and more difficult set of technologies [*Kaplinsky, 1988b*].

Technological innovation has become a fundamental way for companies to face competition. The need for continuous updating of production technology and the decreasing life cycle of the new products and processes are, consequently, leading companies to channel greater resources into speeding up their innovation process in order to gain competitive advantages. The greater costs of R&D investment and the shorter life cycles of products are adding increasing risk to the activities of large companies.[56] In addition, there is widespread concern over protecting intangible assets that result from R&D. One of the major reasons that innovators with good marketable ideas fail to enter or open up markets successfully and profit from their innovations may be that insufficient protection exists for their intellectual property, due either to inefficient legal-protection mechanisms or to peculiarities of the technology that make it easy to copy [*Teece, 1987*]. This is particularly the case of some product technologies based in electronics.

Thus, one of the consequences of the increasing knowledge-intensity in production has been intense international activity towards the enlargement and strengthening of legal regimes of protection of intellectual property. As national regimes of intellectual property rights are territorially limited, bilateral and multilateral initiatives have been taken to ensure world-wide protection of technological assets through the harmonization of such standards of protection [*UNCTAD, 1989: 16*]. Moreover, the current structure of intellectual property protection is not well adapted to the new technologies in use since the 1980s. In particular, developments in IT have opened up new areas for intellectual property claims that cannot be settled by the existing structure of intellectual property protection [*Kaplinsky, 1988a: 13*]. The initiative in bringing this subject to international negotiations was taken by the United States, which, as shown by the evolution of the main aggregate indicators of technological performance, has seen a narrowing of its technological lead over its main industrialized competitors since the 1970s. But interest in a new regime of intellectual property rights is general among the industrialized countries, which now share with the Americans the leadership in technological innovation. As I have shown in Chapter 2, this new issue for multilateral negotiations has been highly controversial from the point of view of the interests of the developing countries.

Summary

General trends in the world economy during the 1980s have created the conditions for the occurrence of various cases of trade friction among the developed economies and between them and developing economies, especially the NICs. The slow-down of world economic growth rates and the declining competitiveness of American exports have pushed American initiatives to open up markets, especially for high-technology products, such as software and services, in the production of which the United States companies can still claim some competitiveness. The higher knowledge intensity in production, with its consequent higher investment costs in R&D, has put the regulation of IPRs and the harmonization of national regulations on the matter high on the agenda of international negotiations. All of these conditions formed the international background to the Brazilian 301 case. The implications that these general trends have had on international trade policies of developed countries, especially the United States, are analysed in the following section.

GROWTH OF PROTECTIONISM AND US TRADE POLICY
IN THE 1980s

In this section I analyse the shift in the United States trade policy towards stronger protectionism or widespread 'management' of trade, a trend that was aggravated during the 1980s. However, as this trend cannot be said to be exclusive to US trade policy but a general trend within the developed economies, I start this section with a discussion of the increase in nontariff barriers to trade among the industrialized countries.

Protectionism in World Trade during the 1980s

Since the Second World War, there has been a great decrease in tariffs brought about by successive multilateral trade negotiations, especially during the 1970s. The beneficial effects of reduced tariffs on international trade was counterbalanced in the 1980s, however, by a large rise in nontariff barriers to trade that had started in the mid-1970s and whose effects on world trade are yet to be assessed.[57] The principles of nondiscrimination and reciprocity that had dominated the negotiations for reducing tariffs seem to have been abandoned by the developed economies or reinterpreted in a rather peculiar way in the 1980s. Developed countries have adopted protectionist trade policies that employ old instruments, such as import quotas, licenses, and prohibitions to import, and newly tailored measures, such as voluntary export restraints, orderly market arrangements, antidumping, and countervailing duty actions, to discriminate against the products of specific countries. Some of these measures are taken in accordance with 'escape clauses' provided by GATT, but many others clearly violate GATT. More than that, however, there has been an increasing trend to use the threat of discriminatory treatment of a country's exports to obtain market access or trade concessions.

Average tariffs on industrial imports by the developed economies, which had fallen dramatically in the previous decades, decreased still further from 7.1 per cent in 1979 to 4.7 per cent in 1988. However, the developed countries increased the proportion of imported manufactured goods subject to nontariff barriers from 18.7 per cent in 1981 to 22.6 per cent in 1987 [*Sassoon, 1990: 4*]. The use of such barriers by developing countries is estimated to be higher, and these barriers may affect more than a quarter of their combined imports [*Grilli, 1990: 152*]. In the case of developing countries, however, the use of barriers to trade is justified by GATT, which gives such countries 'special and more favourable treatment', expressed in Article XVIII and Part IV.

IT goods are among the products subjected to various non-tariff trade restrictions.[58] It is estimated that close to 30 per cent of the international trade of electronics products in the late 1980s was covered by barriers such as quantitative restrictions on imports, export restraints, monitoring systems, and market opening arrangements [*Kostecki, 1989: 18*]. Restrictive measures on the importation of electronics goods by developed economies was, then, higher than that for international trade of manufactured goods in general. Much of those restrictive measures have been imposed against the importation of electronics goods made in Japan and South Korea.

Non-tariff barriers to trade in electronics goods, especially semiconductors and consumer electronics, have been used to restrict what in the United States and European countries is called 'unfair trade'. A paradigmatic case in electronics trade was the bilateral arrangements on semiconductors concluded in mid-1986 between the United States and Japan, after several antidumping cases initiated by American companies against imports from Japan. The two countries, which together have around 90 per cent of the world production of semiconductors, agreed on (i) a process to monitor costs and prices of certain kinds of semiconductor exports from Japan to the United States and to third countries; and (ii) improved access for foreign companies to Japan's semiconductor market. This agreement, which restricted the possibility of diverting low-priced Japanese exports to South Korea or Taiwan from where they could have been forwarded to the United States, created growing concern among other countries that Japan and the United States might agree to fix semiconductor prices for all other user countries. The European Commission decided to observe closely the evaluation of export prices for Japanese semiconductors bound for the EU and requested a GATT panel to examine the US-Japan agreement in light of GATT rules [*Kostecki, 1989: 27*]. This case is a good illustration of a nonlegal purpose of nontariff barriers in the trade of electronics goods. In legal terms, antidumping actions are designed to restrict imports in cases of 'unfair' pricing. Antidumping actions in the electronics trade have, however, often been used also to protect industry from 'fair' foreign competition. As Pugel [*1987*] shows, the semiconductor industry, highly influenced by learning economies, follows a forward or penetration pricing policy. In this strategy, prices are set below current average production cost because the marginal cost is also often below that average level and because additional sales made now will contribute to the achievement of additional learning economies [*Pugel, 1987: 188*]. The price determination model implied in antidumping actions is better suited to industries with falling long-run average costs and less sensitivity to changes in demand. As a consequence, the application of antidumping actions to an industry such as semiconductors may reduce its contribution to national efficiency by forcing a reduction in its price flexibility [*Pugel, 1987: 197*]. Other important 'unfair' trade issues in the electronics trade are patent and copyright protection. Some imports of electronics goods and software have been banned on the grounds of infringement of domestic patent or copyright law.[59]

US Trade Policy in the 1980s

History shows that the United States adopted a free-trade policy only after the Second World War; previously, American trade policy had consistently discriminated against other countries' production.[60] Since the war, American trade policy has been characterized by divergent trends in tariff and nontariff barriers, by an ambivalence towards GATT, and by the opposing trends of supporting multilateralism and dealing unilaterally with trade partners to open up markets.

American tariffs were reduced, as were those of most countries, after various multilateral trade negotiations, but this has not affected the discriminatory features of tariffs imposed by the United States and other developed countries. To start with, although American tariffs are low, they are twice as high on imports from developing countries as on imports from developed countries [*Pearson and Riedel, 1990: 106*]. In 1971, the United States became the last major industrialized country to start implementing the Generalized System of Preferences (GSP) programme, by which favourable conditions were granted to the exports of developing countries. Since the 1980s, US tariff policy has shown a clear departure from this principle.[61] Three important initiatives have illustrated the US move away from nondiscrimination and multilateralism toward preferential treatment and 'plurilateralism': the Caribbean Basin Initiative of 1983, the US-Israel Free Trade Area defined in 1984, and the US-Canada Free Trade Agreement of 1987. Supported by Article XXII of GATT, which provides an exception for customs unions, free trade areas, and interim agreements leading to either, the American initiatives can be justified as bilateralism in a multilateral context.

Nevertheless, some analysts find it difficult to judge whether the overall trend of US trade policy since the Second World War has been toward freer trade or more protectionism [*Jackson, 1988; Pearson and Riedel, 1990*]. There has been wide recognition that in the 1980s the American trade policy has been decisively interventionist. There are many examples of US protectionism in what have been called 'sensitive' sectors, which have been extended from textiles and steel since the late 1960s and 1970s, to automobiles, footwear, television sets, sugar, machine tools, softwood timber, and semiconductors in the 1980s. For all of these sectors, special agreements whereby exporters would 'voluntarily' restrain their selling to the US market were bilaterally negotiated to protect American producers.

Protectionism and discrimination have often been justified in the name of making trade 'fair'. Measures against textile imports from Japan and developing countries, where the wages were lower than in the United States, have been justified because the lower wages would have given these products an 'unfair' advantage. Similarly, restraint agreements on steel imports into the United States from European and most other countries have been based on the argument that governmental subsidies and other targeting policies made their products compete 'unfairly' within the US market. 'Fairness' has become a central idea in American trade policy and has been a powerful tool to promote protectionism in the name of liberal trade. Since 1974, the US Trade Act has given the President special powers to fight for American trade rights, forcing countries whose trade practices are considered 'unfair' or damaging to US interests to change their policies. Section 301 of the 1974 Trade Act made any foreign policy considered 'unreasonable' subject to US action. Moreover, if negotiations do not succeed in changing the 'unreasonable' actions, economic retaliation on the offending country's imports in the American market are to be imposed.

The 1979 amendment to the US Trade Act gave special powers to the President related to the initiation of trade cases.[62] Section 301 authorizes the president to respond to 'any act, policy, or practice of a foreign country or instrumentality' that is 'unjustifiable, unreasonable, or discriminatory and burdens or restricts United States commerce'.[63] The President of the United States is given extraordinary powers to 'eliminate' those acts that violate Section 301. Under the US Trade Act, the United States Trade Representative (USTR) is authorized to request consultations with a foreign country on the issues subject to the investigation and, if these consultations prove to be in vain and a trade agreement such as GATT is involved, the proceedings shall be formally pursued within the framework of that latter organization (US Trade Act, Section 303). Although the Act only vaguely defines the scope of actions the US President should pursue to *'eliminate'* the practices or policies that violate Section 301, economic retaliation or the threat of economic sanctions against the foreign country are among the persuasive instruments used.

Tightening of Section 301 made in the 1979 Trade Agreement Act and in the Trade and Tariff Act of 1984 has not satisfied American legislators. Pressed by their constituencies, they have demanded more explicit punishment for countries that deny to US exports access to their markets comparable to what they enjoy in the American market. This appeal for 'aggressive reciprocity' was satisfied in the 1988 Omnibus Trade and Competitiveness Act. It contains a tougher version of Section 301, now called the Special or Super 301 Section, which requires the US Government to identify foreign practices and countries that offend American interests most strongly. If, at the end of an eighteen-month period, negotiations with them fail, the United States must retaliate. It was under the Super 301 Section that, on 25 May 1989, Brazil, together with India and Japan, were named as 'priority' countries. Some trade policies of these countries would have had to be changed within eighteen months, that is by November 1990, to prevent American retaliation.

'Fairness' and 'aggressive reciprocity' may result in some trade liberalization, but this may not provide widespread benefits as the changes are likely to favour American products. As some analysts have pointed out, American pressure may well result in 'voluntary import expansion' at the expense of other countries' trade, thus subverting the principles of free trade [*Bhagwati, 1988; Pearson and Riedel, 1990*].

Fair trade and reciprocity have thus effectively become rhetorical justifications for a shift in American trade policy from multilateralism to bilateralism or even unilateralism during the 1980s. The US position in relation to GATT and multilateralism has thus been ambivalent for a long time [*Jackson, 1988; Bhagwati, 1989*]. Although the United States has stated strong support for the principles of multilateralism and nondiscrimination, its actual trade policy has pointed in an opposite direction. Not only has US tariff policy been increasingly 'plurilateral', but the United States has also refused to apply most-favoured-nation treatment in its implementation of codes that resulted from the Tokyo Round of multilateral trade negotiations. Also, the United States has shown contradictory attitudes towards GATT, the multilateral forum in trade issues. To begin with, it was criticism by the US Congress that frustrated attempts to create the International Trade Organization after the Second World War. The resulting GATT has been constantly criticized by members of the US Congress. For many years there was no explicit statutory authority even for the US government to pay its financial contribution to GATT. This was finally provided by the 1974 Trade Act, but the Act included the comment that the authorization did not 'imply approval or disapproval by the Congress of all articles of the General Agreement on Tariffs and Trade' [*Jackson, 1988: 380*].

Despite this opposition, the US government has been one of the major parties interested in the multilateral trade negotiations, has particularly committed itself in gathering the agreement of other member countries to open the present Uruguay Round of negotiations, and has made a great effort to achieve a successful conclusion. On the other hand, however, the United States has very seldom agreed to discuss troubling bilateral trade frictions in the multilateral forum of GATT. The inefficiency of GATT procedures may motivate countries to approach trade problems bilaterally, but when trade negotiations are conducted outside the GATT trade-dispute apparatus, sometimes in an environment that is foreign to the parties involved, they tend to deviate from internationally accepted rules and thus lose impartiality [*Grilli, 1990*]. Although the US government has played a dominant role in the establishment of general rules to liberalize international trade, including the new areas of trade in services, TRIMs, and trade-related aspects of IPRs, it has also acted unilaterally to obtain market concessions from others, refused to submit itself to international dispute-settlement procedures, and defined new trading rights through unilateral specification [*Bhagwati, 1989; Pearson and Riedel, 1990*]. American trade policy has been torn between multilateralism and unilateralism.

These shifts in orientation of US trade policy have resulted from a variety of converging processes that reinforced each other, especially during the 1980s.

The prominence of American exports' interests in shaping US trade policy, the 'diminished giant syndrome', and the divergent positions of the US Administration and Congress have been essential forces in the formation of a strategic trade policy, and interventionist trade policy, or export protectionism. The declining relative position of the American economy in relation to Japan, the EU, and even some Asian NICs is considered to have created an ethos favourable to protectionism that has been called the 'diminished giant syndrome' [*Bhagwati, 1989: 451*], whereby fairness and reciprocity in trade gained a central role in national feelings. From another standpoint, the contradictory liberalism and protectionism in American trade policy are seen to arise from a declining hegemony conflict, in which the US government still feels it has a duty to promote liberal trade at the international level, but cannot also betray its commitments to dominant domestic forces that demand protection [*Evans, 1989*]. The opposing directions taken by American trade policy have also been due to the diverging orientations of a free-trade Administration that favours multilateralism and a protectionist or fair-trade Congress that endorses bilateral or even unilateral action. This characterization may oversimplify the political process that has pushed the American trade policy to its present contradictory situation. Congressional sensitivity to protectionist demands may be stronger than the Administration's, but, despite the amount and variety of protectionist bills that have grown significantly since 1983, very few of them made it through both Houses [*Marshall, 1987: 23*].[64] On the other hand, of the hundreds of cases filed by American companies and investigated by the Administration during the period 1975-85, one in four anti-dumping and one in three countervailing duty cases were accepted for investigation [*Pearson and Riedel, 1990: 108*]. Notwithstanding this evidence of a relatively less protectionist Congress and a relatively more protectionist Administration,[65] it is undeniable that both Congress and the Administration have increased their interventionist orientation during the 1980s. There is no better indication of this trend than the 1988 Omnibus Trade and Competitiveness Act and the subsequent action of nominating priority countries and practices that are considered 'unfair' to American interests.

Summary

I have shown in this section that the trend toward increased protectionism in trade policies of industrial countries have been aggravated in the 1980s. The fall in tariff barriers during the 1970s was counterbalanced to a considerable extent in the 1980s by an increase in nontariff barriers to trade in a variety of manufactured goods, including high-technology products such as electronics. In the United States, trade policy has been torn between a commitment to the ideal of free trade and the reality of growing protectionism, established sometimes using escape clauses of GATT, but most of the time in a unilateral pursuit

79

of new markets. 'Fair trade' and 'reciprocity' have been used liberally to justify aggressive American trade policies, most conspicuously expressed in Section 301 of the US Trade Act of 1974 and the Super or Special 301 Section of the Omnibus Trade and Competitiveness Act of 1988. Although the US government has taken a strong position in the establishment of general rules for liberalizing international trade, it has also been ambivalent to multilateralism and to GATT. All these facts have created the conditions for the occurrence of various cases of trade friction in the 1980s, including the Brazil 301 case.

CONCLUSION

In this chapter I have argued that two central points are to be considered as sources of an American offensive against several of its trade partners during the 1980s. Firstly, there were deep changes in the relative position of the United States in the world economy. Secondly, and linked to these changes, there was an aggravation of the contradictory trends of protectionism and liberalism in American trade policy.

After a lengthy period of lowering of tariff barriers to trade and a rapid growth in world commerce, the world economy slowed through the 1980s. In the United States this deceleration was more exaggerated and was reflected by a 'fundamental disequilibrium' in the national trade account. In addition, there was a decline in the competitiveness of American exports, including high-technology products. These trends have nurtured a growing belief - whether or not justified in reality - that other countries have overtaken the United States by either unfairly subsidizing their industries or stealing US technology. It has been a widely supported idea within American society and the Congress that the United States should not allow a repeat of what they took to be the successful use of these two strategies by the Japanese.

According to the analytical framework described in Chapter 1, international bargaining processes are a multiple game in which countries often exploit bilateral disputes either to provoke side-effects in third parties or to 'soften' opposition in multilateral negotiations. The American offensive to open up markets and obtain harmonization of national regulations of IPRs proceeded on two fronts: (i) the multilateral, where the United States pressed for the adoption of internationally agreed rules for trade in the new areas of services, IPRs, and TRIMs; and (ii) the bilateral, including some of the recent cases of trade friction with developing countries. These two fronts were linked since the United States often used bilateral pressure to push through its multilateral objectives.

6

THE EVOLVING DISPUTE

On 7 September 1985, Brazilian Independence Day, the US government announced the beginning of investigations into the Brazilian IT policy and warned that economic sanctions would be imposed against Brazilian exports to that market if unfair trade practices towards US interests were proved. In this chapter, the evolution of the US/Brazil conflict on IT policy is analysed as a bargaining process of exchange of information, promises, and threats by which a mutually agreeable outcome was reached and led to the solution of the conflict. This conflict is an example of a particular type of conflict in international relations in this new technological era. Negotiations between the two countries led to the solution of the conflict only after the Americans threatened to impose punitive tariffs on Brazilian exports. The American pressure resulted not only in increased flexibility in the implementation of the Brazilian policy, but also in the establishment of new legislation on software. The effectiveness of the threat of economic sanctions in changing the target country's policy was due to its effects on the balance of political forces within Brazilian society. The conflict undermined the support the policy had in Brazilian society, uncovering and perhaps even nurturing opposing views on the matter within the Brazilian government and broadening the scope of dissatisfaction with the policy within Brazilian society.

In this chapter I describe the events which developed from September 1985, when the conflict began, until October 1989, when the USTR declared the conflict closed. This discussion focuses on the agenda, concessions, and negotiating strategy for each of the two contenders. First, however, I provide a brief background of the events that led up to the dispute.

BACKGROUND TO THE DISPUTE

In this section I describe the evolution of US/Brazilian economic and political relations during the 1970s and early 1980s. The purpose is to depict the central features of US/Brazilian relations that formed the background to the IT policy dispute. As I show in the present section, the relationship between the two countries had been in a process of continuing deterioration. Several other trade conflicts of small magnitude had already developed, including criticism of Brazil's IT policy by the USTR in 1983. Considering the importance of the

United States as the destination and origin of most of Brazil's foreign trade, conflicts involving trade and threats of trade sanctions would impose heavy potential costs on Brazil, which could not dispense with the commerce with the sanctioning country. The special conditions that led the Brazilians to compromise will be discussed in Chapter 7.

Isolated claims by American firms against the Brazilian IT policy can be traced back to the policy's genesis in the early 1970s. At that time, however, the claims were not as strong and consistent as they became in the early 1980s. Moreover, Brazilian institutions in charge of the policy had more solid domestic support in the early years. Even so, the Brazilian state agencies involved had to act very carefully to overcome these early pressures, which even then had exacted some concessions from the Brazilian government.

The exemplary case that occurred at that time was the response by American companies to Brazil's first tender offer for the local manufacture of minicomputers. IBM had already decided, in 1976, to make and sell a minicomputer model in Brazil in open defiance of CAPRE's Resolution No.1. The Brazilian CDE was required to establish that a proportion of local capital and the use of local technology were conditions for approval of any IT industrial project. Covered by these conditions, CAPRE selected nationally owned firms for the tender to produce minicomputers in Brazil. Data General, a firm that had not bid nor had a significant position in the Brazilian market, wrote to the USTR complaining about Brazilian restrictions on the importation of minicomputers and saying that the IT policy was a bad example to other countries. This last point was the main argument contained in a letter sent in the mid-1970s to President Carter by IBM, Digital Equipment Corporation, Control Data, and Hewlett Packard, in which they asked for the President's intervention to prevent establishment of an IT policy of market reserve in Brazil. Subsequent pressure from the Carter administration led Brazil to compromise and approve the local production and sale of two medium-sized IBM computers. This decision was made by CAPRE in its last meeting before being superseded by the SEI. From that time onwards, claims by American companies against the IT policy have been taken up by the US government, which has demanded changes in Brazilian policy. American pressure against the Brazilian IT policy thus became a constitutive part of the already deteriorating political and economic relations between the two countries, a situation that had started in the early 1970s [*Fishlow, 1982; Lafer et al., 1985*].

From the mid-1970s to the early 1980s, US/Brazil relations shifted from the automatic alignment that had long characterized the Brazilian diplomatic position in relation to the United States. During that period, Brazil's nonaligned orientation strengthened the country's economic and political relations with other developed and Third World areas, especially in Latin America. Throughout President Reagan's first administration, the cooling relations between the two countries evolved into an agenda for the discussion of their divergent political positions.[66] The increasing external vulnerability of the Brazilian economy during the 1980s and the increasingly important US role in negotiating Brazil's foreign debt are amongst the forces that worsened relations between the two countries.[67]

Economic relations between the United States and Brazil changed significantly during the 1970s and early 1980s. It was during this period that Brazilian trade showed the effects of Brazil's strategy to diversify its economic partners. Beginning in the late 1960s, changes in the Brazilian trade pattern made the EU's and Latin America's shares of Brazilian exports larger than that of the United States. The United States maintained its large share of the Brazilian import market, with consequent deficits in the Brazilian trade balance with that country. This situation was reversed between 1981 and 1985, when the financial crisis and the recessionary trend in the world economy, counterbalanced by strong growth in the United States, made the United States the largest market for Brazilian exports. The trade balance between the two countries thus became favourable to Brazil in this period.

As Table 6.1 shows, excluding imports from the Middle East, the United States was the largest single supplier of Brazilian imports in the period 1980-1985, but its share was almost equalled by that of the Latin American region, which was the origin of more than 20 per cent of Brazilian imports from 1981 to 1984.

TABLE 6.1
BRAZILIAN FOREIGN TRADE WITH SELECTED REGIONS, 1980-1985

	Destination of exports (% share)			Origin* of imports (% share)			Overall trade balance (US$ billion)		
	US	EU	LA+	US	EU	LA	US	EU	LA
1980	17.1	27.2	17.8	26.9	23.2	17.9	-0.64	1.95	0.85
1981	17.3	25.5	8.6	22.7	19.4	20.7	0.56	2.96	1.17
1982	19.7	26.9	14.6	22.0	18.9	25.8	1.14	3.00	-0.37
1983	22.8	25.9	9.9	23.7	18.6	22.2	2.61	3.82	-0.06
1984	28.2	22.8	11.0	22.6	17.3	21.6	5.35	4.43	0.82
1985	26.7	24.3	9.3	25.2	18.2	15.9	4.25	4.36	0.73

Source: Banco do Brasil, [1985].
* Total Brazilian imports excluding those from the Middle East
+ LA, Latin America

In fact, during the years which preceded the opening of the IT policy conflict, Brazilian imports from the United States declined in absolute figures from US$ 4.1 billion in 1980 to US$ 2.3 billion in 1984. The year the conflict started, Brazilian imports from the United States increased slightly, marking the beginning of a more recent upswing trend. In any case, these changes did not mean a drop in the significance of the US market for the Brazilian economy. In 1985, the year the IT policy conflict started, the United States was the destination of more than 26 per cent of Brazilian exports and the source of around 25 per cent of Brazilian nonoil imports.

One such Brazilian import from the United States has been electronic goods and computer-related items. As Table 6.2 shows, available data on Brazilian foreign trade with the United States in the three years preceding the conflict show an increase in Brazilian imports of American computer-related goods. Although total electronics imports by Brazil declined sharply during the first years of the IT policy import controls, they grew throughout the 1980s, as shown in Chapter 4, as a consequence of the development of the Brazilian electronics industry.

The US share of total Brazilian imports of electronics goods, which grew from around 50 per cent in 1983 to 60 per cent in 1984, curiously declined in 1985 and continued decreasing in subsequent years to 50 per cent in 1986 and 48 per cent in 1987 [*Paiva, 1989: 119*]. According to these data, the IT trade conflict had no positive immediate effect in increasing the Americans' share of the electronics imports received by Brazil. However, as Table 6.2 shows, Brazilian imports of electronics goods from the United States increased at a larger rate than overall imports from the United States in the period. This is not surprising given the growing share of electronics in global trade.

TABLE 6.2
BRAZILIAN TRADE WITH THE UNITED STATES, 1983-1985
(US$ MILLION CURRENT)

	1983	1984	1985	% change 1983/4	% change 1984/85
Total Brazilian imports	15,429	13,916	13,168	-9.8	-5.4
Brazilian imports from the US	2,398	2,256	2,590	-5.3	14.8
Brazilian IT imports*	153	149	202	-2.6	35.6
Brazilian IT imports from the US	76	89	112	17.1	25.8

Source: Banco do Brasil, [*1985*].
* Computers and peripherals (NBM - Brazilian Nomenclature for Commodities - position 84.53) and electronic parts (NBM position 84-55).

The composition of Brazilian exports to the US market changed during the first half of the 1980s, with increasing significance for manufactured goods.[68] As the decade progressed there was a growing incidence of US/Brazil trade conflicts, of which the most recent, far-reaching, and politically sensitive is being analysed in this study. Since the promulgation of the US Trade Act in 1974, US/Brazil trade relations have become tense in relation to primary goods as well as manufactured products.[69]

It was in this context of deteriorating US/Brazil trade relations that, in the early 1980s, the Americans approached the issue of how to improve co-operative relations with Brazil. In 1982, a number of bilateral working-groups were created at the suggestion of the US government to explore the possibilities of improving co-operation between the two countries.[70] Brazil's IT policy was one of the central issues that the United States intended to be tacked by the groups. The Brazilian authorities did not accept the inclusion of the IT policy in the trade cooperation negotiations, however, and in the end refused to discuss it at all. The Brazilians did, however, favour addressing the issue of scientific and technological cooperation in the IT area. The discussions produced meagre results. In the area of science and technology the poor outcome was due largely to the fact that the most sensitive problem, the Brazilian IT policy, was excluded from the negotiations. In any case, it was clearly in reference to the Brazilian IT policy that one of the conclusions of the report of the working-groups, made public in October 1983, stated that trade restrictions and market reserve would, at best, bring frustrations and, at worst, retaliation [*Azevedo and Zago Jr., 1989: 138*]. The failure of the working-group showed that the conflict between the two countries in relation to the Brazilian IT policy had already begun to surface.

Subsequent events aggravated tensions between the two countries on the issue of the Brazilian IT policy. In March 1983, the USTR made public a report containing strong criticisms of the Brazilian IT policy. In April 1983, in a meeting with the US Treasury Secretary, the Brazilian Finance Minister, and other authorities, the US Secretary of Commerce declared that the IT policy had become a compulsory topic in any negotiation between the United States and Brazil [*Azevedo and Zago Jr., 1989: 135*]. This policy became a strategic point in the negotiations of the Brazilian foreign debt. The IT policy entered what Griffith-Jones [*1989: 22*] calls the 'hidden agenda', wherein political interests of the United States have been made part of the negotiation on debt rescheduling and new loans.

Among the direct pressure the US government exerted on Brazilian IT policy before the 301 case started was the 1983 report by the USTR, which accused the Brazilian policy of being not just protectionist but biased against transnational corporations (TNCs). In that report, the USTR asserted that market reserve for Brazilian companies, discriminatory intervention by Brazilian state agencies, and import restrictions were major obstacles working against the interests of US exporters. At the time, the USTR report was supported in Brazil by the National Federation of Industries (CNI) and the Federation of São Paulo Industries (FIESP). In April 1983, FIESP publicized its critique of the IT policy based on arguments similar to those used in the USTR report. ABICOMP reacted by accusing the two industry groups of voicing the interests of TNC subsidiaries in Brazil.[71]

Escalation of US criticism of the Brazilian IT policy in the early 1980s was an American reaction to legal codification of the market reserve policy but, at the same time, served to reinforce this process. In fact, the nationalist reactions within Brazilian society provoked by US pressure helped to mobilize the social forces that pressed the Brazilian Congress to vote on the matter [*Borelli, 1986; Azevedo and Zago Jr., 1989*]. As pointed out in Chapter 3, discussion of the 'informatics' bill did not bring significant changes into the text introduced by the Brazilian Executive Branch, especially in relation to the principle of market reserve and the SEI's powers. However, the law left some subjects to be regulated by future legislation. This point was crucial not only for subsequent developments of the policy, but also for ensuing negotiations, as was the case in the IT conflict.

I have shown in this section that the US/Brazil IT policy conflict developed in the context of deteriorating political relations between the two countries, and was preceded by various instances of pressure from the US government for changes in Brazilian policy. The conflict analysed in this study was a culmination of all of these previous pressures. Its solution was made possible not only because the American complaints became more focused, as I will show in the next section, but also because of the potential effects of the threatened American economic sanctions on Brazilian economy and society.

US COMPLAINTS AND STRATEGY

In this section I discuss the American complaints and negotiating strategy related to the Brazilian IT policy dispute. The evolution of the agenda's scope from the American point of view, the strategy of fractionating the conflict, and the Americans' threatened economic retaliation against Brazilian exports to the United States are analysed to show the effectiveness of the US strategy in coercing Brazil to agree on the focal point of negotiations (i.e., establishment of Brazilian legislation on software).

The USTR proceedings against the Brazilian IT policy were initiated under Section 301 of the US Trade Act, which allows economic retaliation against discriminatory or unfair trade practices contrary to American interests. More precisely, the Brazilian IT policy came to be investigated by the USTR in order to advise the US President concerning the exercise of his authority under Section 301. Investigation of the Brazilian IT policy was not the only initiative taken by the US President in September 1985. Cases against Japan's restrictions on American tobacco exports, Korea's obstacles to the activities of American insurance companies within its market, Korea's lack of IPR protection, and the EU's production subsidies on preserved fruit were also initiated at the same time. The then ongoing investigation into Japan's import regulations against American leather goods was also accelerated.

These American charges were backed by special presidential powers granted under Section 301 of the 1979 amendment of the US Trade Act. Accordingly, the President was authorised to act to eliminate policies considered damaging to American interests. Such actions could include any kind of economic retaliation. In the Brazilian 301 case, these were the threat to impose punitive tariffs and to exclude some Brazilian exports from duty-free treatment under the GSP programme, the latter threat affecting especially exports of manufactured and semimanufactured goods. Brazilian exports to the United States have benefited from the GSP programme. According to CEPAL [*1985: 71*], Brazilian exports of GSP articles to the United States increased at an annual rate of 36.4 per cent in the period 1976-79; in 1985 the programme granted duty-free treatment to some 3,000 tariff items from Brazil, mainly manufactured and semimanufactured goods. Until 1984, few Brazilian products (hardboard not face-finished, ferrosilicon, ferrosilicon manganese, piston-type compression engines, and motor vehicle body parts) had been excluded in one or more years, affecting a relatively small value of trade [*CEPAL, 1985: 72,87*]. The articles excluded in 1984 were worth US$ 46 million [*CEPAL, 1985: 73*] in Brazilian exports to the US market in 1983, or less than one per cent of the total. The US position related to GSP has been to review eligible articles to identify those beneficiary countries that have reached a sufficient degree of competitiveness in relation to other beneficiary countries to be excluded from the programme. Willingness of benefiting countries to liberalize their imports increases the possibility for some of their products to be considered not competitive, and thus eligible for the GSP. On the other hand, competitive need limits may be waived by the US President if, among other factors, benefiting countries grant the United States access to their markets and basic resources. Thus, Brazilian products were in danger of receiving only restricted duty-free access to the US market in connection with the accusation against the Brazilian IT policy.

The US complaints toward the Brazilian IT policy were outlined by the USTR, which specified US concern with a 'wide array of restrictions on foreign participation in the market'. These restrictions included (1) broad authority to restrict imports for at least eight years, (2) the granting of an exclusive right to Brazilian-owned firms to produce and sell certain types of high-technology products, (3) incentives for Brazilian firms, and (4) restrictions on foreign direct investment through local content and export performance requirements [*Santarelli et al., 1985: 1*].

These complaints, which cover the central points of Law No. 7232, were discussed in general terms in the first consultation between the two countries, which took place in February 1986, six months after the opening of the case.[72] In May of that year, the US Economic Policy Council decided that the Brazilian IT policy constituted a case of unfair trade practice and that retaliation was justified. With the powerful threat of economic sanctions, the Americans concentrated on specifying alterations in Brazilian policy needed to alleviate the alleged unfair treatment of US interests.

It was only almost one year after the announcement of the Brazilian 301 case that the American delegation presented to the Brazilians a more specific list of criticisms against the IT policy. On 2 July 1986, the American delegation to the first Paris meeting presented a list of twenty-six items containing what they viewed as expressions of unfairness in the Brazilian policy. The list of the American complaints was organized into five topics: (a) trade and investment, (b) intellectual property rights, (c) transborder data flow, (d) subsidies, and (e) technical standards.

Related to trade and investment, American criticism was directed specifically to Brazil's definition of IT goods and services, which was considered too wide and vague; to the procedures for the concession of import licenses, which were estimated to be too expensive and complicated; to the concept of *local similar*, which was viewed as nebulous; and to the conditions for the formation of joint ventures and the requirements of local content and export performance, which were deemed to be too restrictive to the activities of American companies in the Brazilian market. The Americans suggested a clear delimitation of the items under reserve, gradual abbreviation of the list of reserved items, and progressive broadening of the list of goods foreign-owned companies could manufacture in the Brazilian market. Import licenses were to be under the jurisdiction of just one agency, which should proceed quickly and explain the justification for both the approval and denial of the licence. They recommended that a technical committee be constituted to define and apply the concept of local similar and to act as a superior forum to which the companies could appeal before any decision was made. They also wanted (i) the approval of joint ventures between American and local companies to be expedited, (ii) equal treatment for both American- and Brazilian-owned companies, and (iii) an end to local-content and export-performance requirements for approval of American investment in the Brazilian market.

The other four sections of the US demands were presented in less detail. Demands related to IPRs were targeted on software, with adoption of the copyright regime being demanded as a way to protect American interests. Calls for free transborder data flow and the end of the requirement that the data be processed in Brazil were the central tenets of section three. Section four dealt with the issue of subsidies given to purchasers of products made by Brazilian-owned companies. The Americans viewed these subsidies as an infringement of Article 3 of GATT, the most-favoured-nation treatment. In the last section, they suggested the adoption of technical standards that could improve international trade. The lack of such standards was deemed to be a more subtle way of enforcing the market reserve.

These American criticisms were subsequently discussed with the Brazilians, and these discussions resulted in a more focused agenda for negotiations. The Americans dropped the issues of transborder data flow, technical standards, and subsidies, and the agenda was confined to three areas: (a) administrative procedures, (b) market access, and (c) IPRs.

Agreement was reached first on the subject of administrative procedures. In August 1986, the SEI announced internal reforms that would expedite the application process for local manufacture and import licences. In September, the association of IBM with the Brazilian company Gerdau for data-processing services was approved by the SEI, and in November a US/Brazil *ad hoc* group was set up to review specific complaints presented by American companies. These actions were considered evidence of the Brazilian government's good will and were followed by the US government's withdrawal, on 30 December, of the part of the Brazilian 301 case which dealt with administrative procedures.

Compromise proved to be more difficult on the issue of market access. *Market access* is the main essence of the IT policy and is enshrined in the market reserve provisions established in Law No. 7232. Negotiations on this issue could progress only if the law was changed, a matter of great political sensitivity in Brazil. The Americans had to be satisfied, at least for the time being, with an interpretation of Article 8 of the Informatics Law that would terminate the market reserve when SEI controls expired in 1992. They were also assured by the Brazilians that the market reserve would not be extended beyond that year, nor to any other product. Brazil's market reserve was maintained for the entire duration of the conflict without any change in the Brazilian policy. In fact, only two significant changes occurred in Brazilian policy in the area of investment and market access: (i) approval of the IBM-Gerdau association; and (ii) CACEX Communication 171, of 11 December 1986, which narrowed the range of products subject to import restrictions and eliminated the SEI's powers to control importation of products containing numerical controlled systems.

Considering Brazil's relatively insignificant concessions in the areas of administrative procedures and market access, the conflict's outcome would not have satisfied the Americans if a focal point were not reached that produced a more substantive result. This focal point was found in negotiations dealing with IPRs for software. It was in negotiating this issue that the Americans used the threat of economic sanctions to make the Brazilians understand the US government's unwillingness to retreat from its position.

As I have shown in Chapter 3, the Brazilians had been concerned with the definition of a policy towards software since the late 1970s. One of the controversial points relating to software was the regime for protection of intellectual property. The Brazilians were inclined to adopt a *sui generis* regime, combining the concepts of patents and copyright. As I have already mentioned, the American suggestion of copyright for software was made in July 1986.

CONIN approved the copyright regime for software in its meeting of 26 August 1986. In December of that year, a software bill was introduced into the Brazilian House of Representatives, which approved it on 24 June 1987. On 30 June 1987, the US government suspended the part of the Brazilian 301 case dealing with IPRs.

Thus, by 1987, the conflict seemed to have been largely settled, although the issue of market access remained unresolved. The question was brought back on to the agenda in July 1987, however, when SEI denied a request by Brazilian companies to license Microsoft's MS-DOS on the grounds that a local equivalent had already been developed. This decision triggered an American reaction. Firstly, on 6 November, the US Senate approved a resolution recommending that the President initiate sanctions against Brazil. Then, on 13 November the US government announced the adoption of punitive tariffs on US$ 105 million worth of Brazilian exports. This announcement hit hardest at producers of the top items in Brazilian exports, especially those who had already faced some trade difficulties with the United States. Among them were footwear producers, airplane manufacturers, and orange juice producers. Less than one week later, the Brazilian Senate voted on the software bill, which was finally turned into Law No. 7646 on 4 December 1987. The Americans were not, however, pleased with the Brazilian regulation, especially because it consecrated the concept of similarity or *functional equivalence* as a mechanism for protection of Brazilian products. Under this concept, filing is a precondition to marketing any software in Brazil, but software developed by non-Brazilian companies can be filed only if there exists no similar software developed in the country, by a national company.[73] In the first months of 1988, American threats showed initial results: Orders for some of the products threatened with additional tariffs were cancelled by American buyers. In January, CONIN reversed SEI's previous decision and approved the licence of the latest version of Microsoft's MS-DOS. This outcome, coupled with pressure from its Brazilian counterparts, moved the American Electronics Association (AEA) to ask the USTR to postpone implementation of sanctions for 120 days, within which the procedures for implementation of the software law were expected to be ready. In February 1988, the US government suspended the retaliatory measures but did not close the Brazilian 301 case and continued to *monitor* Brazilian software policy. It was only in October 1989 that the Brazilian 301 case was finally dropped.

The Americans' general strategy was to keep the Brazilian 301 case on bilateral terms, despite communicating to GATT its intention to impose punitive tariffs on Brazilian exports. The Americans seem to have been confident that direct pressure on what they saw as the offending country would be more effective in producing the desired results. Nevertheless, as I will show in the next section and in Chapter 7, the Brazilians' firm position on not changing the Informatics Law but only discussing specific cases related to its implementation, and the local nationalist reaction raised by US pressure, pushed the Americans to moderate their targets and strategy. In fact, after the initial consultations, the Americans moderated the strategy of 'excessive claims' they had employed in opening the Brazilian 301 case, when they had set about to eliminate the censured central points of the IT policy. As Evans [*1989*] has shown, the tough position of the Department of Commerce was superseded by the diplomacy of the Department of State.

In presenting the list of 26 claims, the Americans realized that Brazil would strongly resist making deep changes in its policy. As a consequence, the United States came to phrase its demands in more cautious terms. As USTR spokesman declared, 'the US, realising the political difficulties, is not asking for a repeal of Brazil's informatics law but wants transparency, an appeals process and a guarantee that it will not be expanded into other products' [*Financial Times, 1986*].

If the Americans could not pressure Brazil to change the Informatics Law, they could at least force its implementation to favour American interests and, most of all, they could influence subsequent legislation. To obtain more favourable implementation of the Law, the United States focused its complaints on SEI, accusing if of being much too strict in interpreting the Law and very inefficient in making any decision on schedule. This criticism gained widespread local support, both among some Brazilian industrialists and within the state apparatus itself. The Brazilian Foreign Minister declared that 'the SEI cannot be an immobilizing agency' [*Jornal do Brasil, 1986a*] and a study was reportedly carried out by the National Intelligence Service and the Army Ministry questioning the benefits that had resulted from the SEI's toughness towards foreign capital.[74] Attempts to reduce SEI's powers produced very limited results, however, expressed mainly in CACEX Communication 171. Administrative reform of SEI, creation of the *ad hoc* group, CACEX communication 171, and the approval of the IBM-Gerdau association were, then, the major results of American attempts to secure more favourable implementation of Brazil's Informatics Law.

It was in the area of influencing new legislation that the American strategy proved to be more effective. CONIN's definition of the copyright regime for software and the subsequent process of elaborating the software bill, discussing it within the Brazilian Congress, and defining the procedures for activating the software law developed under American scrutiny and the threat of economic sanctions. In fact, the first year of negotiations resulted in the regulation of IPRs for software becoming the most significant issue in the conflict. It was only with this specific target that the two parties found a way to resolve the conflict. The relevance of software protection to US interests was expressed clearly by Michael B. Smith, Deputy USTR at the time.

We believe that, if we are to keep our market open to Brazilian labor-intensive products here in the United States, it is only reasonable that Brazil open its markets to American computer software which is symbolic of this country's comparative advantage in hi-tech products and services [*US House of Representatives, 1988: 3*].

The threat of economic sanctions against Brazilian exports was a strategic tool the Americans used very effectively. In December 1986, the USTR excluded 30 Brazilian products from the GSP programme. At the time, Brazilian exports gaining tariff reductions under GSP would have been valued at around US$ 1.3 billion, but this figure dropped to US$ 860 million after the exclusion of the 30 products. The US government declared that this exclusion was not linked to the Brazilian 301 case, but the Brazilian exporters and government interpreted it as a signal of the seriousness of the American threats of sanctions. The US government announcement of punitive tariffs in November 1987 specified the amount of Brazilian export revenues that would be affected but not the list of the products affected. The threat therefore loomed over any significant export item, especially those products against which the United States had already threatened protectionist attacks: orange juice, footwear, and aircraft. In any case, specifying the products to be punished was irrelevant, because the threat of punitive tariffs would produce the desired results even if they were not implemented (indeed they were not). In fact, the less specific, the greater the number of Brazilian groups who would feel threatened by potential sanctions. Thus, by increasing the number of Brazilian social groups potentially dissatisfied with the IT policy, the threat of economic sanctions transformed the balance of forces supporting the existing policy, forcing the Brazilian government to establish more liberal measures towards software.

I have shown in this section the evolution of the American complaints and the strategy they used to combat the alleged unfair trade practices in the Brazilian IT policy. Two conclusions can be drawn from this analysis. One is related to the narrowing of the list of issues that the United States managed to include in the agenda for negotiation. The agenda evolved from the Americans' initial 'excessive claims' for changes in the policy's central points to a feasible set of outcomes consisting of administrative changes and relaxation of restrictions to market access, and finally to the focus on software regulation. It was not that the Americans renounced their earlier claims. Rather, they concentrated on obtaining the more relevant and yet attainable gain of modelling the Brazilian software policy. The second conclusion is related to the American strategy, which coupled the initial 'excessive claims' with the tactics of 'fractionating' the conflict into a number of issues, separating agreeable subjects from contentious ones. For each 'part' of the conflict, the Americans bargained for a 'package deal' involving simultaneous settlement of a number of issues so that losses in some were offset by gains in others. Negotiations on the most contentious 'part' of the conflict - investment and market access - had an outcome that did not fully satisfy the Americans. Therefore, in order to obtain a more significant gain, the Americans led the negotiations to concentrate on the regulation of IPRs for software in Brazil. This issue became a 'focal point' of the conflict: A solution to it involved the Brazilian's awareness of the seriousness of the American's threats, which thereby limited the Brazilians' possibility of retreat.

Evolution of the American position in the Brazilian 301 case is better understood in light of Brazilian strategy and concessions, which I discuss in the next section.

BRAZILIAN STRATEGY AND CONCESSIONS

In this section I analyse Brazil's strategy throughout its dispute with the United States over the IT policy. Evolution of the Brazilian position from refusal to discuss the policy to subsequent negotiation on how to prevent US economic sanctions is described and examined in the light of Brazil's internal political conditions. It is in relation to those internal conditions that I address the issue of Brazilian concessions to US pressure.

Brazil's strategy was initially similar to its opponent's: What I call the Brazilian 'principled objection' to any discussion of Law No. 7232 paralleled the American's 'excessive claims' to repeal the law. In subsequent rounds of bargaining, the Brazilian strategy evolved to 'pragmatic negotiation' of the policy's implementation and of some features of future legislation.

Brazil's refusal to discuss the Law was based on the principles of Brazilian diplomacy and international law. One of the strategic principles of Brazilian foreign policy established in the early 1970s, during President Geisel's administration, had been to discuss international trade disputes in multilateral forums rather than in bilateral negotiations. In Brazil's view, the US government's unilateral action was based exclusively on American internal law. Brazil considered it absurd that some complainant country could decide, without appeal and in accordance with its own criteria, on the 'unfair practice' of another country. According to this reasoning, to accept the 301 case would be tantamount to admitting that US national law has, unlike the legislation of all other countries, universal validity. Brazil's initial course of action was to explain its response in the framework of GATT. In fact, it had already been made evident to the Americans that they had no clear case against the IT policy when, in June 1985, they called the Brazilians for consultation on the issue at GATT. The Brazilians clearly stated their position at the first consultative meeting, which took place in Caracas in February 1986, when they defended Law No. 7232 as being entirely acceptable under GATT rule. The fundamental principles of

GATT are that trade must be conducted on the basis of nondiscrimination and that all contracting parties are bound to grant each other treatment as favourable as they give to any signatory of the treaty. Nevertheless, GATT specifies some circumstances that justify non-compliance with member obligations. The Brazilian IT policy is supported by provisions of Articles XII, XVIII, and XXI of GATT. Article XVIII permits developing countries to impose restrictions when they are justified by balance-of-payment objectives and to protect infant industries. A similar balance-of-payments exception applicable to developed and less developed countries alike is found in Article XII. Article XXI permits a contracting party to take any actions it considers necessary to protect its essential security interests. National security was invoked by the Brazilian military in launching the IT policy in the early 1970s in connection with the need to develop local capability to operate and maintain new frigates equipped with on-board computer systems.[75]

The Brazilians maintained this 'principled' objection to the case during the first twelve months of the dispute. Brazilian president José Sarney then declared, for the first time since the opening of the Brazilian 301 case, that the market reserve was not to be changed. In his words, 'The IT policy which orients the Sarney administration was approved by the Brazilian Congress and reflects our determination to protect national interest. It will not be weakened or modified' [*Jornal do Brasil, 1986b*, my translation].

This position was also evident in a note by the Brazilian Foreign Minister published in the local press:

> In face of the news that the US government may retaliate against Brazilian exports due to the Brazilian IT policy, we say that the law which supports this policy is a legitimate expression of Brazil's national sovereignty and will be implemented in its entirety by the Brazilian government. Such facts do not contribute to an adequate dealing with the matter. The Brazilian Ambassador to the United States received instructions to obtain from the US government detailed information on this issue. [*Folha de São Paulo, 1986*, my translation]

Nationalist reaction to the opening of the Brazilian 301 case and the first consultation meeting was vociferous. The Brazilian Congress passed Law No.7463, which established targets for a triennial programme for stimulating automation and local development of the IT sector (I PLANIN), thus putting into practice the principles defined in the 'informatics' law. A ceremony for the President to sign I PLANIN was set up as a political event attended by fifteen Ministers of State, the leaders of all political parties in the Brazilian Congress, scientists, and the representatives of several professional associations in the IT area. The ceremony was seen as an answer to the American demand for changing

Brazilian IT policy. Senator Severo Gomes (of the Partido do Movimento Democrático Brasileiro, PMDB) introduced Bill No. 99/86 (called the National Self Defence Bill) into the Brazilian Congress. The Bill would have established Brazil's right, in the case of any foreign country restricting the access of Brazilian products to its market, to retaliate against companies from that country operating in Brazil. The Bill would have granted the Brazilian government power to cut off those companies' licenses to remit profits, to register patents, to explore mineral resources, and to receive financial incentives from the Brazilian government; it even granted the government special power to expropriate them. Although never submitted to a vote, this bill shows the extent of nationalist reaction to US pressure.

The 'principled objection' position did not, however, prevent Brazilian authorities from meeting with American delegations in Caracas on 4 February 1986, and in Paris six months later. It was only after the Paris meeting that the Brazilian strategy began to change towards a more pragmatic approach. An observer of the development of the conflict, working at the Brazilian Ministry of Foreign Relations, explained this move as an acknowledgement of the constraints imposed on Brazil by international events.

> Brazil adopted a position of realism and pragmatism. It had four different alternative options to choose: alternative (a) was to deal with the matter only at GATT, alternative (b) was to refuse any sort of conversation on the subject, alternative (c) was to make all changes demanded by the Americans, and alternative (d) was to talk with them in light of our interests. It was the awareness of the dependence of the Brazilian economy that explains the choice of alternative (d) [*Paranhos, interview, 23 Sept. 88*, my translation].

By that time not only was the Americans' intention to impose economic sanctions on Brazilian exports already known, but so were their specific demands for change in the Brazilian policy. At the meeting held in Paris on 11 August 1986, and in Brussels in mid-December of that year, the Brazilians discussed the list of 26 American complaints. According to the Brazilian Minister of Foreign Relations in his report to the CONIN,

> From the twenty-six questions initially raised by the Americans, only four remained. The other twenty-two were eliminated from the agenda of our conversations either because they would imply modifications of the Informatics Law, which we consider unacceptable; because they were based on a misunderstanding of the Brazilian Law; or because they lacked enough factual evidence. The four remaining questions were (1) improvements of the SEI's procedure, (2) import controls, including a new communication

of CACEX, (3) investment, including joint-ventures, and (4) software [*Sodre, 1986:3,* my translation].

This report was intended to define a scope of changes the Brazilians would accept in implementation of the IT policy and in future legislation on the matter. In the same month as the second Paris meeting (i.e., August 1986), SEI announced internal reforms and CONIN approved the regime of copyright for software. In the following month, SEI approved the IBM-Gerdau association for data processing. And in November, CACEX Communication 171 was issued and the US -Brazil *ad hoc* group was set up. Finally, in December 1986, the Software Bill was sent to the Brazilian House of Representatives.

The Brazilian tactical move was justified in light of their previous position. They had not agreed to modify Law No. 7232, but had instead agreed to implement the law in a more flexible way, in some specific cases, for pragmatic reasons. At that point, the Brazilian move towards negotiating a significant part of the IT policy, software regulation, was justified in relation to broader interests of the country, as was stressed by a Brazilian delegate to that meeting. In his words, 'the IT issue is too small a question when compared to the whole interest Brazil has in all areas of international cooperation' [*O Globo, 1986*]. All but one Brazilian concession to American pressure may be analysed in this way, that is, as a result either of a need to be tactically flexible or of an acknowledged requirement of the development of the policy. As the then Chairman of SEI declared when interviewed

> There were not many real concessions to US pressure. Much of what was accepted had already been planned in the past, but not yet implemented. These actions should have been presented as major concessions in order to placate the Americans. The Brazilians had not, however, enough ability to present the changes made in that way [*Rocha, interview, 12 Sept. 88,* my translation].

Approval of the IBM-Gerdau association, the setting up of the US-Brazil *ad hoc* group, CONIN approval of copyright for software, CACEX Communication 171, and internal reforms at SEI may be seen as minor tactical concessions or the strategic anticipation of needed changes. The software bill was, however, a major concession that affected the integrity of the IT policy as it had been defined and implemented to that time. In the words of the Office Chief of the Ministério de Ciência e Tecnologia (MCT) at that time,

> The great loss of the IT dispute was in the area of our software policy. The US pressures forced the elaboration of Brazilian legislation long before it was considered necessary in the context of the overall Brazilian IT policy.

This was completely different from the case of hardware, where a law came only when we all knew what we wanted. The Brazilian Congress itself voted on a matter it did not know about, because the Brazilian representatives did not have time to discuss the subject and understand its implications [*Seligman, interview, 13 Dec. 88*, my translation].

The Brazilian government's reaction to the US accusations was greatly affected by the country's economic crisis and political instability. The extent to which these processes undermined the local social support of governmental action is a subject that I will deal with in Chapter 7. Here, however, it is necessary to point out the implications of political instability and the economic crisis upon the lack of cohesion among the Brazilian agencies involved in the dispute.

The end of military rule in Brazil in 1984 negatively affected the IT policy. Until then, the policy had benefited by being insulated from social pressures within the institutional apparatus; it also benefited from apparent governmental agreement on the subject. Democratization revealed opposition to the policy that existed within the state itself. Criticism already acknowledged from the Ministry of Communications was accompanied by reproach from the Ministry of Commerce and Industry (MIC) and by disagreement from the Ministry of Finance (MINIFAZ), which had been disclosed in connection with the negotiation of Brazil's foreign debt.[76] All were eager for the government to make some change in the policy that could forestall damage to Brazilian exports. The Brazilian Ministry of Foreign Relations had to mediate between MCT and SEI, who wanted to resist the pressure and make the smallest concessions possible, and the American delegation, which pressured the Brazilian government to act. The Brazilian Ministry of Foreign Relations thus had to negotiate in the name of a government within which there were opposing views on the matter. In the middle of the IT policy dispute, for example, another conflict with the United States developed when the Brazilian Minister for Trade and Industry declared, on 19 May 1986, his intention to ask for market protection for Brazilian pharmaceutical companies. This dispute started, and then evolved rapidly from an issue of foreign investment, which is far more extensive in the Brazilian pharmaceutical industry than in the IT sector, to the subject of pressing Brazil to recognize patent protection in the area. In July 1988, the USTR opened another case against Brazil initiated by American pharmaceutical companies because of lack of patent rights in the Brazilian market. The Pharmaceutical Manufacturers Association, claiming losses of US$ 39 million each year since 1979, asked the USTR for an annual increase in tariffs on Brazilian imports to the US market of around US$ 20 to US$ 25 million, which later increased to US$ 100 million [*O Estado de São Paulo, 1988*]. In October 1988, the United States imposed punitive sanctions of 100 per cent tariff on Brazilian exports of paper, electronic goods, and some pharmaceutical and chemical products [*Ricupero, 1989*].

Because of its internal disagreement on the issue, the Sarney administration was clearly too weak to deal with its strong opponents. As the MCT Office Chief at the time observed when interviewed:

> Sarney's administration was not firm enough to face the Americans. The President's inner circle was and still is against the policy. They are prehistoric liberals in their condemnation of any form of state interventionism. Sarney's closest advisers, however, had for some time to conceal their disagreement with the IT policy because of the PMDB majority in the governmental team. And PMDB's position in favour of the market reserve policy was very strong and firm. A poll among PMDB affiliates had showed that 80 per cent of the party backed the IT policy. With the erosion of PMDB participation in the Sarney administration, the governmental position on the policy became malleable [*Seligman, interview, 13 Dec. 88*, my translation].

Basic disagreement over the IT policy within the government, which was to some extent fuelled by the negotiation of the Brazilian foreign debt, added to the government's impotence before US pressure. Some time before the dispute, the debt crisis of the early 1980s had put the IT policy in the hidden agenda of negotiations for Brazilian debt rescheduling and new loans. This link became a strong argument in favour of deregulating the Brazilian IT market, and put the Brazilian Finance Ministry in an opposing stance to interests within the government that resisted changing the policy, namely the MCT and the SEI. According to the then MCT Office Chief. 'The Brazilian Finance Minister negotiated various concessions in the software bill without the acknowledgement or the agreement of the Ministry for Science and Technology' [*Seligman, interview, 13 Dec. 88*, my translation].

While the policy's defenders were clearly concentrated in the MCT and the SEI, the Sarney administration's heterogenous views on the policy could be seen in CONIN where these views were represented. I believe that CONIN came to be the instrument of Sarney's government in achieving a softer approach to the dispute over the IT policy. This council decided to adopt copyright for software, in accordance with the negotiations with the Americans. The SEI then prepared the legal instrument to formalize the decision, the software bill, which in turn established *functional equivalence* as a criterion for protecting software developed locally. While SEI rejected Microsoft's local licence application for MS-DOS because of its similarity to the locally developed SISNE program, CONIN accommodated American criticism by limiting this rejection to earlier versions of MS-DOS.[77]

However, this pragmatism was inadequate to meet the US challenge, and despite Brazilian concessions, the Americans announced economic sanctions.

This announcement induced the Brazilians to change their tactics in order to improve integration with the private sector, which was directly affected by the threat of sanctions. A joint action by state agencies and private companies was launched to prevent implementation of the announced sanctions. Brazilian authorities summoned the managers of the subsidiaries of American IT companies to discuss the issue. Brazilian companies, both state-owned and private, mobilized some of their American commercial counterparts to oppose the sanctions. Their main argument was the interdependence of the two markets, which meant that sanctions would not damage Brazilian interests alone.[78]

Despite these efforts, flexibility in the implementation of the IT policy and the new software legislation were the real justifications for suspension of the economic sanctions and the closing of the dispute. As Meyer-Stamer [*1990*] summarised, a trade war between the United States and Brazil was prevented by Brazil's debt situation, the complex trade links between the two countries, and Brazilian concessions.

I have shown in this section the Brazilian role in defining the agenda for negotiations and in the evolution of the bargaining process. The Brazilian strategy shifted from a 'principled objection' to even discuss the American accusations to 'pragmatic negotiation' of some US demands for changes in the IT policy. The Brazilians' initial refusal to discuss the American claims contributed to the subsequent focusing of the agenda on a feasible set of mutually agreeable outcomes. The Brazilian strategy of 'pragmatic negotiation' led to some concessions which pleased its opponent, but these were insufficient to end the conflict. The Brazilians' awareness of the political implications of sanctions, their impact on the Brazilian economy and balance of payments, and the seriousness of the American threats helped move them towards a more realistic position. The Brazilians' preference ordering of possible outcomes was affected by the lack of cohesion within the state apparatus in relation to the issues involved and by the shift in domestic support for the IT policy due to the American threat of economic sanctions.

The agreement on copyright protection for IPRs of software led to the closing of the conflict. It was reached under the threat of sanctions against Brazilian exports to the US market. It was further facilitated by the conflicting views, within the state apparatus, on the relevance of the IT policy and on the amplitude of adjustments to make in the policy to assuage its opponents. The lack of cohesion characteristic of the Brazilian government helps to explain the duration of the dispute, which was dropped and taken up again various times in connection with conflicting actions taken by the Brazilian agencies involved.

CONCLUSION

The purpose of this chapter has been to analyse the US/Brazil dispute as a bargaining process of exchange of information, promises, and threats that led to a mutually agreeable outcome and closed the conflict. This analysis of the evolution of the bargaining process has shown each player's role in composing an agenda for negotiations, defined in accordance with each one's strategy, which itself shifted as a function of the opponent's moves.

The players first agreed upon the agenda's scope after initial rounds of negotiations in which both players put forward claims higher than they would have been if the negotiations had been limited to one round and higher than what each party expected to gain in the end. The Brazilians' initial strategy was a 'principled' objection to discuss the American claims. Just as the Brazilian party adopted a strategy of 'pragmatic negotiation' and concessions, the Americans moved from their initial demand for repeal of the Brazilian 'Informatics' Law to a more focused agenda. Fractionating the conflict into three parts and negotiating a 'package deal' in each of them, the Americans aimed to settle various issues simultaneously so that losses in some could be offset by gains in others.

The bargaining process resulted in some Brazilian concessions, which, nevertheless, did not fully satisfy the Americans. Negotiations eventually resulted in the definition of a focal point - the Brazilian adoption of copyright protection for IPRs of software - beyond which each player could not retreat. Under the American threat of sanctions, the Brazilian side, which was about to make a concession, became aware of the seriousness of its opponent's threats and both players knew that this situation limited each one's retreat. Thus, the Brazilian Congress approved a Software Law defining copyright protection for IPRs of software and the Brazilian 301 case was closed.

As I will further explore in the following chapter, the American threat of sanctions was effective in changing the target country's policy not only because of the potential costs of sanctions on affected exporters, but also because it altered the domestic balance of social forces in support of the policy. Brazil could not forego its trade with the United States because of the Americans' large share of Brazilian foreign trade. An adjustment to the interruption of trade would have been lengthy and painful. More than that, vested interests affected by the American threats were so wide and strong that they altered the balance of support for the Brazilian government in defining and implementing the whole IT policy.

The Brazilian 301 case was a culmination of deteriorating political and economic relations between the United States and Brazil. It was preceded by various incidents in which the US government pressured Brazil to change its IT policy. As such, this conflict exemplifies the toughness of international relations in this new technological era. The Brazilian position on a number of multilateral issues in the international arena did not facilitate the negotiations, but Brazil, despite the fragility of its government at the time, was not weak enough to jettison its IT policy. The value of its own markets as a resource to American exporters, combined with the value of Brazil's compliance with American positions on new issues in multilateral trade negotiations, gave the Brazilian considerable bargaining power. The Brazilian foreign debt, however, severely restricted the Brazilian state's bargaining power in defence of its policy against threat of economic sanctions.

7

SHIFT IN THE BRAZILIAN SOFTWARE POLICY: RESOLUTION OF THE CONFLICT

In this chapter I analyse the shift in the Brazilian software policy that led the United States to drop the Brazilian 301 case. It offers a deeper and closer look into the process of conflict resolution, emphasising the role of local players, both governmental and non-governmental, within Brazilian society. Considering these internal social forces is critical in understanding the US/Brazil dispute. As discussed in Chapter 1, this type of international conflict is a 'two-level game', in which negotiations are simultaneously made in international and domestic arenas. It is the complex interplay of domestic and international pressures that explain the resolution of such conflicts.

In Chapter 6, the evolution of the dispute and its concentration on the regulation of IPRs for software were analysed in relation to the two players' strategy. The definition of legal protection for IPRs of software in Brazil was the focal point of the US/Brazil dispute. The adoption of copyright protection for software in Brazil was a compromise solution to the conflict. This final solution was achieved, however, only after the Americans had threatened to impose sanctions. At that point, the party that was going to make concessions was led to 'expect to be expected not to retreat'. There was no chance for Brazil to withdraw from the dispute. The Americans' expectations were also that the Brazilians, taking the threat of sanctions seriously, would either adopt copyright protection for software or leave the US government no other choice than to activate sanctions. For both players the conflict would either be closed or changed into an open trade war.

Here, the focus is on the role of social forces internal to Brazil in shaping the government's negotiation strategy. These forces affected the conflict in two ways, either (i) directly, by supporting or opposing the adoption of legal protection for software, or (ii) indirectly, by withdrawing support previously given or joining the opposition to the IT policy. These forces thus altered the preference ordering of the Brazilian government and lead to the acceptance of a compromise solution. The evolution of the Brazilian government's position from rejection of any special legal protection for software to acceptance of a *sui generis* regime and, finally, agreement on copyright protection is analysed in the first section which also outlines key provisions of the software law. In the subsequent section, I will discuss (i) the effects of the threat of economic sanctions upon the balance of domestic social support of the IT policy, especially in mobilizing previously uncommitted groups against it; and (ii) the consequences of these changes for the adoption of the software law.

Copyright protection for software was adopted in Brazil because of American pressure, and in contradiction to previous government opposition. However, the acceptance of a copyright regime for software was a solution to the conflict because it not only satisfied the Americans but was also acceptable to Brazilian interested parties and to all those Brazilian groups that pressed the government for a settlement that prevented economic sanctions. Nevertheless, a significant concession to American pressure was that the software law does not protect locally owned production of computer programs as the informatics law did for locally owned production of hardware.

TOWARDS A COPYRIGHT REGIME FOR SOFTWARE IN BRAZIL

The discussion of legal protection for software was not raised in Brazil until the early 1980s, and even then it was mostly limited to the domestic legal profession. In 1976, domestic debate on what sort of software policy Brazil should adopt did not include the issue of legal protection for IPRs of software. At that time, the Brazilian government had decided that software for DIGIBRAS's (Empresas Digitais Brasileiras S.A.) G-10 computer project was to be developed by Brazilian engineers. Data-processing professionals and entrepreneurs viewed this decision as a controversial resolution. A national policy for software based exclusively on domestic resources and aimed at complete independence was deemed by some of them to be irrational, useless, and doomed to failure. This view was the opinion of the majority of the IT entrepreneurs. Others supported that decision, however, and believed that its major outcome would be accumulation within the country of local capabilities and knowledge in software development [*Dados e Idéias, 1976: 17*].

Probably the first mention of local protection for IPRs of software was in the journal of SUCESU (an association of Brazilian IT users), which in 1975 published a Portuguese translation of Calvin N. Mooers' paper 'Computer software and copyright'.[79] Mooers' paper strongly supported the adoption of copyright protection for software and gave practical advice to software developers. The impact of this publication on the development of Brazil's software policy cannot be traced, and this obscurity may suggest that it had only a limited effect on interested parties.

Among the Brazilian legal profession, protection for software was also not an issue of great interest in the late 1970s and a few specialists who spoke of or wrote about it mostly favoured adoption of some protection, usually the copyright regime. (This would later result in a clash between representatives of the

104

Brazilian legal profession and the agency in charge of the IT policy.) As discussed in Chapter 3, until the early 1980s, CAPRE and SEI had opposed the adoption of any special legal protection for software. However, as governmental agencies in charge of the subject area, they had to consider WIPO's 1978 model-dispositions of legal protection for software. In consequence, and pressed by the recommendation of its Special Commission on Software and Services (SCSS), SEI participated in various discussions on the issue. In October 1981, SEI sponsored a seminar to discuss the legal treatment of software, with the participation of distinguished representatives of the Brazilian legal profession. In this seminar, WIPO's model-dispositions were discussed in relation to copyright, modified copyright, patents, and utility models. Some practical recommendations were made (e.g., the creation of an agency for the registration of software and the adoption of a reciprocal system for protecting foreign software), but the seminar produced no conclusive recommendations about which available legal regimes of protection to adopt [*Manso, 1985: 164-90*]. The clash between the Brazilian legal profession and SEI over legal protection for software was evident at the First Congress of the Brazilian Computing Society in 1981, when lawyer Carlos Alberto Bittar claimed that the legal profession overwhelmingly favoured copyright protection. This idea was met by strong resistance from SEI. This disagreement between the legal profession and SEI helps to explain the exclusion of provisions on software from the Informatics Bill: Not only was the set of measures designed to foster software production in Brazil still immature but the issue of legal protection for software was highly controversial within Brazil - as well as in other nations - in the early 1980s.

By the time the Informatics Bill was being discussed in the Brazilian Congress [*i.e. 1983-84*], the ongoing international debate on legal protection for software and the domestic needs of software producers and users was pressing the Brazilian government to change its rejection of any specific legal regime for protection of software. In response, Brazil sent representatives to WIPO's Expert Committee Meeting in June 1983. This committee concluded (i) that IPRs of software should be subject to legal protection at the international level; and (ii) that, given the complexity of the issue, it was premature to take a definitive position in relation to the regime of protection. Brazil also sent a representative to WIPO's Working Group Meeting in Canberra, in April 1984. Two months later, SEI sponsored an international seminar on the legal treatment of software, which included representatives from Japan, the Federal Republic of Germany, WIPO, the US Computer Law Association, the US Patent Office, and the Hungarian Bureau for Copyright Protection. The Brazilian delegation represented both government agencies and private industrial and business interests. In his opening speech, SEI's Chairman stated the Brazilian government's intention to tackle the issue of legal protection of software.

One of our main concerns at the present is to define a policy for software that conforms to Brazilian interests in the development of this industrial segment. The definition of the legal treatment to give to software is a basic premise of this policy. This new product of the human mind has characteristics that are so peculiar that its treatment by traditional approaches to goods, technology, or services seems to be oversimplistic. The need for legal regime for software is urgent. Without it we cannot improve our production, commercialization, distribution, and production in the domestic market [*SEI, 1984: 4*, my translation].

Except for Japan, most countries at the seminar expressed support for the copyright regime, based on their past experience. The international seminar of 1984 was also an opportunity for Brazilian software producers and users to express their interest in the adoption of legal protection for software. The delegation from SUCESU, representing the interests of IT users, strongly favoured adoption of legal protection for software in Brazil because they believed it would necessarily include dispositions to protect users. SUCESU also represented entrepreneurs in the area of data processing, who voiced many complaints about suppliers of software, especially of foreign origin. SUCESU's principal complaints included incompatibility and lack of portability of software in relation to the equipment available in the country; difficulty of access to the software's source-code, which would allow the solution of problems or adaptation of the product to the user's needs; and the need to make copies of the software for distributing processing.

Domestic software producers were represented at the seminar by the Associação Brasileira de Empresas de Serviços de Informática (ASSESPRO). For ASSESPRO representatives, the main problems to be tackled by Brazilian authorities were unauthorized copying and software smuggling. According to them, these unlawful acts were committed by domestic companies that sell foreign software as well as by hardware manufacturing companies, both locally owned and foreign subsidiaries. They accused hardware manufacturers of importing software without paying proper duty and of selling software, especially operating systems, at symbolic prices, as an accessory to the equipment. Surprisingly, they did not suggest the adoption of one of the available legal regimes of protection or the creation of a specific regime. Instead, they favoured (i) enforcement of existing legislation, that is the civil code for punishment of trade in unauthorized copies and INPI rules for the examination of contracts of technology transfer; and (ii) urgent definition of an overall software policy. Domestic software producers were much more interested in the definition of a policy that could foster their production and strengthen their position in the Brazilian market than in protection of IPRs of software. For these local producers, enforcement of legal measures that could prevent unauthorized copies, especially of smuggled foreign software with which the local product had to compete, was the main immediately beneficial result of the recognition of monopoly rights on computer programs. Protection of property rights, however, would not be enough to foster domestic software production. If the domestic software market were not reserved for domestic producers, their position in the local market would be at risk. They felt they needed market protection for two reasons: Firstly, originality is difficult to achieve for beginners in software development, and secondly, local products would not be price-competitive with foreign software produced on a large scale and with development costs already covered by global sales. This position on market reserve was supported by Brazilian software engineers who, like the electronics engineers during the launching of the IT policy, were interested in preserving the conditions for the exercise of their creative activity in a protected market for locally owned companies.

ASSESPRO's view that available legal dispositions were sufficient to protect the IPRs of software in Brazil was adopted in its entirety by the commission created by SEI in 1983 to prepare a draft software bill. This draft was never introduced into the Brazilian Congress. It was analysed - together with studies made by ABICOMP and SUCESU - by Senator Virgilio Távora, who introduced Bill No. 260/84 into the Brazilian Congress soon after the approval of the Informatics Law. As I have shown in Chapter 3, Bill No. 260/84 proposed a *sui generis* regulation for software based on the Brazilian Code for Industrial Property and Copyright Law. Its most controversial dispositions were the term of protection proposed - five years - and the recommendation of a compulsory licence for domestic use of software that had been registered but not economically exploited within the country. Discussion of Bill No. 260/84 was interrupted by the opening of the conflict with the United States in 1985. Subsequently, CONIN approved the adoption of copyright protection for software in August 1986, accepting the US demand, and for this purpose a new bill was introduced into the Brazilian Congress in December 1986.

Interested parties within Brazilian society mobilized to influence the definition of a software policy: Seven associations[80] representing engineers, hardware producers, lawyers, and employees in software development and data processing jointly sent suggestions for the software bill to the Brazilian government. The main proposals called for (i) a term of copyright protection between 15 and 25 years; (ii) regulation of payment for software imported by subsidiaries of the parent company according to provisions of the Brazilian law of profit remittance; (iii) payments to the software producer to be based upon the number of copies sold; and (iv) all information and relevant documentation related to the protected software to be deposited in a Brazilian public institution.

Clearly these suggestions enlarged the proposed software bill well beyond the mere extension of copyright protection to computer programs. In fact, the bill introduced into the Brazilian Congress in December 1986 did far more than that: It also defined rules for commercialization of software in the Brazilian market, according to the principle of market reserve for locally owned companies, and made provisions to defend user's rights. Besides extending copyright protection to software for 25 years, it legitimized the provisions established by SEI's Normative Act No. 22 of 1982, by (i) creating a software registry (or file) and making registration a condition for marketing any software in Brazil; (ii) making the filing of software of foreign origin dependent on the nonexistence of functionally similar software developed locally; (iii) reserving commercialization of software exclusively to locally owned companies; and (iv) allowing foreign companies to sell software of foreign origin in the Brazilian market only to run in imported equipment or in mainframes manufactured locally by foreign subsidiaries.

Hardware manufacturers either openly criticized or responded vaguely to the software bill. The association of computer users, however, criticized the software bill, stressing technical difficulties in implementing the concept of 'local similar'[81] and asserting that insufficient protection was provided for locally developed software. SUCESU's criticism of the inadequacy of protection granted to local production had profound repercussions among locally owned companies that developed software in Brazil and their association, ASSESPRO. SUCESU's president expressed users' and producers' common interest:

> SUCESU and ASSESPRO understand, and have told the government, that we must have the capability to develop our own software on a large scale. But, as we must have the capability of building our own computers, we need to have access to foreign software, especially those that complement the national production, in order to ensure that we are, in fact, adequately employing IT [*Mussalem, 1987b*, my translation].

SUCESU's declaration was not only a statement of common interest between users and producers of software in Brazil. It was quite clearly intended to attract the support of hardware producers who, as pointed out in Chapter 2, benefited from little state intervention in the software market.

SUCESU and ASSESPRO presented a joint suggestion for the software bill while it was being discussed in the Brazilian Senate. This suggestion took the form of amendments to the bill approved in the House of Representatives. The main suggestion was tariff protection to replace the market reserve established by the concept of 'local similar'. The joint suggestion also recommended creation of a 'licence to sell' foreign software in Brazil, to be issued by the Brazilian authorities and to be stamped on each copy sold in the country. The Senate considered these amendments in preparing its substitute bill, which rejected tariff protection, but introduced a 'contribution fee' to be paid by the copyright owner for a 'licence to sell' foreign software in Brazil. These points were, however, among those vetoed by the Brazilian President.

A comparison between Bill No. 260/84 and the software law as enacted (Table 7.1) shows how the conflict softened the Brazilian position. The software law - Law No. 7646 of December 1987 - makes provisions in four areas: protection of author's rights, filing of software, commercialization of software in the Brazilian market, and users' rights. The Brazilian law, like similar laws in France, Japan, and Spain, made substantial changes in copyright law to adapt it to protection of IPRs of software. Under Brazilian law, the term of protection is 25 years from the launching of the software in any country, independent of registration or filing dates, and protection is granted to foreign authors on a reciprocity basis.

Filing of software is required for commercialization of software in Brazil. Filing categorizes software according to whether it was developed in Brazil or not and by foreign or Brazilian companies. The categories imply no differences in the protection of author's rights but are established only for financial and fiscal purposes. Filing of foreign software is conditional on nonexistence of a functionally similar product developed in Brazil by locally owned companies. Commercialization of software is subject to licensing agreements or contracts of assignment of rights and is authorized only to locally owned companies. The software law also makes provisions to protect user's rights. The owner of software commercialization rights is obliged to correct any mistakes during the period of technical validity of each version, and to ensure the rendering of technical services. The software owner may not withdraw it from commercial circulation without fair indemnification of possible damages to third parties. The owner is also responsible to the user for the technical quality of the software and its recording.

The adoption of this amended copyright regime for software did not fully satisfy the Americans. They suspended economic sanctions after the approval of the software law, but did not drop the case. This was because the Brazilian software law contained a major controversial provision related to the key issue that initially moved the Americans to threaten a trade war against Brazil: market reserve for local producers. This sensitive issue was embodied in the concept of 'functional equivalence', or the idea of 'locally similar'. On this basis, foreign software could be excluded from the Brazilian market.

Between December 1987, when the software law was approved, and May 1988, when the rules for implementing this law were finally issued, at least four different proposals for operationalizing the principles defined in the law were elaborated. These proposals differed in various points, but in all the central subject was definition of criteria to assess similarity.

TABLE 7.1
COMPARISON BETWEEN PROVISIONS OF BRAZILIAN SOFTWARE POLICY
BEFORE AND AFTER THE CONFLICT

Provision	Bill No. 260 - 1984	Software Law - 1987
Regime Of Protection	Established by the bill	Copyright
Term of protection	15 years from the date of application for filing, conditional on filing; 2 years for entertainment software	25 years from the launching in any country, independent of filing or registration date
Rights of foreign producers	According to specific international treaties or conventions signed by their countries and ratified by Brazil; on a reciprocal basis	On a reciprocal basis
Filing restrictions	Necessary condition for granting of rights Information required for filing: source-code; specification of language when not of public knowledge; declaration of the original or derivative nature of the software Approval of contracts involving foreign producer depends on nonexistence of local similar at reasonable price	Necessary condition for trade in Brazil. Valid for 3 years, automatic renewal if there is no local similar Information required for registration: sections of the work and other data considered sufficient to demonstrate independent creation For foreign product registration conditional on nonexistence of 'local similar'. 'Local similar' (functional equivalence) defined as follows: has the same performance; complies with Brazilian standards; carries out same functions
Commercialization	Exclusive rights of producer, transferable to others. Assignment of rights or authorization for trade cannot restrict use, trade, improvement, or export of software or of goods and services in which the software is used	Exclusively by locally owned firms. Of foreign product, only with assignment of rights or licensing agreement. Contracts cannot limit production, distribution, and trade; and cannot exempt parties from responsibility on defects or infringement of copyright. Remuneration of foreign author: price per copy with technical documents
Restrictions to producer's rights	Compulsory licence/expropriation: for reasons of relevant national economic or social interests	None

The least precise suggestion, which introduced no significant clarification, came from the Brazilian government itself. MCT's suggestion was to define as functionally equivalent 'software which produces essentially the same results that could have been obtained from the other in contrast to which the similarity is being examined'. MCT's notorious opponent, MINICOM, recommended considering functional equivalent as 'software equal or superior to the one in contrast to which the similarity is being examined'. Defending local producers of software, ASSESPRO suggested that (i) the association of local software producers be consulted in the analysis of similarity; (ii) there be a 12 month interval after denial of a filing application for foreign software that has a Brazilian similar before filing an application for a new version of that same software, to give Brazilian producers an opportunity to update their version; (iii) communication in the Portuguese language shall be a factor that improves the performance and productivity of software.

The most precise and the strongest suggestion for implementing the software law was presented by representatives of the groups most interested in conflict resolution: FIESP, SUCESU, the Brazilian Association of Software Vendors (ABES), ABDI, and the Association of Brazilian Exporters (AEB). Their proposal specified the following criteria for the assessment of similarity: (i) the similar software shall achieve 95 per cent of the performance achieved by the other software in parameters that are measurable quantitatively; (ii) the similar software shall be compatible with the same equipment, instruments, peripherals, and operating systems commercialized in Brazil with which the other software is itself compatible; the similar software shall also allow access to the same existing resources of equipment, instruments, peripherals, and operating systems commercialized in Brazil; (iii) similar software shall produce the same outputs from the same inputs in the essential functions of the software; in other functions, there shall be 95 per cent correspondence; (iv) resources and additional functions of software developed in Brazil by locally-owned companies to meet Brazilian market requirements as well as differences due to the communication language in which the software is presented shall not be considered as differential criteria; (v) decision on the nonexistence of locally similar for any software shall be based exclusively on consideration of other software filed up to the filing application date.

Decree No. 96036, of May 1988, clarified the main controversial points of the concept of similarity defined by the software law.[82] Most of the FIESP proposals can be easily identified in the decree, which defined the following specifications:

'have substantially the same performance characteristics considering the type of application it is intended for' means that, comparing relevant parameters, the software developed by a locally owned company produces

111

essentially the same effect obtained by the software in relation to which the similarity is being assessed;

'relevant parameters', including those which are measured numerically, comprise memory requirements, processing time, and transaction capacity between user and system;

'operate in similar equipment and processing environment' means that the software developed by a locally owned company is compatible with equipment, instruments, peripherals, and operating systems commercialized in Brazil with which the other software being compared is itself compatible. The locally developed software shall, in addition, allow access to the resources existing in the equipment instruments, peripherals, and operating systems commercialized in Brazil which the other software being compared permits;

'to carry substantially the same functions' means to produce equivalent output for a given set of input data, considering those computer program specifications which are public knowledge [*Decree No. 96036/88, Article 3*, my translation].

Reacting to Decree No. 96036, ASSESPRO and even ABICOMP accused the software law of protecting only foreign software, as a local product would have to be equal, not similar, to be granted protection. Analysts of the software law have reached the same conclusion. Gaio and Segre [*1989*], examining the question of what was the aim of the Brazilian software law, infer that it was to protect foreign software and local users, not to promote local technology. This is because it did not create an environment conducive to the fostering of local production of software. The software law was not, in fact, an instrument for fostering local production of software, but only an instrument for the protection of locally owned companies that commercialize this product. In a nutshell, this legislation was the first formal product of liberalization of the Brazilian IT market.

Summing up the discussion so far, I conclude that the issue of legal protection for IPRs of software was, in Brazil as well as in some other countries, still controversial in the early 1980s. Based on economic considerations, the Brazilian authorities in charge of the IT policy resisted dealing with the matter, leaving it to business associations of interested parties - domestic producers and users - to define a code of conduct and to denounce unlawful practices and acts. Existing legal dispositions, such as the civil code, contract law, copyright law, and the Brazilian Code for Industrial Property, were considered by those authorities good enough to protect property rights on software. Eventually, pressures arising out of Brazil's participation in international organizations, as well as from domestic producers and users, led the Brazilian government to admit the need to give special legal protection for software. Controversy over the appropriate legal instrument of protection among the Brazilian legal profession resulted in a consensus on the superiority of copyright over other possible alternatives. This resulted in a clash with the governmental agency in charge of the IT policy, which preferred the creation of a *sui generis* form of protection. Soon after the approval of the Informatics Law, Bill No. 260/84 was introduced into the Brazilian Congress with dispositions inspired both by the Brazilian Code for Industrial Property and by copyright law. Some of these dispositions were highly controversial, as was the short term of protection and the compulsory licensing provision. This Bill was under discussion in the Brazilian Congress when the conflict with the United States started. The definition of copyright protection for software, made by CONIN in August 1986, resulted clearly from American pressure. Copyright of software would also have benefited domestic producers, however, as long as recognition of property rights was accompanied by measures to reserve the Brazilian market for them. Brazilian software producers did not dislike extending legal protection to IPRs of software, but they were much more interested in a policy that could reserve their share of the market. Mobilization of a large group of interested parties managed to influence the preparation of a software bill, which did much more than simply extend copyright protection to software, but failed to reserve the Brazilian market for domestic producers.

CHANGING ATTITUDES OF DOMESTIC SOCIAL GROUPS TOWARDS THE IT POLICY

The Brazilian IT policy had been marked by a strong nationalist drive, whose ideological foundation was the aim to improve domestic technological capability. This nationalist policy originated from its promoters' awareness of developed countries' dominance, developing countries' dependency, and the resulting inequitable international relationships in science and technology. National independence from foreign suppliers of technology had been a powerful mobilizing idea, around which several segments of Brazilian society gathered during the setting up an institutionalization of the IT policy. Strong domestic support and the compliance of relevant segments of the armed forces in a military regime had given the military administration of SEI wide powers to act strictly according to its interpretation of national interests in the area. Therefore, adoption of copyright protection for software against SEI's will was a surprising outcome. Foreign pressure was decisive in explaining this change: It was clearly due to American pressure that copyright protection for software was adopted in Brazil (as shown in the previous section). One of my central arguments here, however, is that internal conditions in Brazil, through a complex interplay with external forces, also played a prominent role in forcing SEI to yield. The purpose of this section is to analyse the change of social and political domestic conditions that led to this shift in SEI's position.

Changes in the balance of domestic support for SEI and for the IT policy as a whole were the main domestic factors determining SEI's decision to accept a compromise solution for the conflict. Social support had grown throughout the policy's conception and implementation, based on the ideal of domestic technological capability and on the policy's positive achievements. The policy achieved its greatest support during discussion and approval of the Informatics Law by the Brazilian Congress in December 1984. After that, economic and political instability eroded its support, with consequent weakening of the legitimacy of SEI's activities and orientation. The conflict with the United States started at a time when support for the policy, although still strong, was starting to decline. The conflict accelerated this tendency and provided important ammunition to the policy's opposition.

Three phases characterize the development of the Brazilian IT policy from its beginning in 1972 until the formal conclusion of the Brazilian 301 case in October 1989: a setting-up phase (1972-79), an institutionalization phase (1980-84), and a consolidation/adaptation phase (1985-89). The *setting-up phase* of the policy started in 1972, with the creation of a Special Working Group (GTE) to define a strategy for the construction of a computer for military and civilian use in Brazil. This phase covered the whole period of operation of CAPRE, ending in 1979 with the replacement of CAPRE by SEI. This was the time when production of mini- and microcomputers and their peripherals was first reserved for local capital. At that time, the policy was of limited interest to the overall governmental structure, and remained insulated within the state apparatus. Protected by its support in the armed forces, the policy was relatively safeguarded from interference by foreign firms and powerful state agencies. From a political standpoint, the policy's very existence depended mostly on the ability of its supporters to convince relevant players in the governmental structure of the policy's merits. The *institutionalization phase* started with the creation of SEI and ended with the passing of the informatics law in 1984. During this phase, the scope of the policy was enlarged to reserve production of a comprehensive set of IT goods and services for local capital. The policy's success in establishing a locally owned professional electronics industry, combined with Brazil's large potential market for electronic products and services, made the policy more visible and, consequently, more fiercely challenged by its opponents. The subsequent phase, from 1985 to 1989, was one of *consolidation of policy* instruments *and adaptation of* its goals and strategy to changing conditions, both foreign and local. The recent domestic debate on the policy's strategy and long-term objectives, which involves local entrepreneurs in electronics and other industries, was triggered by local macroeconomic factors, but strengthened by the US/Brazil conflict over the Brazilian IT policy. The potential

114

victims of the US threat of retaliation were the most significant newcomers to the list of IT policy critics. A summary of the balance of social support for the policy in each of these three phases is presented in Table 7.2.

TABLE 7.2
BALANCE OF DOMESTIC SOCIAL FORCES IN OPEN SUPPORT OF
THE BRAZILIAN IT POLICY

Setting-up phase (1972-79)	Institutionalization phase (1980-84)	Consolidation/adaptation phase (1985-89)
FOR	FOR	FOR
Scientific/technological, and planning communities inside the state apparatus	Scientific/technological, and planning communities inside the state apparatus	Scientific/technological, and planning communities inside the state apparatus
	Bulk of Brazilian IT industrialists	
Scientific/technological community outside the state apparatus	Scientific/technological community outside the state apparatus	Most Brazilian IT industrialists
		Intelligence forces/military
Military	Intelligence forces/military	
		Brazilian Congress
	Brazilian Congress	
AGAINST	AGAINST	AGAINST
Representatives of foreign capital in the IT sector	Representatives of foreign capital in the IT sector	Representatives of foreign capital in the IT sector
Representatives of industrial users of IT goods	Representatives of industrial users of IT goods	Representatives of industrial users of IT goods
Top executives in the state apparatus (MINICOM)		Top executives in the state apparatus (MINICOM, MINIFAZ, MIC, ITAMARATY*)
		Exporters affected by the threat of sanctions

*ITAMARATY, Brazilian Ministry of Foreign Relations

Balance of Domestic Support in Establishing the IT Policy

Brazil's IT policy was established after the high growth rates of the Brazilian 'economic miracle' had already declined. Unfavourable international conditions following the first oil crisis in 1974 made the goal of promoting economic expansion dependent on greater foreign borrowing. Positive trade balances became of strategic relevance. Governmental policies were oriented toward saving foreign exchange and establishing long-term technological objectives.

The alliance that underlay the setting-up of the Brazilian IT policy consisted of segments of the scientific/technological community within and outside the state apparatus and some navy officers.[83] Members of the scientific/technological community employed by state agencies (also identified as the technical/scientific and planning community) united with navy officers in the common objective of local technological development. Backed by the planning minister, they provided the 'within the state' bunker of IT policy support, exploiting their inside position to convince relevant players within the state apparatus of the strategic opportunity for establishing the policy. Outside it, members of the scientific/technological community, organized in the Brazilian Society for the Progress of Science (SBPC) and, later, in the Brazilian Computing Society (SBC) and the Association of Data Processing Professionals (APPD), constituted a relatively small but highly mobilized force that pressed the government for consistency in the IT policy.

Participation of the scientific/technological community in the alliance has been explained elsewhere by their ideological commitment to overcome dependence and their identification of the central role of local technological capability as the basis for autonomous economic development.[84] Two factors explain the military's participation in the alliance. Initially, some navy officers were motivated by their concern over national security. Lack of local control over new technology employed in the navy's ships risked national security, either because the military would be unable to operate its own defence equipment or would have to rely on foreign maintenance. These strategic considerations were augmented, as soon as the first actions had been taken, by a nationalistic reaction to the behaviour of subsidiaries of transnational corporations that affronted the Brazilian state.

Opposition to the policy during this initial phase was mostly limited to foreign subsidiaries acting in the Brazilian IT market. Within the state apparatus, most of the criticism to the policy came from MINICOM. Foreign subsidiaries in the sector of professional electronics saw their prospects of entering the profitable market of smaller computers blocked by government decisions. Subsidiaries in the Brazilian telecommunications sector became increasingly worried by SEI's interference in decisions that had previously depended on MINICOM's exclusive authority. Criticism by foreign subsidiaries had little effect on other relevant social groups within Brazilian society. Only isolated Brazilian IT industrialists showed their dissatisfaction with the restrictions the policy placed on their association with foreign capital.

New Supportive Forces during the Institutionalising Phase

Recessionary policies adopted in Brazil after the second oil crisis and the rise of international interest rates resulted in strict limits on public spending, and reductions of direct public investment, of spending by governmental agencies,

116

and of imports by public companies. Industrial production and employment declined in absolute figures, as did net foreign investment.

Recessionary policies and the financial crisis had negative effects upon Brazil's scientific and technological policy. Resources became scarce and the process of developing an institutional structure and financing mechanisms slowed down. This 'drought' stage of the Brazilian science and technology policy [*Adler, 1987: 156*] eroded the confidence of the scientific and technological community in governmental effectiveness. However, it was not until the mid-1980s - during the adaptation phase of the IT policy - that reduced resources for science and technology, including the presidential veto of the R&D fund established in the informatics law, led to reduced support by the scientific and technological community for the IT policy. At that time, this support played a crucial role in the policy's institutionalization.

Under the gradual political liberalization of the authoritarian regime, the need to formalize the IT policy became a prime concern for its supporters, who felt the policy too weak to survive the instability of the transition to democracy. Pressure from foreign firms and even from the US government had mounted, and at the beginning of the 1980s the policy's supporters saw clear signs that the end of the market reserve was going to be pressed upon the Brazilian government. A strategy was then launched to enact into law the set of norms that had embodied the IT policy so far.

At that stage, the IT policy's supporting alliance of the previous phase was augmented by three new participants: army intelligence, members of the Brazilian Congress, and national hardware producers. The involvement of army intelligence was precipitated by the nomination of constitutive members of the National Intelligence Service (SNI)[85] to a commission created by the new Brazilian government to study the activities of CAPRE and to make suggestions for the electronics complex. The commission recommended that CAPRE be dissolved, and its functions passed to a new agency, SEI, under the National Security Council (CSN). Intelligence involvement was, at first, highly controversial among the policy's supporters. Mutual suspicion contaminated the relationship between intelligence officers, the planning intelligentsia, and the scientific community. Once established, SEI criticized the narrow scope of the policy (because it did not yet address microelectronics and software) and accused CAPRE of having been too liberal with transnational corporations.[86] Nevertheless, SEI's pragmatic decisions[87] toward licensing foreign subsidiaries, and its intolerance of the civil community that had defined the IT policy up to that time, kept the intelligentsia opposed to SEI for some time. This situation changed when the process of turing the policy into law forced the supporting forces to reunite.

By this time, national hardware producers had entered the political arena, having become a relatively important segment of the industrial sector. In August

1979, some of them defected from the Brazilian Association for the Electric and Electronic Industry (ABINEE), where affiliates of foreign subsidiaries prevented the Association from supporting the IT policy, to create ABICOMP. National manufacturers of hardware were a much more homogeneous and cohesive group at that time than they are today. Satisfaction with the segment's high growth rates and SEI's backing contributed to their cohesiveness. Many of them genuinely supported the technological goal of self-reliance and were investing significant resources in R&D.[88] Their minor internal differences related mainly to the process of technology absorption, since some microcomputer producers had been copying foreign models without much learning effort [*Fregni, 1988*].

The Brazilian Movement for Informatics (MBI), formed while the Informatics Bill was being discussed, was decisive in pressing the Brazilian Congress to vote on the matter before the change of government. The MBI united ABICOMP, SBC, APPD, SBPC, ASSESPRO, SUCESU, and the National Federation of Engineers (FNE) to defend the IT policy principle of a reserved market for local capital.

Opposition to the policy grew stronger during this phase, especially opposition from the US government. American pressure to exclude the market reserve principle from the Informatics Bill took various forms, including putting the issue on the hidden agenda of debt rescheduling. Foreign subsidiaries in the IT sector remained opposed, but during this phase very few Brazilian IT industrialists backed their criticism. The huge social mobilization for the approval of the Informatics Bill overcame all criticism to the policy, including in the Brazilian Congress where the bill was approved with one solitary vote against.

Pressed by foreign opposition and at the political juncture of the transition from military rule to democracy, state action towards institutionalizing the IT policy developed within a situation of economic crisis, foreign indebtedness, and IMF supervision. The policy's supporting alliance, which had been strengthened by new politically weighty participants, mobilized wide social support and gave Congress the backing it needed to turn the IT policy into law.

Changing Social Support in the Consolidation Phase

Since enactment of the Informatics Law, the economic crisis, political and institutional instability, and development problems in the electronics industry have severely weakened the alliance that supported the policy during the institutionalization phase. Support for the policy was eroded due to disaffection of the scientific/technological community, the military retreating to the back stage, and the loss of cohesiveness among IT industrialists. By the end of this phase, open support of the policy was limited to some industrialists in the sector of professional electronics working with the help of a few institutions representing the technological community.

Brazilian annual inflation rates, which had stabilized at around 200 per cent since 1983, began to increase by the end of military rule. The first civilian government in twenty years set up unorthodox antiinflationary programmes that triggered a brief economic surge. Severe financial disequilibria soon reappeared, however, leading to the return of high inflation rates. Economic growth rates declined in 1987 and the economy stagnated in 1988. In February 1987, a drastic fall in Brazilian foreign-exchange reserves led to a unilateral moratorium on all interest payments of its debt to private banks.

Failure of attempts to curb inflation added to the political instability of Sarney's administration. The precarious political coalition of liberal and interventionist forces that formed the basis of the Sarney administration broke apart. Domination of Sarney's administration by liberal forces threatened the IT policy because a wider segment of the government began to criticize it.

The Brazilian electronics industry developed under conditions that divided IT producers, reducing their support for the policy and altering the industry's relationship with the governmental agency in charge of the policy. Conflicting policies towards the various sectors of the electronics industry aggravated inefficient interindustrial relations within the IT industry, especially those involving the production of components and the rest of the industry. Fragmentation in the professional electronics sector resulted in small-scale production processes, which affected price performance and technology strategies [*Tigre, 1988: 117*].[89] Financing for investment in capital and technology, readily available during market growth, became scarce, and the burden of debt became risky, under conditions of diminishing economic growth and high inflation. This moved state agencies to encourage medium-sized and smaller firms to merge, which created a trend toward great local conglomerates and increased the willingness of many smaller firms to associate with foreign capital

During this phase, administrators of various agencies within the state apparatus and the potential victims of the threatened US retaliation joined the policy's opposition. Within the state apparatus, MINICOM, which disagreed strongly with SEI over conceptions and strategies of action, continued to oppose the policy. They were joined by MINIFAZ and ITAMARATY, whose negotiation of Brazil's foreign debt and of a solution to the US/Brazil conflict led their top executives to criticize the IT policy. In addition, the Minister of Industry and Commerce started to view the IT policy as an obstacle to his intention to create 'export processing zones' of IT products.

Although opposition to the policy grew and diversified within the state apparatus, changes within the private sector had a more significant impact on the Brazilian government's, and particularly SEI's, positions. In Brazil, domestic managers of IT user companies, especially the larger industrial ones, were natural allies of the managers of foreign IT subsidiaries who opposed the policy. Larger industrial producers in Brazil complained that the policy's restrictions on importation of IT goods and the alternative of less developed 'domestic similar' hindered their modernization programmes. The US/Brazil conflict added powerful new critics to this group of industrialists. Producers of industrial goods such as orange juice, shoes, textiles, plywood, steel products, and aircraft, whose interests and activities had never before been disturbed by the policy, were led to oppose it because of the American threats of economic sanctions against their exports.

The American threat to retaliate against groups of exporters with no connection to IT production strengthened the opposition. They accused the policy of aggravating Brazilian industry's isolation from international markets. Thus, for the first time in the IT policy's short history, the conflict pitted the local IT sector against the whole Brazilian economy. 'Will Brazil defend an *island policy* in order to save the informatics sector and to condemn all local exports to stagnation'? asked an important newspaper's lead article [*Jornal do Brasil, 1985*]. Referring to the conflict, another leading newspaper article commented that

> The problems Sarney's administration faces are related to the whole country. Their solution depends on the technological evolution of the industrial sector, the international competitiveness of Brazilian manufacturing, and the openness of the local economy [*O Estado de São Paulo, 1986*, my translation].

Local technological capability in IT, the major justification for a protectionist industrial policy, was blamed for Brazil's lack of modernization in the industrial sector and for the potential loss of Brazilian exports. Moreover, local R&D in information technology itself was also censured.

> The road that leads to the independence of Brazil includes cooperation with other countries and the assignment of high priority to technological development. It is essential for the country to invest in areas such as research on tropical diseases, on deep-water oil extraction, on selected seeds, and on genetic adaption of cattle to tropical conditions. We cannot let the idea of technological advance be reduced to electronics, computers, software [*Jornal do Brasil*, 1986c, my translation].

The alleged misplaced emphasis on IT compared to other relevant technologies revealed another idea present in this criticism: Brazil's acceptance of a subordinate role in a new international division of labour. Delays in industrial modernization, blamed on SEI's import controls, were said to make Brazilian producers non-competitive internationally in the production of manufactured goods that were once made in developed countries. It was said that the developed economies' abandonment of traditional manufacturing and the subsequent shift to production of more knowledge-intensive goods and services would create greater export opportunities for other countries. In the trade war for these newly opened markets, only countries that harmonized technological modernization of their industrial sector with commercial reciprocity would have a chance of winning. The goal of attaining local capability and keeping a locally reserved high-technology industrial market was seen to jeopardize the goal of increasing industrial exports [*Jornal da Tarde, 1986*].

In this section I have described changes in the balance of domestic social support for the Brazilian IT policy and the shifts in it that resulted from the US/Brazil conflict. A crumbling supportive alliance, a strengthened opposition, high political instability, increasing disarticulation within the state, and the general economic crisis narrowed the limits for the state agencies' actions, including negotiating a solution to the conflict. Among all these unfavourable conditions, the shift in the balance of domestic social support for the policy was the most relevant. The main changes in this balance were fewer proponents, decreased willingness of the remaining supportive groups to fight, and strengthening opposition to the policy with the progressive integration of top executives of several governmental agencies and exporters potentially affected by the threat of economic sanctions. Along with the involvement of previously uncommitted groups, the threat of sanctions gave the opposition the opportunity to mobilize social support in the name of eliminating the international isolation the policy was imposing on the whole Brazilian economy.

CONCLUSION

Brazil had managed to maintain its firm stand to grant protection for IPRs of software only by trade secret, regulated by contract law, from CAPRE's time until 1986. At that time, CONIN decided, under American pressure, to adopt the copyright regime. The Brazilian software law, however, does more than extend copyright protection to computer programs. It is, most of all, a set of principles to regulate commercialization of software in the country, some of which had been in force, in a less polished form, since the early 1980s. Expansion of locally controlled microcomputer production in the 1980s, enhanced by the protection of a reserved market, would have been jeopardized by similar protection of the local software market. Clearly, then, the policy was directed mostly toward the claims and aspirations of national hardware producers. This provoked disaffection in the scientific/technological community, and damaged the policy's legitimacy among other segments of the industrial sector.

As discussed in Chapter 1, government players in international bargaining have to take into account expectations of their constituencies. This makes international negotiations 'two-level games' [*Raiffa, 1982; Putnam, 1988*]. In this context, Brazil sought outcomes to the conflict that would maximize the government's ability to manage the conflict between the IT industry and the rest of the nation's economy, while simultaneously minimizing domestic damage from the possible solutions to this international conflict. This 'two-level game' approach implies that the outcome that solves an international conflict belongs not only to a set of feasible outcomes that can satisfy both governments. The outcome must also belong to a 'win-set', or a set of international agreements that can also be accepted by domestic constituencies.

In the Brazilian IT conflict, Brazil had to negotiate on an international level, while simultaneously dealing with strong domestic political constraints. Domestic support for the policy, although still strong, was beginning to erode. Conflicting interests within the alliance supporting the policy revealed the weakness of its support, and widened the range of conflicts the Brazilian government had to manage with respect to the policy. In addition, the US/Brazil conflict impacted domestic groups that were previously uninvolved in the policy. The conflict thereby revealed, and in some cases intensified, the belief that the IT policy either did not serve or actively damaged the interests of the majority of the Brazilian industrial sector. In a nutshell, the conflict jeopardized the policy's legitimacy.

The shift in social support for the policy decisively affected public respect for SEI, whose actions had been in strict accordance with the Informatics Law. Thus lacking the domestic support it enjoyed throughout most of its existence, and pressured to make significant concessions to prevent a trade war, SEI could do no more than yield and accept the adoption of copyright protection for software contrary to its previous stance. However, in order for this outcome of international bargaining to be a 'win-solution' it had to be accepted at the domestic level. Brazilian exporters potentially affected by the threat of sanctions were satisfied with any solution that could end the conflict. Brazilian hardware producers, especially microcomputer industrialists, were relieved by the prospect of closing the conflict without opening the market. Domestic software producers, despite gaining - at least in a long-term perspective - with the adoption of copyright protection, were convinced that their position in the domestic market would be threatened unless they had this market reserved for them. The concept of 'functional equivalence' was intended to provide such protection for Brazilian software producers and, therefore, to make adoption of copyright protection for software a 'win-solution' to the conflict. In the end, when the concept of 'functional equivalence' was operationalized in accordance with American interests, domestic software producers - a weaker member of the Brazilian IT producers group - were 'sacrificed' for the benefit of stronger domestic interests. The solution agreed upon at the international level was thus accepted at the domestic level. The 'focal point' solution achieved at the international level (as described in Chapter 6) was thus a 'win-solution' as well.

The analysis in this chapter has shown that, although costs imposed by the threat of economic sanctions may help to explain their effectiveness, it was the effect of these costs upon the domestic balance of forces in support of the policy that finally moved the Brazilian government to change it. The effectiveness of the threat of trade sanctions was not due, as would have been expected in Kaempfer and Lowenberg's [*1988*] approach, to the concentration of losses on groups benefiting from the IT policy. The threat of sanctions was effective because it was directed to uncommitted interest groups: It 'tipped the balance' by providing arguments for the policy's opposition and, more significantly, making new groups join the opposing team.

PART III:

UNDERSTANDING CONFLICT RESOLUTION

8

HOW THE RESOLUTION WAS
NON-ZERO SUM

The purpose of this chapter is to analyse the balance of gains and losses for each player in the US/Brazil conflict. My central argument in this respect is that the conflict had a non-zero-sum solution, in which there was no absolute winner or total loser. Both players gained. But the Americans reaped more benefits than the Brazilians.

As I have shown in Section 6.2, the list of American complaints against the Brazilian IT policy presented in the first meeting of the delegations of the two countries consisted of twenty-six items. After the first round of negotiations, the two parties agreed on an agenda confined to three sets of issues, which became the constitutive 'parts' of the Brazilian 301 case. Part one contained all issues related to administrative procedures in the implementation of the policy; part two organized all American complaints against restrictions on market access; and part three referred to protection for IPRs of software. The analysis of each country's balance of gains and losses in this chapter refers to these three parts.

The balance of gains and losses of any player can be determined only in relation to the player's utility function, which gives his/her preference ordering of desired outcomes. However, as I have pointed out in Chapter 1, the utility function of each player is not clearly expressed, usually changes during the negotiation, and must often be inferred by his/her moves. This difficulty is circumvented in axiomatic approaches to bargaining, in which the analyst defines the utility function of each player. In this study, using a descriptive approach to bargaining, I make some inferences on the utility function of each player, based on their moves, to complement available information on their preference ordering of outcomes.

BRAZILIAN BALANCE OF GAINS AND LOSSES

From the opening of the conflict in September 1985, until withdrawal of part one of the Brazilian 301 case by the Americans in September 1986, the Brazilians took the following actions in response to American claims: (i) internal reforms at SEI to expedite the process of issuing authorization for importation of IT goods; (ii) authorization of a joint-venture between IBM and the Brazilian company Gerdau; and (iii) establishment of an *ad hoc* group to review specific complaints by American companies against the Brazilian IT policy. These initial measures taken by the Brazilian government were the easiest and held the fewest implications for the Brazilian ideal of making no substantial changes in their IT policy. These measures pleased the Americans and demonstrated the Brazilians' willingness to cooperate. They implied no changes in the policy's guiding principles. Instead they represented attempts at increasing efficiency in policy implementation either by improving SEI's procedures or by permitting exceptions on a case-by-case basis. This last point was evidenced by the approval of the IBM-Gerdau association and by the creation of the *ad hoc* group to examine other complaints by American companies.

Negotiation of part two of the Brazilian 301 case (i.e., market access complaints) was extremely difficult and was never resolved conclusively. Only a change in the Brazilian Informatics Law could have completely satisfied the American demands for market access. The Brazilians convinced the Americans that such alteration was impossible at that time. But the Brazilians also assured them that the reserved market for IT goods would not be extended beyond 1992, nor to any other product. Nevertheless, the Brazilians granted two significant concessions: (i) approval of the IBM-Gerdau association, and (ii) definition of a narrower list of IT goods under import control (CACEX Communication No. 171). The Brazilians treated the association of IBM with a Brazilian company as an exception agreed upon for pragmatic reasons. Association with foreign capital was allowed by Law No. 7232/84 only when the foreign partner held a minority share - which was the case of IBM-Gerdau - and when technological control was exercised by the Brazilian partner - which was not the case in that association. The acceptance of this joint-venture was, on one hand, a minor concession in the sense that it was treated as an isolated exception. But, on the other hand, it set a major precedent in the implementation of the central provision of the IT policy. CACEX Communication No. 171 of December 1986 represented a much more significant concession. Although not eliminated by the CACEX disposition, the open-ended concept of IT items reserved under Article 3 of the Informatics Law was limited by it . However, even in this major concession, the Brazilians managed to give the Americans something, but not exactly what they had asked for. The Brazilians refrained from publishing a list of nonreserved items, which might have severely limited the prospect of implementing the protective policy. Instead they issued a new list of items whose importation required SEI authorization. A list of nonreserved items would have had greater consequences: It would have excluded some IT goods not only from SEI import control, but also from the control of manufacturing in the Brazilian market. The adjustments made by the Brazilians in market access were more significant than those made in administrative procedures, but they were still far less than what the Americans had demanded.

The practical measures analysed above implied flexibility in implementing the policy, but the Brazilian commitment to terminate the reserved market in 1992 and to restrict its use to IT goods meant a deeper and more far-reaching compromise.

It was in part three of the Brazilian 301 case - IPRs - that the Brazilians made the most significant concessions. The introduction of a bill extending copyright protection for software into the Brazilian Congress in December 1986, and its approval by the House of Representatives in June 1987, were followed by suspension of part three of the case at the end of that month. However, SEI's denial of licensing for MS-DOS on the basis of the existence of a similar software developed in Brazil triggered the threat of sanctions. This threat was suspended only after approval of the software law in December 1987 and publication of rules for its implementation in May 1988. The main concessions made by the Brazilians in relation to IPRs were (i) adoption of copyright protection for software; (ii) authorization for the licensing of the latest version of MS-DOS; and (iii) operational definition of 'functional equivalence' that practically eliminated the Law's ability to protect the Brazilian market for locally developed software. Adoption of copyright protection for software was counterbalanced by the establishment of commercialization rules, which reserved domestic trade of software for locally owned companies. The software law failed, however, to protect local software production from foreign competition as the Informatics Law did for local hardware production. Brazilian software producers might have been protected by the concept of functional equivalence if it had not been operationally defined in the strict terms of Decree 96036. In addition, CONIN's decision to license the latest versions of MS-DOS nullified SEI's attempt to foster local development of software through its Normative Act 026/83, which required local development of the operating system for approval to manufacture microcomputers. It had been in compliance with this disposition that the Brazilian company Scopus developed SISNE, an MS-DOS-like operating system, whose existence justified SEI's denial of licensing for MS-DOS. The Brazilian concession on this issue was as significant as the approval of a software law that, unlike the Informatics Law, provided no preferential protection for locally developed software. Thus, Brazilian software policy was significantly changed by American pressure. CONIN's reversal of SEI's decision on licensing of MS-DOS and the subsequent strict definition of 'functional equivalence' reduced the prospects for development of a Brazilian software industry.

In sum, the Brazilian gains in the negotiations were (i) initial maintenance of the orienting principles of its IT policy by agreeing to address American companies' complaints on a case-by-case basis; (ii) issuance of a reduced list of IT goods under import control instead of a list of nonreserved items; (iii) definition of rules that reserved the commercialization of software in Brazil for locally owned companies; and (iv) maintenance of the IT market reserve until 1992. Brazilian losses were (i) the Brazilian government's reduced freedom to extend the reserved market beyond 1992 or to other goods, in accordance with the new Brazilian constitution (Article 219); (ii) establishing the precedent of flexible interpretation of the reserved market principle for IT goods; and (iii) renunciation of the intent to foster a locally owned software industry.

In order to determine the balance of Brazilian gains and losses in the negotiation it is necessary to weigh them in relation to the Brazilian's utility function, which changed from the beginning of the conflict to its end. Consequently, the Brazilian balance of gains and losses varies depending on what scale of values is used in the analysis. As I argued in Chapter 6, the Brazilian strategy changed from a 'principled objection' to deal with the American complaints at all, to a 'pragmatic' negotiation. These two positions are parallel and reflect two utility functions: (i) maximization of local control over technological development, reduction of technological dependence, and increased domestic capability in high-technology; and (ii) maximization of local production of IT goods and services, and minimization of damage to IT and other business. These two utility functions, which were not necessarily opposed throughout the IT policy history, received different emphasis during the development of the Brazilian 301 case.

If the first utility function, which prevailed during the policy's setting up and institutionalization phases and oriented the Brazilian delegation in the first rounds of negotiation, had dominated until the end of the conflict, then Brazilian losses would have to be considered larger than its gains. Brazil would have lost sovereign command over its future technological development in IT and other high-technology areas. Moreover, the sustained development of what had already been acquired in domestic technological capability would have been jeopardized. Some members of the Brazilian intelligentsia within an outside the state apparatus, some military, and domestic software producers are among the Brazilian groups for whom the final outcome of the conflict was not favourable.

The technological component of the IT policy lost prominence as domestic social support for the policy changed, and it was almost ignored during negotiation of the Brazilian 301 case. Therefore the dominant 'pragmatic' utility function should be used to assess the Brazilian balance of gains and losses. Gains exceeded losses when assessed according to the utility function that oriented the Brazilian delegation during most rounds of negotiation leading to solution of the conflict. For this utility function, the IT policy was not a nationalist flag, nor was the establishment of an electronics industry in Brazil a means to promote domestic technological capability and reduce technological dependence. In this pragmatic utility function, the electronics industry was only a business, as any other, and the role of the delegation to the negotiations was not to defend principles but to minimize damage to business in Brazil. Oriented by this scale

130

of values, Brazilian losses were compensated by its gains: Not only was the threat of economic sanctions suspended and the conflict closed, but the domestic electronics industry established by the policy remained functioning and almost untouched. Brazilian exporters, industrialists of other sectors, and domestic hardware producers are among the groups who viewed the final outcome as not too unfavourable.

AMERICAN BALANCE OF GAINS AND LOSSES

The central focus of American complaints against the Brazilian policy was the restrictions to market access for products and capital and the lack of protection for IPRs. Most of the American criticism focused on the first point. In part one of the Brazilian 301 case (i.e., complaints about administrative procedures), the Americans sought more flexible interpretation of the legal dispositions restricting access to the Brazilian market. Toward these goals, American negotiators aimed to induce SEI to adopt less strict rules for implementation of such dispositions and of the principles established in Law No. 7232. Brazilian actions in relation to these claims were gains for the Americans. In fact, American gains were greater than one would assess based directly on the Brazilian actions alone. These extra gains accrued due to SEI's loss of domestic image and its reduced ability to deal with vested interests. SEI had built a reputation of seriousness and honesty, based on strict implementation of legal dispositions. SEI's acquiescence in interpreting legal provisions so that they could be implemented with 'flexibility' (i.e., sometimes counter to what had been established) weakened SEI's resistance and displayed its vulnerability to pressure from interested parties. In a nutshell, Brazilian concessions on administrative procedures indicated that SEI had been forced to give in.

Negotiations on Part Two of the case did not turn out so favourably for the American side. They had demanded market access - which would mean repeal of the Informatics Law - but instead obtained (i) a narrower list of IT items under import control, (ii) authorization for IBM to enter the reserved market through its association with a locally owned company, and (iii) the Brazilian promise not to extend the restrictions beyond 1992 or to other areas.

American gains in the negotiations of Part Two of the case were more significant than they might seem when compared to their initial demands. In fact, the American delegation soon realized that to insist on a repeal of the Brazilian Informatics Law would not lead to any deal and could even push the Brazilians to withdraw from the negotiation. The Americans, therefore, changed their strategy. Instead of asking for changes in the law, they demanded its interpretation in terms more favourable to American interests. Despite this strategic move, the American delegation still managed to obtain more resounding gains in relation to the policy's restrictions on access to the Brazilian market:

Brazilian authorities agreed not to prolong the reserved market for IT products nor to extend this principle to other areas (possibly biotechnology, pharmaceuticals, or advanced materials).

Thus, although Brazilian actions taken at the time in response to the American demand for wider market access were not of great direct significance, there was a large gain for the Americans in this area. But it was to be reaped in the future.

How justified is it to consider this promise by the Brazilian government as a gain for the Americans when it was a mere statement of intention? Why did the Americans accept this agreement without any apparent guarantee against it not being honoured by future Brazilian governments? That the Brazilians were cheating when they made such a promise is not a reasonable assumption. Cheating, however justifiable it may have been in this situation, was a highly implausible course of action for two reasons. Firstly, Brazilian authorities were already convinced that the ending of import control by SEI in 1992 might be used as a push for the Brazilian electronics industry to improve its competitiveness relative to the international market. At the same time, the need for foreign investment in the Brazilian electronics industry had been previously acknowledged; some policy measures had already been taken to stimulate the merging of domestic companies into stronger conglomerates that would be better prepared to negotiate with foreign investors. Adaptation of the IT policy to the new conditions in the domestic and international markets after 1992 would probably result in some liberalization of Brazilian trade and investment rules. Secondly, Brazilian authorities widely acknowledged the US government's prominent role in negotiations on rescheduling Brazil's foreign debt - on whose agenda the IT policy has been placed as a 'hidden' item. This put the Americans in a privileged position to enforce the terms of this agreement.

The American delegation's largest gain was in relation to IPRs. The Americans were successful in coercing Brazilian authorities and social groups to make SEI accept the adoption of copyright. But with this gain the Americans also had some losses. The Brazilian software law, besides extending copyright protection to IPRs of software - which pleased the Americans - defined a reserved market for domestic trade of software and attempted to protect domestic software production through the concept of 'functional equivalence'. These protectionist features of the software law escaped American 'monitoring' during the whole process of drafting. Congressional debate, and approval of the law. The American threat of sanctions abbreviated the process of approval of the software law, with its protectionist features, but was decisive in defining strict rules for implementing the law that left practically no protection to foster Brazil's domestic software industry.

American gains in the Brazilian software policy also benefited the US government in other simultaneous negotiations. The United States gained strategic advantage in multilateral trade negotiations, in which trade-related aspects of IPRs were included on the agenda at the initiative of the United States and against the opposition of developing countries, including Brazil. Brazilian agreement to grant legal protection for IPRs of software and to adopt the copyright regime for software improved the US position because of the influence these decisions could have on other developing countries. In fact, it was not only in relation to IPRs of software that the negotiations with Brazil bore fruit in other American negotiations. The conflict also had side-benefits for the Americans in other US/Brazil negotiations (particularly the one over IPRs for pharmaceutical products). Moreover, the conflict reinforced the American reputation of toughness in international relations dealing with trade and technological issues. Thus, the conflict may have paved the way for future American gains in negotiations with Brazil and other developing countries.

Summarizing the analysis of American rewards, I argue that whereas the Americans' immediate gains were relatively insignificant compared to what they had demanded, there were substantial benefits to be reaped in the future. Adapting Galtung's [*1967*] terminology for the functions of economic sanctions, I contend that the Americans' gains were of both an 'instrumental' and 'expressive' type. Instrumental gains were all those that gave the Americans at least the possibility of larger access to the Brazilian IT market. Americans' gains of this kind were (i) the setting of precedent in the 'flexible' interpretation of the Informatics Law (approval of IBM-Gerdau association, CACEX Communication 171); (ii) the agreement not to prolong the reserved market for IT nor to extend it to other high-technology areas; and (iii) the copyright protection for IPRs of software. Expressive gains were those that, despite not ensuring direct market access, eroded institutional and political basis for protectionist measures. Americans' expressive gains were (i) SEI's spoilt reputation for seriousness and strictness; (ii) reinforcement of liberal economic positions; and (iii) a softened Brazilian position in GATT negotiations.

The Americans also suffered significant losses in this negotiation, some related to the specific issue at stake and others of a more general character. Besides the protective dispositions of the software law and a disappointing list of IT items under import control, the Americans may be said to have been worn down by a strenuous four-year negotiation with relatively few practical results. Considering the asymmetry in the structural power of the two players, the long duration of the conflict and the nature of the gains obtained may be counted as a loss, despite a minor one, for the stronger party. In addition, this conflict did not improve the already troubled international relations of the two countries. For other developing countries, particularly in Latin America, the Brazilian 301 case was a reminder that the Americans had revived their big-stick policy. In this case, the 'exemplary' effect of the conflict with Brazil might be seen as a gain for the United States.

Paralleling the Brazilian government's strategic move from a principal rejection to negotiate to pragmatic bargaining, the American delegation changed its initial goal of forcing market access to obtaining flexible interpretation of legal procedures and influencing the drafting of new legislation. However, whereas the Brazilians rejected their nationalist utility function in favour of more pragmatic values, the Americans did not alter their orientation toward maximizing market access. This does not mean that the Americans ignored the sensitivity of the issues under negotiation for Brazilian society. The Americans' fear of strong Brazilian nationalist reaction may even have led them to step back from their initial demand for repeal of the Informatics Law. Nevertheless, this move did not imply a significant alteration of the Americans' utility function to substitute economic for diplomatic preference ordering. According to the Americans' orientation of maximizing opportunities of market access, their gains more than compensated their losses. Present and future wider access to the Brazilian IT market, the softening of Brazilian opposition in GATT negotiations on new issues, and the international display of what could happen to any other country that tried to emulate the Brazilian policy more than compensated for the protectionist features that remained in the policy and any loss in international image, particularly among Latin American countries.

CONCLUSION

In this chapter, I have argued that each player's balance of gains and losses shows that the Brazilian 301 case ended with a non-zero-sum solution. Both parties gained something, but the Americans probably reaped more benefits.

Brazil's largest gain was to preserve its Informatics Law untouched and maintain the reserved IT market for locally owned companies until the time established in the law (i.e., 1992). Brazil's largest loss was in the software policy, which was left without any significant instrument for fostering a Brazilian domestic software industry. In addition, the Brazilian government agreed not to extend the reserved market for IT beyond 1992 or to any other high-technology area. According to the dominant pragmatic utility function, in which maximization of domestic production took precedence over development of domestic technological capability, Brazilian gains exceeded losses.

American gains were both 'instrumental' and 'expressive'. In the first case, their immediate gains in wider access to the Brazilian IT market were not as significant as gains they were assured to receive in the near future. They also reaped the promise of no protectionist policy for other high-technology areas. Adoption of copyright protection for IPRs of software not only satisfied American intentions to diffuse this regime of protection internationally, but also benefited American interests in the GATT multilateral trade negotiations. Expressive gains were debilitation of protectionist ideals and of institutions identified with this orientation and the international display of the Brazilian example to other developing countries who might try to emulate it. The Americans lost some face by being seen to struggle so hard and for such a long time with a much weaker opponent for relatively small immediate gains, and by aggravating their international relations with other developing countries, particularly in Latin America, who saw that any attempt at independent technological development would not be tolerated. However, as commercial interests dominated over diplomatic considerations, Americans' gains were almost certainly larger than their losses.

As I have argued in Chapter 1, the descriptive approach to bargaining used in this study does not allow any assessment of the final outcome of this conflict in relation to other possible outcomes. There is no empirical justification for an analysis of what each player could have done to produce a more favourable outcome for itself. I have no basis by which to assess whether or not the final solution of this conflict was Pareto efficient. I do argue, however, that the final outcome seems to express a quasi-equilibrium solution in the sense that it made both players better off. This does not mean that the final solution was the most beneficial to both players or that their gains had similar significance for each of them, but only that the solution was the best they both were allowed to get within the bargaining situation. This conclusion also does not imply that the equilibrium solution was reached by purely rational players choosing among clear alternatives with all necessary information. On the contrary, alteration of strategies and the exploitation of power positions that restricted the choices for the weaker player were the mechanism by which the final solution for the conflict was achieved.

9

BEYOND THE DISPUTE

When the Brazilian 301 case was dropped in October 1989, two other cases over market access and IPRs involving Brazil and the United States already existed, and another would be opened one month later. In July 1988, the USTR opened a case initiated by American pharmaceutical companies over lack of patent rights for pharmaceutical products in Brazilian legislation. By mid-June 1989, the USTR initiated investigations on 'quantitative restrictions and import licensing of agricultural and manufactured products' in Brazil, one of the three 'priority countries' identified by the United States for negotiations on liberalization of trade policies. The other two countries were Japan and India. The American objectives and conditions for these negotiations were established in accordance with the 'Super' and 'Special' Section 301 of the Omnibus Trade and Competitiveness Act of 1988. Brazil also headed the American 'Priority Watch List' with respect to protection of IPRs. In November 1989, the USTR began to review the status of Brazil and seven other countries on the list to identify to what extent they denied adequate and effective protection of IPRs in order to focus bilateral negotiations on situations considered most harmful to American economic interests.

The closing of the Brazilian 301 case and the opening of investigations on IPR protection in Brazil occurred a few months before the first democratic direct presidential elections in Brazil in 27 years. The day after taking office, the newly elected president, Fernando Collor de Melo, started an aggressive programme of economic stabilization, liberalization, and deregulation. His administration identified various protectionist policies as one of the causes of Brazil's economic crisis. His main objectives for reform therefore included elimination of all forms of market reserve, reduction of staff in public administration, and elimination of state intervention in the economy. There was no doubt that some important changes would be made in the IT policy. In fact, the Collor government took its first measures towards liberalizing the IT policy at the end of 1990. In September of that year, the government announced a Foreign Trade and Industrial Policy, with the main objective of integrating Brazil competitively into the world economy. To do that, important changes in the IT policy were anticipated. Together with institutional reforms, which included the elimination of SEI and its substitution by DEPIN (a department of the Secretariat for Science and Technology), the liberalizing measures seem to be effecting most of the promises the Brazilian government had made to the American delegation during negotiation of the Brazilian 301 case.

The purposes of this chapter are (i) to give an overview of changes in the IT policy being defined and implemented during the early 1990s and (ii) to interpret them in connection with the issues dealt with in this study. I will conclude with a tentative analysis of the Collor government's liberalizing measures in the IT policy, taking into account domestic as well as foreign pressure to change the policy.

RECENT CHANGES IN THE BRAZILIAN IT POLICY

Many major changes in Brazilian IT policy were made in the early 1990s. They affected both the institutional structure and content of the policy. Institutional changes were made to keep CONIN under firm control and to reduce SEI's power. SEI's demotion to a department in the Secretariat for Science and Technology (SCT) was accompanied by dispersion of the government's cadre in IT policy. CONIN became responsible for many strategic decisions and was therefore a central instrument in the implementation of policy changes. Consequently, CONIN's composition was altered by Decree No. 99406 of 19 July 1990 before any other changes were made. The central points of Decree No. 99406 were to (i) define government representatives as CONIN majority members; (ii) eliminate the existing list of governmental organizations (NGOs) with representation in CONIN;[90] and (iii) alter the process of selecting representatives who are not appointed directly by their organizations but chosen by the President from persons nominated by NGOs. Because the majority of CONIN's members are part of the government, and because the government chooses both the NGO representatives and the NGOs eligible to nominate representatives, CONIN was strengthened as a governmental decision-making board where NGO's representation was made largely symbolic. Demotion of SEI and the alteration of CONIN's composition gave the President, through the Secretary for Science and Technology, complete control over implementation of the IT policy. This control was further evinced when CONIN Resolution No. 21/90, which outlined CONIN's compositional functioning rules, gave the Secretary of SCT (who presides at CONIN meetings) the power to make urgent decisions without calling a council meeting.

Changes in the policy's content aimed to end the market reserve by 1992, if not sooner. The government's initiatives were directed to (i) limit import control, and (ii) reduce or eliminate restrictions on foreign direct investment in the Brazilian electronics industry. In relation to import control, changes were made in (a) the time-limit of its use; (b) the IT items under such protection; and (c) the criteria for excluding items from protection. In relation to restrictions on foreign direct investment, liberalization of the Brazilian electronics market meant (a) new rules for association of local with foreign capital; (b) a new definition of *locally-owned company*; and (c) the elimination of privileges granted exclusively to locally owned companies.

The Collor government took several measures of different legal character to set in motion the intended changes in the policy's content. Immediate liberalization was put forward by one presidential decree and SCT issued several resolutions; none was formally contingent on approval by the Brazilian Congress. Despite dealing with issues regulated by the Informatics Law, these resolutions had already been in force before the Brazilian Congress started discussing changes proposed by the government. Notwithstanding the government's urgency to liberalize the IT policy immediately, parliamentary approval is the only legitimate way to effect the changes. For this purpose, three bills were introduced into the Brazilian Congress to (i) alter the Informatics Law (Bill No. 5804 of 1990); (ii) define the policy's strategy and targets for the period 1991-93 - II PLANIN (Bill No. 002 of 1991); and (iii) alter the software law (Bill No. 997 of 1991). I will come back to these bills later.

Changes in import and manufacturing control were launched in September 1990, when previous SCT authorization for importation and domestic production was made necessary only for a selected list of IT goods and services; all items not included on the list were free of importation and domestic manufacturing control (Decree No. 99541 of 21 September 1990). The list of protected items was defined by CONIN Resolution No. 26/90 and DECEX 'Portaria' No. 03/91. The list consisted of more than fifty items, including video monitors, floppy and hard disk drives, magnetic tape of low to medium capacity, printers, modems, plotters, microcomputers, super-microcomputers, workstations, multiplexors, front-end processors, computers for motor vehicles, equipment for data communication by satellite, keyboards, and facsimile machines. Electronics components, 8-bit microcomputers (used mainly for entertainment purposes), and minicomputers were the most significant items excluded from the list of protection. The exclusion of electronics components was soon revised. Complementing the list, two other regulations were issued: (i) SCT 'Portaria' No. 02/91, which required SCT authorization for importation of parts and components of the IT goods included on the list; and (ii) SCT 'Portaria' No. 01/91, which required companies manufacturing goods not included on the list to submit annual programmes of production and technological development to show their compliance with the requirement to invest five per cent of their billings in R&D activities.

The immediate changes in import control were complemented by definition of criteria for excluding items from the protected list until complete liberalization in 1992. For this purpose, SCT issued a programme (CONIN Resolution No. 22/90) for improvement in the price/performance ratio of goods produced in the reserved market. According to this programme, IT goods would be kept on the list of protected products until October 1992 only if their domestic production improved significantly so that their prices became competitive with prices of equivalent foreign products. The price in the Brazilian market for each domestic IT good on the list was to be compared to the landed price of equivalent imported products every six months from January 1991 to June 1992. If this ratio exceeded parameters defined in the programme, the IT good would be excluded from the list and its equivalent could be imported without previous SCT authorization. Domestic prices could not exceed the landed price of an equivalent by more than 20 per cent in the period July to December 1991; 13 per cent in the period January to June 1992; and six per cent in the last period, i.e., July to October 1992.

Measures restricting foreign direct investment in the electronics industry could not be amended without the approval of the Brazilian Congress. Even so, the government took immediate action in this area. In October 1990, CONIN decided to change the established conditions for associations of national companies with foreign capital in the protected area. CONIN decided that a foreign company associated with a locally owned one may sign contracts of technology transfer with its Brazilian associate. This was a major modification of the policy, made not as an isolated exception but as a change in the orienting principle stated in the Informatics Law. According to the law, the power to make decisions in nationally owned companies on what technology to use, what to change, and when shall be in Brazilian hands. Participation by a joint-venture of a locally owned company with a foreign one in the reserved market could not violate the definition of 'national' company. In consequence, association with a foreign partner that would keep technological control of the joint-venture had not been allowed. An exception to this rule was the approval of the IBM-Gerdau association. Now, by CONIN Resolution No. 19/90, this case-by-case strategy was changed to a general policy orientation. The required technological control by the Brazilian associate was to be assessed by CONIN at the time of the approval of the contract for technology transfer.

Changes in the definition of a locally owned company and the elimination of privileges granted exclusively to them were proposed by Bill No. 5804/90. This bill replaced the concept of 'national' company defined in Article 12 of the Informatics Law by the one defined in Article 171 of the Brazilian constitution. Article 171 defines 'Brazilian national corporations' as ones in which the majority of voting shares are in the hands of individuals domiciled and residing in Brazil who have the power to administer the corporations' activities. According to Article 171, domestic control of technological activities and a majority Brazilian share of capital are required for Brazilian national corporations to receive temporary protection and privileges as stimuli for technological development. Bill No. 5804/90 also proposed suspending all articles of the Informatics Law that grant fiscal incentives to locally owned companies, effective on

140

29 October 1992. The same suspension was proposed for Article 22 of the law, which establishes conditions under which non-locally-owned companies may produce in Brazil the IT goods that locally owned firms are not capable of producing. This disposition of the Informatics Law was intended as a way to exchange access to the Brazilian market for R&D investment in the country.

All changes described so far, some already in force and others yet to be discussed in the Congress, were part of Bill No. 002/91 - II PLANIN - which defined the following objectives for the period 1991-93: (i) to improve competitiveness in the production of IT goods and services by the adoption of up-dated technology that meets international standards of price and quality; (ii) to develop technologically, i.e., to improve the capability to generate, develop, advance, absorb, and select technologies that lead to innovative design, production, and trade of goods and services; and (iii) to diffuse IT throughout Brazilian society with emphasis on social use and automation of industrial processes. The priority sectors during II PLANIN's duration were proposed to be microelectronics and software. In relation to the former, Bill No. 002/91 proposed stimuli to increase the use of microelectronics components designed and made in Brazil (ASICs), particularly by articulation of policies aimed at various sectors of the electronics industry. In relation to software, the Bill proposed stimuli for the local development of application software, based on open operating systems and support for the development of managerial capabilities in the domestic software industry.

While domestic software production was defined as a priority sector for the period 1991-93, Bill No. 997/91 proposed elimination of the following elements from the software law: (i) the filing of software; (ii) the market reserve for domestic trade of software; and (iii) the protection for domestic development of software. The central point of Bill No. 997/91 was the exclusion from the law of the concept of 'local equivalent', which seeks to protect domestic software production by preventing the registration and trade of foreign products in the Brazilian market. This reinforces the Brazilian authorities' previous decision to sacrifice the majority of the software industry - basic and package software - and maintain only the niches of customized production.

DID BRAZIL WIN A BATTLE TO LOSE THE WAR?

The changes described above in the IT policy, suggest that the gains the Brazilian authorities had battled for during the conflict with the United States are now being lost. During the negotiations, Brazilian authorities adamantly resisted changing either the policy's orienting principles of the law that established them; while the software bill was being prepared, they fought to make the fewest concessions possible in order to maintain consistency within the overall policy. At that time, Brazilian authorities effectively used negotiating power that was linked directly to the existing restrictions on the participation of foreign capital. Their promise of not extending the market reserve beyond 1992, however, cut two ways: It gave them some time to prepare the transition from the protected to the open market; but it also created the risk that this transition would be made under future conditions that might be out of their control. The conflict was halted in late 1989, and in the subsequent year the first democratic presidential elections in 27 years monopolized political debate in Brazil. There is no sign that the proximity of 1992 provoked a systematic discussion of the future of the IT policy. Nor did the presidential candidates make clear proposals for this area in their political campaign. All groups who opposed the IT policy, for whatever reasons, enthusiastically support the present liberal government. As I have shown in the first section of this chapter, the Collor government's measures were designed not only to ensure that the market reserve would end in 1992, but also to promote immediate liberalization of the market. The present government does not seem inclined to reopen negotiation of the opening of the market reserve and, consequently, it has lost the bargaining power to face international pressure in this direction.

There is strong evidence that changes in the Brazilian IT policy in the early 1990s were linked to American pressure. It was not only the pending promise made by the preceding administration to end the market reserve in 1992, but also latent threats emanating from the 'Super' Section 301, that pressed the new Brazilian government for immediate liberalization. American pressure had also persuaded the Collor government to introduce a bill into the Congress that amends the Brazilian Code of Industrial Property to grant patent rights to pharmaceutical products, food, and chemical processes. Brazil may thus have won a battle to lose the war.

It would be a mistake, however, to interpret that changes in the IT policy as if they resulted exclusively from foreign pressure or from the conflict with the United States. The Brazilian macroeconomic crisis and its effects on industrial production have increased industrialists' demands for less control over foreign investment in the electronics industry and of access to foreign technology. At the same time, crisis management has made short-term concerns dominate over long-term technological considerations within the Collor government [*Cassiolato et al., 1991*]. In addition, the predominantly neoliberal orientation of the Collor administration predisposes the choice of measures to restore market forces to correct what are seen as government failures.

Based on the government's intent to face the macroeconomic crisis with economic deregulation and liberalization, there seems to be little chance for the Brazilian IT policy to flourish. There is no doubt that some alteration would have been needed in the policy to adapt it to changing international and domestic market conditions. Many analysts - referred to in Chapter 4 - have pointed out the policy's major challenges, which stemmed mainly from development problems within the electronics industry and from the disarticulation of policies designed individually for the various IT sectors. Some of these problems seem to have been tackled by II PLANIN. Disarticulation among sectors of the electronics industry is to be reduced by stimulating the purchase of domestically made electronics components and domestically developed software by other IT sectors. However, the programme to improve price/performance ratios may liberalize importation of such products within a few months - particularly electronics components, because currently there is practically no import control of software. Thus, disarticulation will persist and a decline in domestic microelectronics production will become more likely. Solving the most serious problem affecting the electronics industry, the nonexistence of an overall industrial policy, requires more than economic liberalization. The stabilization programme has created the deepest recession the Brazilian economy has ever known. Without investment in industrial production, there is no hope of modernizing Brazil's industrial production, with or without linkages with the domestic electronics industry. At this recessionary juncture, liberalization of the Brazilian IT market may reduce even further the already limited opportunities for domestic producers who might be expelled from the market by selling their business either to another locally owned company - which will increase concentration - or to foreign investors. From a liberal point of view, this is not a negative result, but it does not guarantee increasing modernization of Brazilian industrial production in the electronics industry or in industry as a whole.

Considering the variety of interests involved, it might have been better to promote substantial changes in the IT policy only through open discussion of alternative strategies and courses of action. The government's strategy has not, however, been conducive to open debate within Brazilian society about the future of the policy. Nevertheless, the Brazilian Congress has challenged the government's strategy to insulate the process of policy alteration and fragment restructuring of the policy into piecemeal changes, which sought to prevent participation by interested parties.

In fact, the Brazilian Congress seemed to be virtually the only major institution still concerned with the IT policy in Brazil and with its contribution towards domestic technological capability. It is in the Congress that could, in the early 1990s, be found the only combative group in support of the IT policy, although it also contained forces that opposed the policy. All other supporting groups had either defected or been effectively neutralized by the domestic economic crisis and international pressure. Even in Congress, however, weak articulation among those groups within the various political parties that opposed the government diminished support for the policy. The lack of a strong political basis for the government in the Brazilian Congress - which made it difficult to enact governmental measures - gave the opposition a bargaining power that could have been used in favour of the IT policy. However, opposition parties were themselves divided over the future of the IT policy. Some members were highly concerned with the American threat of retaliation and the potential effects of American sanctions on Brazil's deep economic recession.

The resistance by some factions of the opposition parties in Congress to the dismantling of the IT policy was evidenced in the Committee of Science and Technology, Communication and Informatics (CCTCI) of the House of Representatives. All bills dealing with the IT policy and being discussed in the CCTCI were transformed into substitute bills in which some of the liberal dispositions of the original versions were altered. Bill No. 002/91, II PLANIN, is an exemplary case. The substitute bill prepared in the CCTCI, despite giving a new direction to the policy (e.g., by a 'careful use of mechanisms of protection' meaning 'adaptation of the tariff system for imports of electronics inputs'), used the bill to reject important changes already made by the government. For example, the CCTCI substitute bill for II PLANIN rejected CONIN Resolution No. 19/90 by prohibiting, throughout the duration of the plan, the foreign associate in a joint venture from signing a contract of technology transfer with its Brazilian partner. It also rejected Decree No. 99541/90 by restoring SCT's authorization control over importation of IT goods throughout the duration of the plan (i.e., until 1993 and not until 29 October 1992, as established by the presidential decree). Finally, the CCTCI substitute bill for II PLANIN created a group within the House of Representatives to follow up on the plan's implementation. This follow-up group would be composed of members of the CCTCI, representatives of IT industry NGOs, IT users and workers, and the scientific/technological community. The CCTCI substitute bill was approved by the Committee of Finance and Taxation with amendments restoring the presidential decree and the SCT Resolution. In June 1991, the CCTCI substitute and amendments were awaiting debate and vote on the floor of the House.

But first, other battles were being fought in the CCTCI. As of December 1991 a substitute for the government's bill on proposed alterations in the Informatics Law was being discussed by the Committee. In addition, the substitute for the government's bill on proposed changes in the Brazilian Code of Industrial Property (prepared for CCTCI by Deputy Luiz Henrique da Silveira, who was Minister for Science and Technology during the Brazilian 301 case) was to have been discussed in August 1991. Debate over the scope of alterations to be made by CCTCI in the government's proposed changes in the Informatics Law showed the division within the opposition parties in Congress: The leadership of the two larger opposition parties, PMDB and PSDB (Brazilian Social Democratic Party), pressed PMDB's Deputy Luiz Henrique to delete most of his proposed substitute bill, in which the end of the market reserve in 1992 was balanced by extending fiscal incentives for a longer period. President Collor de Melo's visit to the United States in mid-June 1991 was said to have been facilitated by CCTCI's approval of a liberalizing Informatics Bill.

Fifteen years of market reserve policy in Brazil have nurtured an infant domestic electronics industry and generated valuable human skills in the country. This infant industry has been maturing, and the developmental problems of this growth have been a challenge for the Brazilian IT policy since the mid-1980s. There is no doubt about the need for important changes in the policy to improve the Brazilian electronics industry's competitiveness. There are also positive grounds for reducing market protection for this infant industry: Some Brazilian companies will probably survive liberalization, and domestic production of some electronics goods will benefit from incoming foreign investment. The problem is that the adjustment period may be too short: the suddenness and extent of changes suggest the prospect of major losses.

145

ENDNOTES

1. This was an essential point for developing countries, which feared that the industrial countries might threaten retaliation in the area of trade in goods to wrest concessions in the new areas of services, intellectual property, and investment [*Sassoon, 1990: 21-2*].

2. Specification of activities included in the service sector has been one of the difficulties of the negotiations. There has been a consensus related to banking, insurance, transport and maritime transport, computer and data-processing services, construction and engineering, and tourism; two-thirds of the countries would include telecommunications; disagreement is found on air transport, investment, re-insurance, general consulting services, accounting, advertising, management consulting, hotels, travel agencies, and catering services [*Sassoon, 1990: 26-7*]. As negotiations progress, some alterations are expected to emerge in the scope of activities to be included in GATS. Interests linked to U.S. maritime transport, backed by American legislation that reserves coastal transport to American vessels and crew, are lobbying to exclude the activity from GATS. The United States has not yet decided its position related to the inclusion of financial services in GATS [*Hindley, 1990: 142*].

3. Four separate draft framework agreements have been proposed by the United States; the European Economic Community (EEC); a group of developing countries, including Brazil, Chile, Colombia, Cuba, Honduras, Nicaragua, Mexico, Peru, Trinidad and Tobago, and Uruguay; and another group of developing countries formed by Cameroon, China, Egypt, India, Kenya, Nigeria, and Tanzania. For a summary of the negotiations and prospects for agreement in the new areas under discussion in the Uruguay Round see Hindley [*1990*]; Graham and Krugman [*1990*]; and Maskus [*1990*].

4. Special protection for IPRs of software seems not to have mattered much to the initial development of this industrial segment. In the United States, the copyright law of 1909 had been used to protect rights on software until 1976 when a new law was approved extending copyright protection to all 'original works of authorship fixed in any tangible medium of expression, now known or later developed'. This broader concept facilitated the use of copyright law to protect software. It was only in 1980 that the law was changed to include in its Article 101 a definition of software. The American policy for software protection is, however, being made in the courts, on a virtual case-by-case basis.

5. Up to 1969, when IBM first distinguished hardware and software as different components, software had been sold as part of the computer system.

6. Due to developing countries' pressures, a Protocol was appended to the text of the Berne Convention as revised in the Stockholm Conference in 1967. Developing countries were accorded the right to reduce the period of copyright protection by up to 25 years, to cut back severely the rights of translation, and to augment considerably the various forms of free use of educators, broadcasters, and other users of copyright. Developed countries declined to accept the protocol and developing countries threatened to withdraw from the Berne Union. It was only in the Paris revision of 1971 that a solution was found with concessions from both parties.

7. A recent precedent-setting court decision in the United States has reinterpreted the principle that confines copyright protection to the software's expression. Correa

146

[*1989a: 29*] views this American court's decision in Whilan Associates vs Jaslow Dental Laboratory, in which copyright was interpreted to cover the sequence, organization, and structure of the code-program, as an indication of the application of copyright to the underlying idea of the software.

8. Until the mid-1980s South Korea had adhered to none of the international copyright conventions, changing its position as a result of US pressure in this direction [*Correa, 1989a*].

9. In its broad sense, protection of IPRs of 'software includes not only the programmes themselves, but also documents and operating manuals, together with the papers relating to the programming of the computer' [*McFarlane, 1982: 91*]. The source code is the set of detailed instructions used in the composition of a specific computer program. Anyone with expertise in the area would be able to rewrite the software by using the source code. The object code is the set of instructions in binary language that translates logic commands into electronic signals that are processed by the hardware.

10. Nonpatentability of pharmaceutical products in Brazil is now being reexamined. Exclusion of these products from the IPR protection granted by the Brazilian Industrial Property Code was used by the US government to justify the threat of economic sanctions against Brazil in 1988.

11. This change in the government's position is analysed in Chapter 7. Bill no. 260, of 1984, was based on studies made by various interested parties, including SEI. The bill was distributed to the Senate Committees of Constitution and Justice, Economy, and National Security. Approved by the first two of these committees during 1985, the bill was abandoned in April 1986.

12. A detailed description of the conflict's evolution is presented in Chapter 5.

13. Brazilian policy measures towards local development of software are described in Chapter 3. Sisne, a MS/DOS-like operating system developed by the Brazilian company Scopus, entered the market in 1986. This locally developed operating system played a significant role in the Brazilian 301 case, as will be shown in Chapter 6. Because of its existence, the application for MS-DOS to be sold in Brazil was rejected, affecting the interests of some local microcomputer producers and fuelling American pressure when negotiations between the two countries had almost concluded.

14. The principles governing the Brazilian IT policy before the changes introduced by the Collor administration in 1990-91 have been described extensively in the literature. Recent appraisals of these principles are found in Dantas 1988; and Paiva 1989. See also Adler [*1987*]; Piragibe [*1985*]; and Helena 1980.

15. Ministry of Communications, Directive 622, 19 June 1978, section I, point 3.1.

16. The equating of *open capital company and national firm* was complemented by Decree-Law 2203, of December 1984, which specified that at least two-thirds of the companies' common stock and a like proportion of their voting stock, *and at least 70 per cent of their equity or share capital*, shall lie in Brazilian hands.

17. See Decree 77118, of 9 February 1976, summarized in Appendix I.

18. The only decision that shows an attempt to integrate governmental actions towards the electronics industry during CAPRE's existence is Resolution 01, of 2 May 1978, by CAPRE's Plenary Council, which required prior CAPRE approval for establishment of international links on tele-informatics systems.

19. National Security Council, Presentation of Motives 008, of 1 October 1979, summarized in Appendix I.
20. Besides the notorious institutional conflicts between the entities in charge of the telecommunications policy (the Ministry of Communications or MINICOM), a significant part of the consumer electronics production (the Manaus Free Zone Administration, or SUFRAMA), and the overall informatics policy [CAPRE in 1972-1979 and SEI from 1979 to 1990], the case of IT production in the Free Zone of Manaus illustrates the difficulties involved in implementing a policy towards the whole electronics industry. Industrialists located in other areas of the country feared that the extra benefits stemming from the location of an industrial plant in the Free Zone would either cause a massive move of production out of other Brazilian regions into Manaus or force producers from outside that region out of the market. This case was publicized shortly after the Informatics Law came into force and was solved through CONIN Resolution 001/85 (Appendix I), which forbade the concession of additional benefits to any IT company in connection with its location in the Free Zone.
21. Market reserve and import control are central instruments of the IT policy and will be examined later in Chapter 3.
22. See Decree 84067, of 8 October 1979, for SEI's objectives and tasks; and Decree 90755, of 27 December 1984, which adjusted SEI's institutional tasks to the provisions of the Informatics Law. These decrees are summarized in Appendix I. Under the administrative reforms made by President Collor de Melo in early 1990, SEI became subordinated to the Special Secretariat for Science and Technology, which is linked directly to the President's Office. In late 1990, SEI was eliminated and some of its tasks were carried out by the Department of Informatics and Automation (DEPIN) of the Secretariat for Science and Technology.
23. See SEI's Directives 003, of 20 March 1980, and 007, of 15 July 1980, in Appendix I. Measures taken by the Brazilian government towards the software segment are discussed in later in Chapter 3.
24. The products listed in Normative Act 016/81 were mini-and microcomputers, small- and medium-sized electronic computers and their peripherals, electronic cash registers, electronic word processing machines, electronic accounting machines, bank terminals and their controllers, electronic ticket dispensers and readers, modems, video terminals and their controllers, data-base remote-access terminals, data-entry devices, electronic communication processors, digital signal multiplexors for data communication, digital signal concentrators for data communication, teleprinters with transmitting and receiving speeds greater than 75 baud, facsimile machines, instrumentation for process control, numerical control equipment, secrecy equipment, and equipment using encryption techniques.
25. Since 1978 MINICOM has had the power to regulate the policy for the telecommunications industrial sector, using the monopsony power of Telebras (Brazilian telecommunications holding company) in the area of telecommunications services. Most telecommunications equipment has at least some digital components, which made the area dependent on SEI decisions.
26. See SR-59, of 29 June 1988.
27. See CONCEX Resolution 104, of 3 December 1975, summarized in Appendix I.

Endnotes

28. SEI's powers were extended to control the importation of electronic parts, spare components, other inputs, capital goods for use in research and development (SEI Normative Act 019/81), and some other electronic equipment for general use (see CACEX Communications 41 of 24 January 1983, and 171, of 11 December 1986). See Appendix I for a summary of these acts.
29. See SEI Normative Act 001/80 and SEI Communication 115 of 24 June 1988, summarized in Appendix I.
30. The Brazilian Association of Computer and Peripheral Industries (ABICOMP) estimated that Brazilian IT imports would have been eight-and-half percent smaller between January and August 1986 if CACEX Communication 41 had still been in force [*Paiva, 1989: 114, footnote 10*]. The Collor administration initiated in 1990 made important changes in the scope of IT import controls with a view to open the Brazilian economy to the international market. An appraisal of these changes in the IT policy is presented in Chapter 9.
31. In this respect, what happens in the telecommunications sector contrasts sharply with the sector of professional electronics: The guidelines to orient the acquisition of telecommunications equipment restricts suppliers to a minimum of two and a maximum of four and requires prior selection of suppliers for the acquisition of equipment whose manufacture requires large-scale investment (MINICOM Directive 622, of 19 June 1978, summarized in Appendix I).
32. See SEI's Normative Acts 003/80, 005/80, 015/81, and 025/83, summarized in Appendix I.
33. Some measures show the possibility of a more effective use of this instrument in the near future, as a set of technical specifications has been set up for the acquisition of local computer networks for use in the Brazilian federal administration [*SEI, 1988a*].
34. Article 21, which makes dispositions on incentives to capitalization of IT national companies, was regulated by Decree 92181, of 19 December 1985. See summary in Appendix I.
35. For detailed information on these fiscal incentives, see Appendix I.
36. Many national companies were eliminated from the consumer electronics sector during the 1970s. At the beginning of the decade there were about twenty companies manufacturing television sets in Brazil, only three being foreign subsidiaries. The introduction of colour television, government fiscal and credit incentives, and the import facilities provided by the state to foster development of this industry were accompanied by a dramatic reduction in the number of companies operating in the area. In the mid-1970s there were just eight companies manufacturing television sets in Brazil (two foreign subsidiaries, five joint-ventures, and one nationally owned), and these were dominated by Japanese capital and technology.
37. This restriction was changed by the initiative of the Collor administration. All changes made by this administration in the Brazilian IT policy to June 1991 are analysed in Chapter 9.
38. CAPRE Resolution 01, of 15 July 1976, reserved for local capital the manufacture of mini- and microcomputers and their peripherals in Brazil. IBM decided to enter the local market with its minicomputer /32. The foreign subsidiary rejected CAPRE's suggestion for it to export all /32 production and, taking advantage of its privileges in obtaining a generic import licence, imported the /32 components, started a marketing campaign, and even collected 400 statements of interest. It was

only in January 1977 that a decision from CDE gave CAPRE the authority and strength to curb IBM's initiatives.

39. The IBM subsidiary, for instance, has settled business links with national manufacturers either by agreements for technical cooperation or by the purchase of parts or final products to be exported. In 1986, a joint venture with a national company was established for IT services in the Brazilian market. In October 1988, the first technology transfer agreement involving the Brazilian subsidiary of IBM and the national company SID Telecom was established for local manufacture of communication controllers. These recent moves seem to be in tune with a change in IBM's international strategy towards some adaptation to national protectionist policies. DEC and Data General have also agreed to license the technology for the manufacture of superminicomputers to some national companies.

40. INPI's Normative Act No. 15, of 1975, was used to regulate software imports. Agreements for customized and software services were treated as specialized technical services and packaged software as supply of industrial technology [*Gaio 1990: 231*]. INPI's Normative Act No. 15 established very strict conditions for the approval of technology transfer agreements. All technical data about product and process engineering should be supplied; the supplier would not be able to claim industrial property rights in relation to the technology being transferred, except for future innovations linked to the same technology and when such rights are recognized by Brazilian law; any contract clause aimed at interfering in production, sales, prices, distribution, commercialization, or export would not be accepted; clauses that oblige or condition the purchase of inputs, components, or machinery from the supplier or other stipulated sources would not be admitted; clauses that limit or hinder the R&D activities of the purchaser were prohibited; and clauses that impede the free utilization of the technology after a period of time considered reasonable would not be accepted [*Gaio, 1990: 234-5*].

41. Details about the Brazilian software law are given in Chapter 7.

42. SEI has collected extensive data for a sample of both multinational and national companies covering the various sectors of the electronics industry, but excluding consumer electronics. Since 1984, SEI - later DEPIN - has been collecting information on industrial automation and digital instrumentation. In 1985 it started collecting data on IT services and in 1986 on microelectronics. Data on production and marketing of software collected for the period 1986-1988 was first published in 1989. GEICOM - an agency of the Ministry of Communication - collects data on telecommunications and SUFRAMA on consumer electronics. State agencies differ in their figures for the output of the telecommunications and professional electronics sectors. GEICOM and SEI tend to underestimate the figures related to each other's area. Production of professional electronics equipment in 1980, for instance, was estimated at US$ 425 million by GEICOM and US$ 860 million by SEI. In the same year, production of telecommunications equipment was estimated at US$ 364 million by SEI and US$ 674 million by GEICOM. A possible explanation for these discrepancies may be the methodology for data collection. SEI's figures are obtained in a sample survey of representative companies in the segments observed. I decided to use data gathered for the institution in charge of each segment, that is, GEICOM for telecommunications; and SEI for professional electronics, components, services, and software.

43. In 1987, the US Department of Commerce ranked the Brazilian microcomputer market in sixth place, a position ahead of Italy [*Piragibe, 1988: 102*].

44. This decrease was sharper than the fall in production and also reflected changes in US income tax legislation that stimulated capital repatriation. Net foreign investment in Brazil continued to decline during the years of production growth: In 1985 it was US$ 765 million and in 1986 US$ -204 million [*Serra, 1988: 126*].

45. In 1984, 63 percent of the domestic production of components was directed to consumer electronics and telecommunications. However, data-processing production is increasing the demand for domestic components: This demand was estimated to have been 23 per cent in 1987 [*Paiva, 1989: 198*].

46. In Chapter 3 it details the development of Brazil's software policy in the period leading up to the conflict.

47. See OECD [*1988*].

48. Quoted by Gaio [*1991: 160*].

49. See Gaio [*1991: 163*].

50. Analysts report that the price of an IBM 4381 is 2.4 or even 3 times higher in Brazil than in the US market [*Tigre, 1989: 120*].

51. In 1989 the average price in England and France was US$ 1,203 for a PC-XT with twin disk drive and monochrome monitor. The models taken as reference were Amstrad PC 512K, Commodore PC-10, Phillips NMS 9000XT, and Samsung SPC-3000. The average price in Brazil for a comparable computer was US$ 1,473, converted by the parallel exchange rate, which is effective for eventual transactions including acquisition of illegally imported goods. The Brazilian models taken as reference were ATS THOR PC-XT 640K, BASIC Diginet XT II-BSC/204 704K, Digitron PC-XT 704K, Itautec IS-30 Plus 640K, and Scopus Nexus 2602 704K [*Tigre, 1989*].

52. Brazilian printers were compared to Epson LX800 150cps, Panasonic KX-P1180, Brother 1109 100cps, Citizen MPS 15E 160cps, and Amstrad DPM-4000 200cps. Brazilian floppy drives were compared to models of 360K and monitors to Samsung 12-inch monochrome [*Tigre, 1989*].

53. The Itau conglomerate includes the second largest Brazilian private bank, Itau Bank, whose strategy is to increase its investment in the electronics industry to change its present 75:25 ratio of financial to industrial assets to a 50:50 ratio. This group recently acquired Philco, with which it has entered the consumer electronics segment. The Machline conglomerate is linked to the largest Brazilian private bank, Bradesco Bank, through SID Informatica, which is its professional electronics subsidiary. The recent move to merge smaller companies with these conglomerates is exemplified by the case of Scopus, one of the innovative national firms in the professional electronics industry, which sold 70 per cent of its voting shares to Digilab (Bradesco group) in April 1989. One year before, Digilab had joined Itautec (Itau conglomerate) as shareholder of Sistema/Rima, a firm that manufactures printers.

54. There is no consensus on which developing countries are NICs nor on how to label them. The list ranges from the four core members, that is, the Asian NICs of Hong Kong, South Korea, Taiwan, and Singapore (some researchers add Brazil and Mexico), to twenty or more, including India, Argentina, Spain, Portugal, Israel, Yugoslavia, Malaysia, The Philippines, Greece, Turkey, and Egypt. These countries

are also sometimes referred to as the semiperiphery, semiindustrial countries, advanced developing countries, intermediate and subimperial, reflecting different theoretical as well as normative perspectives. I follow those authors who limit the NICs to the four East Asian countries (South Korea, Taiwan, Singapore, and Hong Kong), Brazil, and Mexico [*Moon, 1990: 159*].

55. The rate of growth in productivity was lower in the United States than among its competitors: in the period 1973-79, the growth rate of manufacturing output per hour was 1.6 per cent in the United States, compared with 6.35 per cent in Japan, 4.40 per cent in West Germany, 4.99 per cent in France, and 3.25 per cent in Italy [*Teece, 1987: 2*].

56. One way of coping with these risks has been to adopt a 'global strategy' designed to penetrate multiple major global markets with the new product simultaneously. This strategy leads the firm to reap the benefits of large investments in R&D before competitors can follow suit. Another strategy to reduce risks has been to form cooperative arrangements, especially with regard to R&D and the introduction of new production methods. International joint ventures and nonequity arrangements were used in the past, especially in low-technology industries, but have recently been occurring among two or more transnational corporations in developed economies where each party has advantages in different areas of specialization [*UNCTC, 1988: 54-59*].

57. There have been eight multilateral trade negotiations since the creation of GATT in 1947: Geneva [*1947*], Annecy [*1949*], Torquay [*1950-51*], Geneva [*1955-56*], Dillon [*1961-62*], Kennedy [*1964-67*], Tokyo [*1974-79*], and the Uruguay, which started in 1986 and was due to be closed in December 1990. As of December 1991 these talks were continuing. The preceding round of negotiations, the Tokyo Round, resulted in five new codes of conduct to regulate world trade in the areas of subsidies and countervailing duties, customs valuation, import licenses, and government procurement. These new codes and the existing antidumping code were not successful in reducing or limiting the use of nontariff barriers to trade.

58. The average tariff levels on electronics products are in line with the average tariff rates on other industrial imports. Tariffs imposed by developed countries are lower than those imposed by developing countries, and tariffs are generally lower for electronics components than for consumer electronics [*Kostecki, 1989: 20*].

59. This was the case the US imports of semiconductors made by Samsung, a South Korean company, which was accused in 1987 of infringing patents held by the American company Texas Instruments. The case was solved by a licensing agreement between the two companies.

60. Throughout the nineteenth century, the main concern of US trade policy was to secure the domestic market for American manufacturers. The 'most-favoured-nation' principle was only accepted in a 'conditional' version by which there was no obligation for two contracting parties to extend to each other trade concessions granted to a third country unless the other party reciprocated with equivalent concessions to those conceded by the third country. It was only in 1934 that the Reciprocal Trade Agreement was approved allowing the President of the United States to lower tariffs in return for reciprocal cuts by other countries [*Pearson and Riedel, 1990*].

152

61. This shift was, however, signalled as early as the mid-1960s by the US-Canada Automative Agreement, which granted Canadian exports to the United States duty-free treatment.
62. Section 301 of the 1974 Trade Act was intended to allow American companies to petition the US government to act in order to correct unfair trade practices. The 1979 amendment gave the President a stronger hand in protecting American interests, as he does not need to wait for American businessmen to claim damage, but can 'self-initiate' investigations. The theoretical implications of this point for alternative explanations of US government actions in the Brazilian 301 case are analysed by Evans [*1989*].
63. The critical terms of Section 301 were defined in the 1984 amendments. *Unjustifiable* is 'any act, policy, or practice which is in violation of or inconsistent with the international legal rights of the United States, including, but not limited to, a denial of national or most-favored-nation treatment, and the right of establishment or a denial of protection of intellectual property rights'. *Unreasonable* is defined as 'any act, policy or practice which, while not necessarily in violation of or inconsistent with the international legal rights of the United States, is otherwise deemed to be unfair and inequitable'. As Santarelli *et al.* [*1985: 5*] observe, the phrase 'unfair and inequitable' is not defined as leaving to the President's discretion the power to determine when circumstances exist that require action under this provision.
64. This fact may be interpreted more as a sign of the political need of many US Congressmen to comply with their constituency's call for protectionism than deep Congressional support for protectionism. In this sense, they would have been much more interested in presenting protectionist bills than in having them approved. Another way to explain the behaviour of Congressmen on this issue is to focus on the variety and contradiction of interests that are represented in the Congress [*Marshall, 1987*].
65. Opposing orientations within the US state apparatus on trade issues are not surprising as there is no basis to assume consensus and homogeneity inside any state. All administrations have to deal with this fact of life in politics. In the United States, the growth of export lobbies was encouraged by the Administration as a strategy to offset the import protectionist lobbies [*Bhagwati, 1989*]. And transfer to the Administration of the authority to carry forth trade policy is interpreted as a deal between the Congress and the Administration to insulate that policy and legislation from the effect of pressure groups who are likely to confront the Congress [*Marshall, 1987*].
66. A little earlier, the emphasis of President Carter's administration on human rights, nuclear nonproliferation, and disarmament built a wide area of tension with the Brazilian military government. President Geisel's administration dealt cautiously with the issue of 'state terrorism' in Brazil to avoid disrupting the precarious support within the state apparatus for the process of internal political liberalization. The US pressure in defence of human rights in Brazil was seen as inconvenient by the Brazilian authorities. The US refusal to guarantee the processing of fuel for the nuclear reactors then under construction by Westinghouse was a severe blow to the infant Brazilian nuclear energy policy. American interventionism in Central America, which developed during President Reagan's administrations, worsened tensions between the two countries. These tensions were aggravated by Brazil's support for

the Contadora Group, by Brazil's collaboration with Nicaragua, and by US support for Great Britain in the Malvinas (Falklands) war.

67. Brazil's external indebtedness has become an item on the agenda of US/Brazil relations since the rise of international interest rates in 1979. American direct interference became clear when the US government advised American private banks not to lend new money to Brazil in 1979 and pressed the Brazilian government to abide by International Monetary Fund (IMF) rules to control the Brazilian economy. This interference increased after 1982 when the Reagan administration, fearing a Brazilian default that would have been disastrous to American private banks, authorized the US Treasury to participate jointly with the Bank for International Settlements and various commercial banks in a rescue operation for Brazilian finance [*Lafer et al., 1985: 20*].

68. Primary goods, which had already been surpassed by manufactured products in Brazilian exports to the United States in the late 1970s, were reduced to 18 per cent of exports in 1985. On the other hand, the share of manufactured products in Brazilian exports to the United States between 1983 and 1985 was more than 70 per cent. The composition of Brazilian exports to the United States in 1985 included machines, instruments, and other mechanical devices accounting for 9.4 per cent; footwear, 8.7 per cent; concentrated orange juice, 6.3 per cent; electrical machines and other electrical devices, 4.2 per cent; petrol, 5.3 per cent; manufactures of steel, 4.2 per cent; fuel-oil, three per cent [*Banco do Brasil, 1985: 112*].

69. During 1974, the United States found Brazil at fault in a countervailing duty action brought by American footwear manufacturers. To compensate for export subsidies, the US government imposed a customs surcharge, which drove Brazil to present a formal note of protest [*Fishlow, 1982: 907*]. In the framework of the subsidy code of the multilateral trade negotiations, Brazil committed itself to phase out its export credit premium by June 1983. However, due to problems in the Brazilian balance of payment, the United States agreed, in November 1982, with the maintenance of the premium until April 1985. An appraisal of US/Brazil trade conflicts prior to the IT policy case can be found in CEPAL 1985.

70. The groups were organized to improve cooperative efforts in the following areas: (1) science and technology, (2) space research, (3) military activities, (4) economic and financial matters, and (5) nuclear energy.

71. The content of FIESP's criticism of the IT policy is discussed in Chapter 7 in an analysis of the IT policy's opposition within Brazil and its main arguments.

72. A chronology of the main events in the development of the Brazilian 301 case is found in Appendix II.

73. The content of the software law will be analysed in Chapter 7.

74. The existence of this study was published in the Brazilian press on the same day the Brazilian Foreign Minister criticized SEI. My search for a copy of the mentioned study was, however, fruitless.

75. For an account of the initial stages of the Brazilian IT policy, see Helena 1980; Piragibe 1985; Adler 1987; and Dantas 1988. A political analysis of the IT policy's evolution is found in Bastos 1992.

76. Evolution of support and opposition to the IT policy within Brazilian society, including the state apparatus, is detailed in Chapter 7.

77. Whereas the MCT and the SEI were gradually isolated within the Sarney administration throughout the development of the dispute, they gained important support in the Brazilian Congress, which was then writing the new Brazilian constitution. A chapter on Science and Technology was for the first time included in a Brazilian constitution, which consecrated the principle that is a basic justification for the market reserve policy. Article 219, Chapter IV, establishes that 'the internal market is part of the nation's endowment and will be stimulated in order to promote cultural and social and economic development, the well-being of the population, and the technological autonomy of the country, in terms to be established by federal law' (my translation).

78. The White House Trade Office called a public hearing in December 1987 to discuss the matter and to define the list of products to be subjected to punitive tariffs. The majority of participants stressed that not only American customers, but also American workers and companies, would be hit by the sanctions. Even American IT executives asked the Trade Office not to include electronics products made in Brazil in the list for punitive tariffs because this would affect their Brazilian subsidiaries.

79. Originally published in *ACM Computing Surveys*, Vol. 7, No. 1, March 1975.

80. The National Federation of Engineers, ABICOMP, the Brazilian Association for Informatics Law (ABDI), the Association of COBRA (Computadores e Sistemas Brasileiros S.A.) Employees, the Brazilian Association for Process Control and Industrial Automation (ABCPAI), ASSESPRO, and the Society of Workers in Data Processing in the State of São Paulo (SEPROESP).

81. SUCESU's president warned of the many relevant technical features involved in assessing functional equivalence, and suggested that this ought to be taken into consideration. The following traits of a software would have to be looked at: operating environment; language; means and format of input, output and storage; speed; and used capacity of the main and secondary memories [*Mussalem, 1987b*].

82. A decree is issued by the Executive Branch to operationalize abstract dispositions defined in a law approved by the Legislative Branch.

83. For a detailed account of the participation of the Brazilian scientific/technological community, the planning community, and the navy in this initial phase of the IT policy, see Adler [*1987*]; Dantas [*1988*].

84. See Katz [*1981*]; Westman [*1985*]; Adler [*1986, 1987*]; Evans [*1986*]; Botelho [*1988*].

85. SNI's National Intelligence School (ESNI) had been doing experiments, since the early 1970s, to develop a cryptograph that could enhance information security. From this experience resulted the conviction that the IT policy's goals would never be achieved if the development of microelectronics was not also stimulated.

86. The group in charge of investigating the activities of CAPRE was composed of two members who later became chairmen of SEI. The group was not impressed by the fact that, in 1977-78, the central agencies in charge of the IT policy considered the convenience of a joint enterprise between Fujitsu and SERPRO as a way of allowing a foreign firm other than IBM to act in the local market of medium-sized computers. The group also judged as too liberal the decision made by the planning minister at the end of the Geisel administration to allow the local production of medium-sized computers by IBM.

87. One of IBM's proposals to produce and sell medium-sized computers for the Brazilian market, which was rejected by CAPRE at its last meeting, was presented to SEI, which approved local production and trade under very strict conditions. A similar situation occurred with a Hewlett-Packard desktop microcomputer. SEI justified its decisions on pragmatic grounds. Local demand for that size of computer could be met only by imports at that time.

88. Domestic computer firms were investing a significant amount of their sales in R&D, reaching an average of 11 per cent in the period 1979-82. Although impressive in relative terms, research investment was still minimal by international standards. In 1982, COBRA, the only state-owned and the then biggest computer manufacturer in Brazil, had a research budget of $10 million, which is only 12.5 per cent of Data General's R&D spending during that year [*Peritore, 1988: 33*].

89. Price performance in the reserved segment of the Brazilian electronic complex was used to justify both supporting and opposition positions in the struggle over the IT policy, with opposing sides using different data as evidence. More balanced assessments are now being made. In Chapter 4 I presented some details on this subject.

90. By Decree No. 90754 of December 1984, the following NGOs were to be represented in CONIN: ABICOMP; ASSESPRO; SUCESU; APPD; one representative appointed jointly by the National Federation of Industries, the National Federation of Commerce, and the National Federation of Credit Enterprises; one representative appointed jointly by the National Union of Industrial Workers, the National Union of Commerce Workers, and the National Union of Credit Enterprises Workers; one representative appointed jointly by SBPC and SBC; and one prominent Brazilian citizen chosen by the President from a list of three individuals nominated by the National Council of Brazilian Lawyers and the Institute of Brazilian Lawyers. Decree No. 99406 of July 1990 changed this composition. By this new decree, NGO representatives are to be appointed by national organizations of industry, of users of IT goods and services, of IT professionals and workers, of the scientific/technological community, of the press, and of the legal profession.

APPENDIX I

SUMMARY OF RELEVANT REGULATIONS TOWARDS THE BRAZILIAN ELECTRONICS INDUSTRY[1]

(A) REGULATIONS ISSUED BEFORE LAW No. 7232/84

Law no. 4117 (27 Aug. 1962)

Brazilian Telecommunication Law. Establishes two institutions: the National Telecommunication Council (CONTEL) and the Brazilian Telecommunication Company (EMBRATEL). Creates the National Telecommunication Fund.

Decree 70370 (5 April 1972)

Creates the Coordinating Commission for Electronics Processing Activities (CAPRE), under the authority of the Ministry of Planning, with the task of proposing and adopting measures aimed at rationalizing government investments in the sector and increasing productivity in the utilization of data-processing equipment already installed and to be installed. CAPRE is composed of the Secretary General of the Ministry of Planning, as Chairman, and representatives of the General Staff of the Armed Forces, Ministry of Finance, National Economic Development Bank, Federal Data Processing Service, IBGE Foundation Centre for Computer Science, Department of Modernization and Administrative Reform.

---

1. *Source:* Secretaria Especial de Informatica, *Boletim Informativo*, v. 3, n. 10, 1983; Secretaria Especial de Informatica, *Legislacao*, 1987; Special Secretariat for Informatics, *Transborder Data Flows and Brazil: The Role of Transnational Corporations, Impacts of Transborder Data Flows and Effects of National Policies. Brazilian Case Study*, 1982; *Diario Oficial da União; Departamento de Política de Informatica e Automação (DEPIN).*

Law no. 5792 (11 June 1972)

Creates the Telecomunicacoes Brasileiras S.A. (TELEBRAS) in order to rationalize Brazil's telephone service.

Minicom's Directive 301 (3 April 1975)

Regulates the implementation of public telex and data-communication networks. EMBRATEL is entrusted with data transmission and telex services.

CONCEX Resolution 104 (3 Dec. 1975)

Establishes that up to 31 December 1976 the issuing of import licences for electronic computers and their peripherals shall be conditional upon the prior approval of CAPRE. This provision does not apply to imports connected with drawback operations, pertaining to used equipment intended for reconditioning and reexportation.

Decree 77118 (9 Feb. 1976)

Restructures CAPRE and gives it the objectives of identifying needs in the field of information processing; determining priorities and mechanisms for satisfying these needs; furthering the sectoral integration of resources used, while optimizing investments, with more efficient utilization of already existing resources; encouraging the establishment of information flows based on electronic processing, in order to facilitate government decision-making processes. CAPRE is composed of a Plenary Council and an Executive Secretariat. The Plenary Council has the responsibility of proposing the National Informatics Policy and the Integrated Informatics Plan; examining the decisions of the Executive Secretariat at the appellate level; and resolving specific cases. It is composed of the Secretary General of the Department of Planning of the Office of the President of the Republic [Ministry of Planning] as Chairman, the Chairman of the National Council on Scientific and Technological Development (CNPq); a representative of the General Staff of the Armed Forces; a representative of the Ministry of Communication; a representative of the Ministry of Education; a representative of the Ministry of Finance; a representative of the Ministry of Industry and Commerce. CAPRE's responsibilities are to guide government activities in the various fields of information science, to keep the detailed census of the private and governmental computer population constantly updated, to express its opinion on proposals for the acquisition of equipment and software in any form by state agencies, to coordinate human-resources development programmes, and to propose measures aimed at the formulation of a programme of government financing to the private sector for data-processing activities.

CAPRE's Resolution 01 (15 July 1976)

Recommends that the national informatics policy for the medium- and large-size computer market be aimed at rationalizing investments and optimizing already installed facilities through their more efficient utilization; that the national informatics policy for the market for mini- and microcomputers, their peripheral equipment, modern data transcription and transmission equipment, and terminals shall be aimed at facilitating the control of initiatives for the consolidation of an industrial machine population with total dominion and control of both technology and decision-making within the country.

CDE's Resolution 05 (12 Jan. 1977)

Establishes criteria for the concession of fiscal incentives for the manufacture of computers, including smaller systems, peripherals, and components. The same criteria apply to the analysis of import requests. The criteria are (a) level of nationalization of equipment used in production and the goods manufactured; (b) export potential; (c) complete technological openness to national companies in the cases of joint-ventures; (d) companies' participation in the local market.

CAPRE's Resolution 01 (1 June 1977)

Invites companies to present projects for local manufacture of minicomputers.

CAPRE's Plenary Council Resolution no. 01 (2 May 1978)

The establishment of international links on tele-informatics systems shall be conditional upon CAPRE's prior approval.

Minicom's Directive 622 (19 June 1978)

Establishes objectives, instruments and guidelines for the *Policy on Equipment Acquisition and Technological Development of Telecommunications.* The specific objectives are to develop a local capacity in technology management with regard to telecommunications materials, components, equipment and systems; to develop a local capacity for the elaboration and execution of telecommunications equipment and systems design; to develop within the country an adequate capacity for the production of the materials, components, equipment, and systems necessary for the telecommunications sector; to set up and consolidate Brazilian industries for each type of equipment and material used in the sector, resting on technology developed locally or transferred from abroad; to make sure that consolidation of industries producing telecommunications materials and equipment is accompanied by creation or expansion of their own capacity to elaborate and execute designs and projects of telecommunications systems and equipment; to achieve the highest index possible of telecommunications systems and equipment produced domestically, taking into account the requirements of quality and competitive price of the end product; to provide for the training of the human resources required for industrial R&D in the sector. Instruments for the implementation of the policy: acquisition of equipment and materials, sectoral regulation and standardization, selective importation of components and materials of interest to the sector, R&D activities in the

TELEBRAS R&D Centre (CPqD), training and specialization of human resources. Guidelines to orient the acquisition of telecommunications equipment: (1) import equipment only when there is no locally made similar, (2) prior selection of supplier for the acquisition of equipment whose manufacture requires large-scale investment, (3) competitive bidding for the acquisition of equipment whose manufacture does not require large-scale investment, (4) limit the number of suppliers per product line to a minimum of two and a maximum of four. Brazilian industry, for the purpose of this Directive, means that which is established in the country, the majority of whose stock with the right to vote belongs to Brazilians or foreigners established in Brazil, and whose statutes, shareholder agreements, and technical assistance or cooperation agreements contain no clause restricting the full exercise of the prerogatives inherent in the said shareholders majority.

CAPRE's Resolution 02 (19 Dec. 1978)

Defines detailed criteria for establishing the priority of a project for local manufacture of computers larger than mini- and microcomputers, and their peripherals. The following criteria are to be considered: it is necessary to ensure that the projects do not interfere in the protected segment of mini- and micro-computers; projects under local decision power (control of capital, management, and technology) are to be stimulated; capability of absorption of technology of hardware and software; local content; nationalization requirement; companies shall have industrial experience in electronics, fine mechanics, and software production.

Minicom's Directive 337 (28 Dec. 1978)

Approves regulation for providing of Private-Use International Circuit Leasing Services.

Minicom's Directive 109 (25 Jan. 1979)

Approves regulations governing the operation and use of data-communication services. Defines that this service shall be operated by EMBRATEL within the national boundaries. The purpose of the regulation is to establish the conditions under which the service is to be operated and used within the country, defining the rights and obligations of the company operating the service, its leasing customers, subscribers and users, and the companies operating other public telecommunications services.

National Security Council Presentation of Motives 008 (1 Oct. 1979)

Guidelines for National Informatics Policy. (1) Government incentives and participation in the generation and absorption of the technologies involved in the inputs, components, equipment, software, and services: coordinating the activities of the organizations responsible for human-resource development;

uniting and coordinating the differentiated efforts of laboratories and university groups, research and development groups, and institutes; creating and strengthening university laboratories and groups responsible for pioneering research and development activities and human-resources development; creating a system of technological research and development coordinated by a specialized and autonomous institute constituted as a corporation. (2) National development in the production of linear and digital electronic components and of their basic inputs: study and utilization of mechanisms of control and follow-up in the production and marketing of those inputs that are considered essential to the strategy of national development; use of protection mechanisms for the production of electromechanical components and integrated linear and digital circuits; should it become necessary, extend the activities of the state into the creation of companies in the sector of microelectronics and like areas. (3) Make feasible both the technology and marketing of national companies which produce equipment and systems: maintain market reserve and import control in the areas of microcomputers, minicomputers, and their peripherals and extend these instruments to the production of small and medium-sized equipment by national companies. (4) Incentives, encouragement, and guidance to the development of software and services by national industry: further the development of operational systems; the elaboration of support and application software, systems of distributed processing, and data communication networks; software for data banks; software for making differentiated equipment compatible. (5) Norms, standards, systems of approval, and granting of quality certificates to products and services elaborated in Brazil or imported shall be gradually institutionalized. (6) Implementation of national data communication networks by the Ministry of Communications and its subordinate companies. (7) Creation of legal and technical mechanisms for the protection of the secrecy of stored, processed, and transmitted data when this is in the interest of the privacy and security of individuals and legal entities: elaborate specific legislation and promote domestic manufacturing of devices which will ensure the attainment of these objectives. (8) Complementary participation of the state in productive sectors, when demanded by national interest and when the national private sector is either unable to act or disinterested: verification of the desirability of continued government stock participation, either direct or indirect, in industrial undertakings and the examination of the necessity of furthering or expanding this participation, when the activities of the companies in question so demand. (9) Appropriate implementation of the policy through coordinated mobilization and use of financial resources: creation of an Informatics Activities Fund (FAI) and granting the authority to manage the Fund to a single entity. (10) Improved systems of international cooperation to strengthen technological development and the defence of national interest: in the cases in which private foreign concerns show a willingness to participate according to the demands of national interest; in bilateral and multilateral centres qualified for an exchange of information and experiences. (11) The direction of activities in the field of informatics by a single entity, occupying the highest hierarchical position compatible with current legal norms. The government shall grant the political support demanded to produce the best possible performance on the part of this entity, by conferring upon it the autonomy corresponding to the importance of its responsibilities and the right to administer the Informatics Activities Fund. (12) The guidance provided to informatics activities shall have a predominantly political character and, aside from the technical aspects, shall also take into consideration the greater necessity of preserving and improving Brazilian cultural traditions and supporting the effort to achieve higher standards of living.

Decree 84067 (8 Oct. 1979)

Creates the Special Secretariat for Informatics (SEI) with the powers to (i) provide advisory services; (ii) elaborate and propose the National Informatics Plan; (iii) directly or indirectly implement the Plan; (iv) administer the resources and funds for the development of the sector; (v) orient, approve, and supervise the Informatics Master Plans of state agencies; (vi) propose measures for adequately dealing with specific needs of the Armed Forces and strategic and national security areas; (vii) express opinion on drafts of international treaties and the like, on the creation and restructuring of data-processing agencies, on the granting of tax and other benefits, on contracts for services rendered abroad, on the suitability of granting channels for data-communication links at the national and international levels, on patent applications, on the criteria of product similarity, on the importation of informatics items, on the regulation of professions, and on customs tariffs; (viii) further and encourage production, service and business activities, the utilization of computer science, prospective studies, and the exchange of ideas and experiences; (ix) promote and encourage scientific and technological research in the data-processing sector and the training of human resources; (x) supervise agencies in the indirect administration connected with the field of information processing; (xi) elaborate and institute norms and standards governing equipment, programme, and service contracts to be negotiated by state agencies; for national similarity of products; and on the structure of data-processing organizations to be created; (xii) establish preferential lists of electronic components importation; (xiii) promote the creation of a census of data banks operated by state agencies; the institution of a census of the private and government computer population with regard to human resources, equipment, and programmes; the institution of a registry of companies in the sector with follow-up on their evolution as regards stockholder control, products, and technology; and the setting up of a system of scientific and technological information for the sector.

162

Appendix I

Decree 84266 (5 Dec. 1979)

Establishes SEI's structure: the Office of the Secretary, Sectoral Advisory Boards, Executive Secretariat: Under-Secretary for Studies and Planning, Under-Secretary for Industry, Under-Secretary for Services, Under-Secretary for Strategic Activities, Under-Secretary for Administration and Finance. An Informatics Commission is created with the following composition: representatives of the Ministries of Foreign Relations, Finance, Education, Industry and Commerce, Interior, Communication, and a representative of the National Security Council, National Intelligence Service, General Staff of the Armed Forces, Secretary of Planning, and presided over by SEI's Chairman.

SEI's Normative Act 001/80

Defines import priorities and criteria for the examination of requests for imports of electronic data-processing equipment. Criteria for the import of electronic data-processing equipment: (1) import requests will be analysed taking the following basic factors into consideration: the utilization of national alternatives; the software assets which have already been developed in the country by the petitioning entity, which, due to tits complexity, may make the use of noncompatible national equipment unfeasible; the utilization of software that is specific and indispensable to the activities of the user, when it may not be opportune to develop the same within the country, aggregated to the equipment to be imported; (2) import requests of state agencies will only be considered with the prior approval of the informatics commission or secretariats of each agency; (3) import requests of those state agencies which possess state councils of data processing or informatics shall only be considered with the previous approval of the aforementioned councils; (4) import requests of the organs and entities of the Public Administration in general should involve electronic data-processing equipment to be used in rendering the services of their specific area; (5) import requests presented by institutions of higher learning should have the priority objective of being used in the development of teaching, research, and academic activities. Authorization for the import of electronic data-processing equipment is limited to the following priorities: (1) equipment considered to have priority standing in keeping with the National Development Plan in force at the time; (2) equipment destined to Federal, State, and Municipal companies involved in electronic data processing and which render services preferentially to related governmental organs; (3) equipment to be utilized in the end activities of private companies to be used in production planning and control in the industrial sector; (4) equipment to be used in the independent bureaux services; (5) the installation of intelligent terminals, which avoid the installation of electronic data-processing equipment of considerable size, on the condition that the central equipment be reserved for the exclusive use of the petitioning entity;

(6) the importation of devices or peripheral equipment of small value in relation to the overall value of the equipment to which it will be aggregated.

SEI's Normative Act 002/80

Establishes the obligation of the registration at SEI of all projects for local manufacturing of electronic equipment.

SEI's Directive 003 (20 Mar. 1980)

Creates the Special Commission no. 003/Software and Services, for the purpose of examining the situation of the segment of software and services within the country and providing assistance to SEI with a view to the development and consolidation of the domestic industry of software and service.

SEI's Normative Act 003/80

Defines the prior approval of SEI as a condition for state agencies' acquisition or leasing of automatic data-processing equipment in the local or foreign markets.

SEI's Normative Act 005/80

Establishes the preference to national alternatives in competitive bidding procedures for the acquisition of informatics equipment and services by state agencies.

SEI's Directive 007 (15 July 1980)

Creates the Special Commission no. 05/Process Control.

SEI's Normative Act 009/80

Establishes the obligation of state agencies to request their suppliers of informatics equipment to submit a copy of their registry at SEI.

Decree 85790 (6 Mar. 1981)

Extends SEI's tasks to coordinate the research, development, and production of electronic semiconductor and optoelectronic components as well as their inputs.

Minicom's Directive 81 (21 May 1981)

Approves regulations governing the use of the Public Telephone Network for Data Communication.

Minicom's Directive 172 (18 Sep. 1981)

Establishes that the protocol for access to the Switched Public Data-Communication Network shall be standardized and shall be the one defined in the Serie-X recommendations of the International Telegraph and Telephone Consultative

Committee (CCITT) of the International Telecommunication Union. TELE-BRAS shall define the specifications of such standard protocols.

Minicom's Directive 215 (9 Nov. 1981)

Modifies the guidelines regarding the introduction of Telephone Exchange with Stored Programme Control into the National Telecommunications System and establishes that contracting on new centres of this nature be restricted to the CPA-T type, manufactured within the country. Installations of CPA-T shall be effected during the initial stage in defined metropolitan areas. It shall be permissible for the Brazilian companies to make use of the technology trans-ferred from their foreign associates or licensors in the production of CPA-T models, provided that the characteristics of language, protocols, interfaces, and other applicable specifications established by the Ministry of Communications are met. As soon as they are available for installation, Brazilian CPA-T models developed by TELEBRAS'CPqD shall be used in the National Telecommuni-cations System. Once the Brazilian medium-sized CPA-T model is available for installation, the system of competitive bidding on the national market shall be adopted, with preference being given to technologies developed within the country, subject in all cases to the suitability of limiting the number of techno-logies present in the system.

SEI's Normative Act 012/81

Approves the forms for submitting prior consultations to SEI in connection with the importing, or the acquisition on the domestic market, of informatics pro-ducts.

SEI's Normative Act 013/81 (joint with INPI)

Creates an Equal-Representation Commission made up of INPI and SEI repre-sentatives for the purpose of jointly examining and recommending the approval of technology-transfer contracts in the informatics area. Establishes a procedure for patent application in the informatics area and mechanisms for the exchange of technical information and mutual consultation in technological matters.

SEI's Normative Act 014/81

Establishes preference for domestic alternatives in contracting for automation and process-control systems by both state agencies and private companies.

SEI's Normative Act 015/81

Defines the obligation of state agencies to present to SEI their annual Informa-tics Master Plans. These plans are to be approved and followed up by SEI.

SEI's Normative Act 016/81

Substitutes Normative Acts 004/80 and 006/80. Defines prerequisites for the examination of new projects for local manufacture of informatics products. The companies have to prove (a) that the effective control of the operation and the activities of the concern, including the control of the corporate capital, lies permanently and exclusively in the hands of individuals born, residing, and domiciled in Brazil; (b) the compatibility of the formation and structure of the corporate capital with the scope of the project; (c) that the technology used is developed within the country, unless it is not available locally and the products to be manufactured are assessed as being highly relevant for the economy. Defines a list of products whose authorization for local manufacturing is dependent on the fulfilment of the above conditions: mini- and microcomputers, small-sized and medium-sized electronic computers and their peripherals, electronic cash registers, electronic word processing machines, electronic accounting machines, bank terminals and their controllers, electronic tickets dispensers and readers, modems, video terminals and their controllers, data-base remote-access terminals, data-entry devices, electronic communication processors, digital signal multiplexors for data communication, digital signal concentrators for data communications, teleprinters with transmitting and receiving speeds greater than 75 baud, facsimile machines, instrumentation for process control, numerical control equipment, secrecy equipment, or equipment using encryption techniques.

SEI's Normative Act 017/81

Complements Normative Act 016/81 and replaces Normative Act 011/80. In the analysis and evaluation by SEI of projects for local manufacture of informatics products not listed in Normative Act 016, the following factors shall be grounds to eliminate a product: (a) compatibility of the formation and structure of the corporate capital with the project's scope; (b) the product described in the project does not interfere in the market segment of the machines and equipment listed in Normative Act 016/81, and (c) use of domestic products and detailed schedule for the substitution of imported components and parts. The condition of the company's local control shall be applied whenever there is the possibility of developing projects in which both local technology and capital are considered sufficient. Whenever local technology and capital are insufficient, local manufacturing will be authorized for foreign companies that do not increase their monopoly nor excessively fragment the market, that show export potential, and, in the case of foreign technology, only if it could be opened to other local producers under conditions internationally accepted.

SEI's Normative Act 018/81

Defines a model form for presenting projects for local manufacture of informatics products. The project is a previous condition for the issuance by SEI of import licences. Replaces Normative Act 010/80.

Appendix I

SEI's Normative Act 019/81

Establishes the obligation of submitting to SEI research and development projects by individuals or institutions that need to import parts, spare components, other inputs, and capital goods destined to the research.

SEI's Normative Act 020/81

Establishes that the Import Permit Application shall be included among the documents to be submitted for the prior consultation of SEI when the items to be imported are finished products.

SEI's Normative Act 022/81

Creates a registry for software at SEI. They are to be classified in three categories: A - locally developed by Brazilian nationals or companies constituted under Brazilian law, with the headquarters within the country and the control over capital and technology by Brazilian nationals; B - foreign developed, without local equivalent, transferred to national companies through contract approved by INPI; C - all other cases. Registration of software in category C will not be issued when (i) there is a national alternative or correspondent software registered as B; (ii) there is the possibility and convenience of using or developing similar software in the country. The registration is a precondition for state agencies contracting software, SEI's agreement with the concession of fiscal or any other kind of incentives to projects referred to software, SEI's approval of the Informatics Master Plans of state agencies, SEI's authorization for importation of data-processing equipment, SEI's analysis of projects for local manufacture of informatics products. The registration is valid for two years and can be renewed if, in the case of C, there is no local equivalent.

Decree 87980 (23 Dec. 1982)

Enlarges SEI's autonomy to hire specialists and consultants, to have its own budget, and to administer the Fund for Informatics Activities (FAI) to finance its activities.

Decree 88010 (30 Dec. 1982)

Creates the Technological Centre for Informatics (CTA), to promote the development of scientific and technological research in the informatics area.

SEI's Normative Act 023/83

Establishes conditions for state agencies to contract informatics services. They would be allowed to contract services with foreign subsidiaries only if there is no national firm qualified for the service required. Informatics services are defined as data processing; software design, development, trade, operation, and maintenance; consultancy in informatics; training in informatics techniques. Companies offering informatics services are to be registered at SEI.

SEI's Normative Act 024/83

Enlarges the list of reserved items to include digital technical instruments for measurement testing (instrumentacao de teste-medicao), analytical instrumentation (instrumentacao analitica), and biomedical equipment.

SEI's Normative Act 025/83

Establishes that in any purchase or leasing contracts (including importation) of data-processing systems, automatic machines, digital data-processing equipment, and their peripherals by state agencies (inclusive for the purpose of process control and automation) operations related to the equipment itself, its maintenance, software, and any other informatics service shall be treated as separate operations.

SEI's Normative Act 026/83

States that projects for local manufacturing of microcomputers with the logic structure based on microprocessors will be approved only if the operating system is developed by a locally owned company.

CACEX Communication 41 (24 Jan. 1983)

Lists 52 items that require prior SEI approval for the issuance of an import licence. The list replaces the one established by Resolution 121, of 1979, issued by CONCEX. This communication also replaces CACEX Communication 18 of 13 April 1982. It includes, among others, doped crystals, electronic printers, electronic typewriters, electronic calculators and accounting machines, electronic stored-programme automatic telephone exchange, multiplexors, electronic teleprinters, facsimile machines, nonlinear semiconductor resistors, printed circuit boards, automatic data-processing machines, transistors, electronic home appliances, electrocardiograph, electroencephalograph, magnetic disks, and magnetic tapes.

SEI's Normative Act 001/84 (joint with STI)

Establishes that the approval of projects for local manufacture of instruments or equipment with digital electronic technology for exclusive use in automobiles is dependent on the provisions defined by, among other regulations, Normative Act 016/81.

(B) REGULATIONS ISSUED AFTER LAW 7232/84

Decree-Law 2203 (27 Dec. 1984)

Makes provisions about equating open capital companies to national companies as they are defined in Article 12 of Law No. 7232, for the objective of qualifying for the fiscal and financial incentives and other provisions of the aforementioned law. In relation to the requirement of control upon the capital, at least two-thirds of their common stock and the like proportions of their voting stock and fixed or minimum dividend stock, and at least 70 per cent of their equity or share capital shall be held by (I) individuals born, residing, and domiciled in Brazil; (II) private law corporations, constituted and with seat and venue in Brazil, which fulfil the requirements for being considered national companies; (III) domestic public law corporations; (IV) foundations constituted and administered by the individuals mentioned in the previous lines.

Decree 90754 (27 Dec. 1984)

Specifies the organization and functioning of the National Council for Informatics and Automation (CONIN) in accordance with Articles 6 and 7 of Law no. 7232. CONIN is composed of (1) the ministers of the Navy, Army, Foreign Relations, Education, Finance, Labour, Air Force, Health, Industry and Commerce, Mining and Energy, Interior, and Communication; the Chief-Secretary of Planning; and the Secretary of the National Security Council; (2) one representative of each of the following associations: the Brazilian Association for Computer and Peripheral Equipment Industries (ABICOMP), the Association of Data-Processing Services Enterprises (ASSESPRO), the Society of Computer and Subsidiary Equipment Consumers (SUCESU), the Association of Data-Processing Professionals (APPD); one representative jointly appointed by the National Federation of Industries, the National Federation of Commerce, and the National Federation of Credit Enterprises; one representative jointly appointed by the National Union of Industrial Workers, the National Union of Commerce Workers, and the National Union of the Credit Enterprises Workers; one representative jointly appointed by the Brazilian Society for the Advancement of Science (SBPC) and the Brazilian Computation Society (SBC); (3) one highly regarded Brazilian citizen chosen by the President of the Republic out of a list of three individuals appointed by the National Council of Brazilian Lawyers and the Institute of Brazilian Lawyers. CONIN's members (2) and (3) are nominated by the President of the Republic for a three-year term. CONIN will meet each two months and when necessary, always on convocation by the President of the Republic, or by solicitation from any of its ministerial members.

Decree 90755 (27 Dec. 1984)

Specifies SEI's tasks and structure. SEI is subordinated to CONIN and its tasks are (1) to support CONIN in technical matters; (2) to implement CONIN's resolutions; (3) to elaborate a proposal for a National Plan for Informatics and Automation (PLANIN) to be submitted to CONIN and to implement the Plan in its area of competence; (4) to take the necessary measures to implement the National Informatics Policy in its area of competence; (5) to analyse and make decision on projects for local development and manufacture of informatics goods; (6) to decide upon the importation of informatics goods and services for eight years from the date of publication of law no. 7232.

Decree 90756 (27 Dec. 1984)

Approves the norms governing the Technological Centre for Informatics (CTI).

Decree 91171 (22 Mar. 1985)

Alters Decree 90754 to include the Minister of Science and Technology in the composition of CONIN and to make him the coordinator of the subjects under the competence of that council.

Decree 91229 (6 May 1985)

Alters Decree 90754 to include the Chief of the General Staff of the Armed Forces in the composition of CONIN.

CONIN Resolution 001/85

Establishes that activities in the area of informatics shall not be limited by nor create privileges in connection with the place in which they are exercised. Concession of fiscal, financial, and any other kind of incentives to informatics activities carried out in any part of the country shall be decided by CONIN in accordance with the National Plan for Informatics and Automation.

Decree 92181 (19 Dec. 1985)

Approves specifications of Article 21 of Law no. 7232 on the subject of incentives for the acquisition of new shares of national informatics companies. Corporations are allowed to deduct up to one per cent of the income tax due provided they apply directly an equal amount in new shares of private national companies, the application of such benefits being forbidden to companies belonging to the same conglomerate and/or whose capitalization plans have not been approved by CONIN.

Decree 92187 (20 Dec. 1985)

Approves norms for concession of fiscal incentives established in Articles 13 to 15 of Law no. 7232. *Incentives to research and development activities:* deduction of up to double the amount spent in research and development activities under the limit of 50 per cent of the taxable profits; waiver of the import duties on goods without local equivalent and necessary to the development of research projects; waiver of the Industrialized Product Tax on either imported or locally manufactured goods to be used in research and development; waiver of the Credit, Foreign Exchange, and Insurance Operations Tax and of the Tax on Stock Exchange Operations on foreign exchange operations to pay for importation of goods to be used in research activities; annual rate of depreciation of 33.33 per cent for fixed assets. *Incentives for the development of human resources:* deduction of up to double the amount spent with training under the limit of 15 per cent of the taxable profits for companies that have training programmes previously approved by CONIN. *Incentives for the production of informatics goods and services:* waiver of import duties on equipment, machines, and instruments, including their accessories, spare parts, and tools; waiver of the Industrialized Product Tax on goods which are part of the business' fixed assets; waiver of the Credit, Foreign Exchange, and Insurance Operations on foreign exchange operations to pay for importation of goods or for technology transfer contracts; annual rate of depreciation of 33.33 per cent for fixed assets. *Incentives for donations of informatics goods and services:* donation of goods and services produced by national companies to teaching institutions for training activities will be accepted as project of R&D in respect to the incentives. *Incentives for export of informatics goods and services:* waiver of the export tax for national companies that export the mentioned goods and services. *Incentives for the development of software:* reduction in the taxable profits, for income tax purposes, by a percentage equivalent to the share in the business' total revenue represented by the gross revenue derived from the marketing of such software. *Incentives for the microelectronics sector:* projects for manufacturing of semiconductor electronic, optical-electronic, or similar components, as well as their inputs, which involve physical-chemical processing, will benefit from the following incentives: (I) reduction of the bands of import duties and of the Industrialized Products Tax in the case of importation of (a) processed inputs - 75 per cent, (b) semifinished goods - 50 per cent, (c) final products - 25 per cent; (II) reduction of the bands of the Industrialized Products Tax in the case of acquisition of inputs or intermediate locally made products - 80 per cent, and in the case of selling final products locally made - 80 per cent; (III) reduction of the bands of Credit, Foreign Exchange, and Insurance Operations Tax and the Tax on Stock Exchange Operations on foreign exchange operations related to the payment of (a) processed foreign inputs - 75 per cent, (b) semifinished foreign products - 50 per cent, (c) final foreign products - 25 per cent; (IV) waiver of the taxes referred to in item I and III above in the cases of importation or acquisition in the local market of (a) machines, equipment, instruments, and apparatus with their respective accessories, spare parts, and tools which are part of the business' fixed assets and (b) unprocessed inputs; (V) waiver of the tax referred to in item III on foreign exchange operations for the payment of technology transfer contracts in the microelectronics segment; (VI) depreciation of goods which are part of the business' fixed assets in 3 years; (VII) deduction, as operational expenditures, in the percentage shown, of the amount spent in (a) projects of R&D contracted with public or private research institutions - 200 per cent; contracted with others - 170 per cent; (b) programmes of development of human resources - 200 per cent. Companies that use microelectronic goods locally made by national companies with projects approved by SEI and CONIN may deduct, for the determination of taxable profits, twice the amount spent in the acquisition of those goods effectively used as intermediate products.

Communication SEI/SEINF 006/86 (27 Feb. 1986)

Defines preliminary rules for presentation of application for fiscal incentives.

Communication SEI/SEINF 66 (18 Aug. 1986)

Alters the model for elaboration of the annual capitalization plan by national informatics companies.

Communication SEI/SEINF 120/86 (12 Nov. 1986)

Establishes a maximum period of 60 days beyond which projects for R&D and for local manufacture, with pending complementary information solicited by SEI, will be rejected.

CACEX Communication 171 (11 Dec. 1986)

Replaces the list of goods presented in CONCEX's Resolution 121, of 17 December 1979, with a list of twenty-five items whose import licence is dependent on previous authorization by SEI.

Law 7463 (17 April 1986)

Defines the First National Plan for Informatics and Automation (I PLANIN).

Decree 93295 (25 Sep. 1986)

Approves CONIN's Resolution 026/86.

CONIN's Resolution 026/86

Specifies Article 23 of Law no. 7232. Provides basic definition; establishes guarantees for the technical quality of informatics products; defines rights of customers and obligations of producers related to information upon interface and connected to maintenance, including any product that ceases to be manufactured; defines CONIN as the arbiter of any conflict that could result from implementation of present Resolution and the penalties on its infraction.

Communication SEI/SEINF 068/87 (2 June 1987)

Publishes criteria and parameters for use in the analysis of applications for fiscal incentives.

Communication SEI/SEINF 069/87 (2 June 1987)

Publishes criteria and parameters for use in the analysis of plans for capitalization.

Decree 94424 (10 June 1987)

Specifies the concept of small- and medium-sized informatics companies and the procedures for these companies to follow in order to apply for incentive resources. They shall require CONIN to approve their annual capitalization plan.

Decree 92779 (13 June 1987)

Approves norms for the functioning of CONIN.

Law 7646 (18 Dec. 1987)

The *Software Law*. Makes dispositions for the protection of intellectual property and the marketing of software in Brazil. Copyright relative to software is granted for a period of 25 years counting from their launching in any country. For marketing software in Brazil, the previous filing of it is mandatory by SEI who will classify it into different categories according to whether it was developed in the country or abroad, in association or not with foreign or Brazilian companies. The filing of software developed by non-Brazilian companies is conditional on the nonexistence of similar software developed in the country by a national company. In relation to the protection of copyright, differences are not established between these categories. The registration of a software at SEI is a previous and necessary condition for the production of fiscal and exchange effects and the legitimization of corresponding payments, credits, or remittance. The filing is valid for a minimum of three years and shall be automatically renewed by SEI if there is no similar software developed in the country by a national company. Software is considered similar to another when it is functionally equivalent (original and independently developed, have substantially the same performance characteristics, operate in similar equipment, and in a similar processing environment), complies with established Brazilian standards, and carries out the same functions.

Decree-Law 2433 (19 May 1988)

Makes provisions related to financial instruments for the industrial policy. The IT area is to continue to be ruled by the provisions defined in Law No. 7232/84.

SEI's Communication 115 (24 June 1988)

Makes dispositions for the analysis and decision-making on the importation of goods which are dependent on the previous approval by SEI. For this approval the following factors are considered: availability of local similar, convenience of use of local similar, need of specific software linked to the item to be imported, availability of import quota.

SEI's Communication 116 (24 June 1988)

Makes dispositions for the analysis and decision making on local manufacture and integration. Defines specific criteria for projects with local or foreign technology, for manufacture by national or foreign subsidiaries.

Decree 99541 (24 Sep. 1990)

Makes dispositions for the authorization of IT imports.

CONIN Resolution 19/90 (11 Oct. 1990)

Establishes that a foreign associate to a domestic company in a joint-venture in the IT area is allowed to sign contracts of technology transfer with the domestic associate. Establishes operational definition of disposition of Law 7232/84 in relation to the requirement of 'technology control' by Brazilian national company.

CONIN Resolution 20/90 (26 Oct. 1990)

Approves a list of IT items which are subject to SEI's previous authorization for importation and for manufacture in Brazil.

CONIN Resolution 21/90 (21 Nov. 1990)

Approves CONIN composition and rules of functioning. New composition: twelve representatives of the government; eight representatives of NGOs to be chosen by the Executive Branch from lists elaborated by each entity. CONIN is to meet at least twice a year or when called by one-third of its members. The Secretary of Science and Technology presides at CONIN.

CONIN Resolution 22/90 (28 Dec. 1990)

Approves programme for improvement of the price/achievement ratio. Between January 1991 and October 1992, achievement of each product will be assessed, and if the ratio proves to be higher than that established by SEI, their importation will be considered free from control.

'Portaria' SCT No. 01 (9 Jan. 1991)

Makes dispositions for the presentation of annual programmes for production and development of IT goods by locally owned and foreign subsidiaries to the SCT. Foreign subsidiaries which are producing goods not included in the list approved by CONIN Resolution 20/90 are required to present their programmes for production only in order to prove their compliance with the following: (i) use of a given share of their earnings for R&D in Brazil; (ii) export planning; (iii) programme for development of local suppliers.

'Portaria' SCT No. 02 (9 Jan 1991)

Makes dispositions for the importation of IT goods which shall receive previous authorization by the SCT. The analysis of the existence of local similar will consider the ratio of the price of the good in the domestic market and the landed price of the imported equivalent according to given parameters.

'Portaria' DECEX No. 03 (31 Jan. 1991)

Communicates that the importation of a list of IT items is dependent on previous authorization by the SCT. Gives the list of CONIN Resolution 20/90.

APPENDIX II

CHRONOLOGY OF THE
BRAZILIAN 301 CASE

1985 September, 7 - Announcement of the USTR proceedings.

1986 January - The US Department of State asked the Brazilian Ministry of Foreign Relations for formal explanation on the Brazilian Law No. 7232, the Informatics Law.

1986 February, 4 - Caracas: consulting meeting. Deputy USTR headed the American delegation and the Executive Secretary for Informatics, the Brazilian delegation. Brazilian delegation discussed the IT policy under GATT rule.

1986 April, 17 - Brazilian Congress voted on Law No. 7463, the First Informatics Plan (I PLANIN).

1986 April - Letter from the US Secretary of State to the Brazilian Minister of Foreign Relations suggesting they should personally devote their attention to the case.

1986 May, 9-10 - Seminar, held in the United States and organized by ABI-COMP and the American Electronics Association (AEA), for Brazilian and American IT businessmen.

1986 May, 14 - The US Economic Policy Council decided that the Brazilian IT Policy constituted an unfair trade practice and that retaliation was justified.

1986 May - Brazilian Ambassador to GATT informed of the government's intention to appeal to GATT if there is retaliation against Brazilian exports to the United States.

1986 May - Brazilian Senator Severo Gomes (PMDB-SP) introduced Bill No. 99/86, the National Self Defence Bill, establishing sanctions against foreign interests in Brazil in the case of restrictions against Brazilian exports to foreign markets.

1986 May - Brazilian Minister for Commerce and Industry declared himself in favour of an extension of the market reserve principle to the area of pharmaceutical products.

1986 May - Microsoft Corporation announced its intention to sue four Brazilian companies for infringement of copyright on its MS-DOS operating system.

1986 May - The US Deputy Secretary of State visited Brazil.

1986 July, 2 - Paris: second meeting. The US delegation, headed by the USTR, presented a list of twenty-six items, organized in five sections, expressing their demands. The sections were trade and investment, intellectual property rights, transborder data flow, subsidies, and technical standards. The Brazilian delegation was headed by the Brazilian Secretary General of the Ministry of Foreign Relations.

1986 July - The Chairman of SEI visited Japan and met potential suppliers or electronics components to Brazilian IT companies.

1986 August, 11 - Paris: third meeting. The Brazilian delegation discussed some of the twenty-six items. The US delegation demanded positive actions towards more flexibility in the implementation of the policy.

1986 August, 17 - SEI announced internal reforms.

1986 August, 26 - CONIN approved the regime of copyright for software.

1986 September, 10 - The Brazilian President visited the United States.

1986 September - SEI approved the IBM-Gerdau association for data processing.

1986 September - Brazil announced its intention to publish a list of nonreserved items.

1986 September - The US government postponed the conclusion of the proceedings to January 1987.

1986 November - The SEI began to institute administrative reforms designed to speed up its processing of company applications.

1986 November - A US-Brazil 'ad hoc' group was set up to review individual complaints by American companies.

1986 November - CACEX Communication No. 171 was issued, narrowing the range of products for which imports have been restricted and eliminating SEI's powers to control the importation of unspecified products as long as they contained commands or controls or other systems with digital logic of the numerical control type.

1986 December - The software bill was sent to the Brazilian House of Representatives.

1986 December, 13-14 - Brussels: fourth meeting. Brazilian delegation declared its mission completed as all information required was given. The US delegation asked for further discussion on the software bill.

1986 December, 16-17 - Meeting ABICOMP/AEA in Rio de Janeiro to discuss the following agenda: economic and business climate in Brazil, Brazilian perspective on current informatics issues, US perspective on current informatics issues, the state of Brazilian technology, policy issues relating to hardware, policy issues relating to semiconductors, policy issues relating to software.

1986 December, 23 - The USTR declared no trade retaliation related to the IT conflict would occur until July 1987.

1986 December, 26 - The USTR announced the exclusion of thirty Brazilian products from the GSP list of concessions.

1986 December, 30 -The US government announced the suspension of the part of the Brazilian 301 case which dealt with administrative procedures. The parts referring to software and investment were kept and action on those parts was postponed until July 1987.

1987 March, 12 - The USTR public hearing on intellectual property rights for software in Brazil, on the rules for software trade in Brazil, and on restrictions to foreign investment in the Brazilian IT sector.

1987 June, 17 - Mexico City: discussion on the changes made in the software bill by the Brazilian House of Representatives.

1987 June, 24 - The Brazilian House voted on the software bill.
30 - The US government suspended the part of the Brazilian 301 case dealing with intellectual property rights and asked the USTR to continue to pursue the investment part, but without deadline.

1987 July, 15 - Hearings before the US Subcommittee on Commerce, Consumer Protection, And Competitiveness of the Committee on Energy and Commerce, House of Representatives.

1987 July - The SEI turned down a request by Brazilian companies to license Microsoft's MS-DOS on the grounds that a local similar had already been developed.

1987 November, 6 - Some US Senators from the Democratic Party introduced a resolution recommending that the White House start sanctions against Brazil because of the IT policy.

1987 November, 13 - The US government announced retaliation by imposing punitive tariffs on US$ 105 million worth of Brazilian exports to that market. The list of the products affected was not announced.

1987 November - Brazilian authorities called local subsidiaries of foreign companies to discuss the imposition of punitive tariffs against Brazilian products.

1987 November, 18 - The Brazilian Senate voted on the Senate substitute for the software bill approved by the Brazilian House.

1987 December, 4 - The Brazilian House voted on the Senate substitute and approved Software Law No. 7646.

1988 January - CONIN discussed the SEI's previous decision against local trade of Microsoft's MS-DOS. The decision was to allow local trade of version 3.3 of that operating system.

1988 January - The AEA asked the USTR to postpone economic sanctions for 120 days.

1988 February - The US government announced the suspension of retaliatory measures.

1988 May, 13 - The procedures for implementation of the Brazilian Software Law were published.

1988 June, 6 - The Brazilian President José Sarney went to the United States for the UN General Assembly's opening session. In a press conference he criticized the Brazilian IT policy and declared he would not vote for it again as he had done in 1984.

1989 January - The Ministry for Science and Technology, under which the SEI was placed, was extinguished and its tasks were transferred to the Ministry of Industry and Trade at the time being headed by a notorious opponent of the IT policy.

1989 March - Creation of the Special Secretariat for Science and Technology directly subordinated to the President's Office.

1989 October - The US government dropped the Brazilian 301 case.

APPENDIX III

PERSONS INTERVIEWED
(Date of interview)

Roberto Campos - Brazilian Senator (PDS-MS), the most combative opponent of the Brazilian IT policy in the Brazilian Congress (2 March 89).

Celso Cordeiro - President of ABES (Brazilian Association of Software Vendors) (1 Sept. 88).

Ivan da Costa Marques - Director of COBRA (Brazilian Computers and Systems plc) (10 Jan. 89).

Carlos Antônio da Rocha Paranhos - Chief of the Eastern Europe Division, Brazilian Foreign Relations Ministry, member of the Brazilian delegation - as observer - to the bilateral negotiations (23 Sept. 88).

Joubert de Oliveira Brízida - General of the Brazilian Army, Directory for Material, Communication and Electronics, SEI Chairman from 1981 to 1982 (19 Oct. 88).

Descartes de Souza Teixeira - Director of ABCPAI (Brazilian Association for Process Control and Industrial Automation) (18 Nov. 88).

José Rubens Dória Porto - Director of Sistema (industrial automation equipment manufacturing company), SEI Chairman from 1985 to 1986 (25 Oct. 88).

Edson Dytz - President of Dytz Informatica, former SEI Chairman from 1982 to 1984 (15 Sept. 88).

Severo Fagundes Gomes - Brazilian Senator (PMDB-SP), author of the 'National Self-Defence Bill' introduced into the Brazilian Senate in reaction to the US threat of economic sanctions during the Brazilian 301 case (10 Dec. 88).

Octavio Gennari Neto - Advisor to PRODAM (Data-Processing Service for the City of São Paulo), SEI Chairman from 1980 to 1981 (25 Oct. 88).

Jorge Panazio - Deputy Executive-Secretary of SEI from 1982 to 1984 (15 March 89).

Arthur Pereira Nunes - ABICOMP's Executive Director (27 Jan. 89).

Ricardo A.C. Saur - President of SAUR Associados (consulting company), member of the Brazilian delegation to various negotiating meetings with the Americans during the Brazilian 301 case, Executive Secretary of CAPRE (10 Jan. 89).

Milton Seligman - President of PMDB's studies centre, the Pedroso Horta Foundation, former President of MBI (The Brazilian Movement for Informatics), MCT Office Chief in the administration of Dep. Luiz Henrique da Silveira (13 Dec. 88).

Euclides Tenório Junior - Deputy Secretary-General of the Brazilian Finance Ministry, former SEI member during Gennari Neto administration (14 Sept. 88).

José Ezil Veiga Da Rocha - SEI Chairman from 1986 to 1989 (12 Sept. 88).

APPENDIX IV

INTERVIEW STRUCTURE

1. Professional background of the person interviewed. How long involved with the Brazilian IT policy? Within which organization and in which institutional position(s)?

2. What caused the pioneering role of the Brazilian Navy in the Brazilian IT policy? Was the Navy the only force concerned with IT development in Brazil in the early 1960s?

3. How was the military assessment of the role of civil participants in the government in relation to the IT policy? Had people in the Planning Ministry and the military very different positions related to domestic IT development? Was there some signal of Brazilian companies' interest in starting a domestic production of IT goods in the early 1970s?

4. How to explain the institutional changes in the Brazilian IT policy in the late 1970s and early 1980s? What led to CAPRE's end? What were the main justifications for the creation of SEI? What led to the extinction of DIGI-BRAS?

5. The Brazilian IT policy seems to have shifted orientation from an initial acceptance of association with to exclusion of foreign capital. Is this statement correct? What can be argued as an explanation for this change in orientation?

6. What have been the most critical periods SEI faced since its creation? Has SEI had to make concessions to the IT policy opponents? What were they?

7. Considering the diverging views related to foreign direct investment in the domestic IT complex within the Brazilian government, how did SEI manage to make the market reserve strategy dominant?

8. When did the idea of legalizing the IT policy by a law approved by the Brazilian Congress first appear or start to grow within the government? How strong has been the commitment of the Brazilian Congress to the IT policy?

9. What are the greatest challenges to be faced by the Brazilian IT policy in the near future? In relation to the policy's scope, is the policy likely to keep

the broad definition of items under protection? In relation to the institutional structure, are CONIN and SEI satisfactory as, respectively, the central decision board and the central executive agency? Related to the justification of the whole IT policy do 'national sovereignty' and 'autonomous technological development' still have the same appeal they had in the 1970s? At present, how would maintenance of an unchanged IT policy be best justified? And how would its change be justified? In relation to the role of foreign investment in the IT complex, should any change be made in the present orientation of the IT policy?

10. Which social groups or social segments support the maintenance of an unchanged IT policy? Which groups support the policy with some changes? Which groups oppose the policy? Which are the main arguments used by those supporters to justify changes in the policy? Are supporters and opponents homogeneous groups?

11. How do you assess the behaviour of the Brazilian government during the US/Brazil IT policy conflict? What was the conflict's final balance of gains and losses: Who had the greater gain and who had the greater loss? What were these gains and losses?

12. How did the Brazilian and the American strategy develop throughout the conflict? How did the governments involved relate to the issues at stake during the conflict? Did the delegations to the negotiating meetings act in accordance with a clear-cut strategy? Did the Brazilian delegation show a coherent orientation throughout the negotiations? Was there any sort of disagreement among the Brazilian delegation or within the Brazilian negotiators?

13. How did the Brazilian IT entrepreneurs (or their associations) participate in the negotiations? Who took the lead in pressing American trade partners of Brazilian companies against the threat of economic sanctions?

14. What have been the major results of this conflict related to (a) what is to be reserved to locally owned companies? (b) reduction of SEI's power? (c) permission for foreign direct investment in the Brazilian IT market? (d) adoption of regulation of IPRs for software?

15. How did the conflict affect the local balance of power in support of the IT policy? How have the following social segments positioned in relation to the IT policy since 1985: (a) Brazilian manufacturers of microcomputers and peripherals? (b) Brazilian manufacturers of equipment for industrial automation? (c) Other Brazilian industrialists? (d) Brazilian software vendors? (e) Brazilian software producers? (f) Brazilian banking sector? (g) Brazilian building contractors? (h) Brazilian industrialists in other high-

technology areas (e.g., pharmaceutical, aviation)? (i) IT users? (j) Data-processing professionals? (k) Others (who?).

16. How much domestic support does the Brazilian IT policy have nowadays compared with the period of discussion of the 'Informatics' Bill? Are the ideas of 'national sovereignty' and 'local autonomous technological development' still strong as main arguments for justifying the IT policy as they were in the setting-up of the policy?

17. Do you think the Brazilian IT policy will change in the near future? If yes, in what sense or in what direction is this change more likely to occur? What would be the main justification for the change (or for keeping the policy as it is now)?

BIBLIOGRAPHY

Adler, E. (1986), 'Ideological guerrillas and quest for technological autonomy: Brazil's domestic computer industry', *International Organization*, Vol. 40, No. 3, pp. 673-705.

Adler, E. (1987), *The Power of Ideology. The quest for Technological Autonomy in Argentina and Brazil*, Berkeley, University of California Press.

Azevedo, C. and G. Zago Jr. (1989) *Do tear ao Computador. As lutas pela industrialização no Brasil*, São Paulo: Política Editora.

Baldwin, D.A. (1985) *Economic Statecraft*, Princeton, NJ: Princeton University Press.

Banco Central do Brasil (1990), *Boletim do Banco Central do Brasil*, Vol. 26, No. 10, Oct.

Banco do Brasil (1985), *Brasil - 1985, Comércio Exterior, Séries Estatísticas*, Brasília.

Baptista, M. (1987), 'A Indústria Eletrônica de Consumo a Nível Internacional e no Brasil', M.Sc. dissertation, Universidade de Campinas.

Baptista, M. (1988), 'The Consumer Electronics in Brazil: Current Situation and Outlook', in Clelia Piragibe (Coord), *Electronics Industry in Brazil. Current Status, Perspectives and Policy Options*, Brasilia: MCT/Center for Studies in Scientific and Technological Policy.

Bastos, M.I. (1992), 'State Policies and Private Interests: The Struggle Over Information Technology Policy in Brazil', in H. Schmitz and J. Cassiolato (eds.), *Hi-Tech for Industrial Development*, London and New York: Routledge.

Bhagwati, J. (1988), *Protectionism*, Cambridge MA: MIT Press.

Bhagwati, J. (1989), 'United States Trade Policy at the Crossroads', *The World Economy*, Vol. 12, No. 4, Dec., pp. 439-79.

Borelli, M.H.C. (1986), *Grupos de Interesse e Informática*, Brasília: Universidade de Brasília.

Botelho, A.J.J. (1988), *The Political Economy of Professionalization: the Birth of the Brazilian Informatics Policy*, paper presented to the 4S/EASST Joint Meeting, Amsterdam, 16-19 Nov.

Camargo, S. and G. Moura (1984), 'Uma visita pouco frutuosa', *Brasil Perspectivas Internacionais*, Rio de Janeiro, Pontifícia Universidade Católica do Rio de Janeiro, No. 1, pp. 5-8, junho/julho.

Campos, R. (1985), *Além do Cotidiano*, São Paulo: Record.

Cardoso, F.H. (1979), 'On the Characterization of the Authoritarian Regimes in Latin America', in David Collier (ed.), *The New Authoritarianism in Latin America*, Princeton, NJ: Princeton University Press.

Carneiro, D.D. (1986), 'Perspectiva del Endeudamiento Externo Brasileño 1986-1990', in Ricardo Ffrench-Davis and Richard E. Feinberg (eds.), *Mas Alla de la Crisis de la Deuda. Bases para un movo enfoque*, Santiago do Chile: Ediciones CIEPLAN.

Cassiolato, J., Hewitt, T. and H. Schmitz (1992), 'Learning in Industry and Government: Achievements, Failures and Lessons', in Hubert Schmitz and Jose Cassiolato (eds.), *Hi-Tech For Industrial Development*, London and New York: Routledge.

CEPAL (1985), *Trade Relations Between Brazil and the United States*, Santiago, Chile.

Ciência hoje (1989), Vol. 9, No. 51.

Cline, W.R. (1987), *Informatics and Development: Trade and Industrial Policy in Argentina, Mexico and Brazil*, Washington, DC: Economics International Inc.

Cline, W.R. (1989), *American Trade Adjustment: The Global Impact*, Washington, DC: Institute for International Economics.

Colson, F. (1985), 'New Perspectives on the Brazilian Computer Industry: 1985 and Beyond', *Multinational Business*, EIU, UK, No. 4, pp. 1-9.

Conybeare, J.A. (1987), *Trade Wars. The Theory and Practice of International Commercial Rivalry*, New York: Columbia University Press.

Correa, C.M. (1989a), *The Legal Protection of Software - Implications for latecomers Strategies in Newly Industrializing Economies (NIEs) and Middle-Income Countries (MICs)*, Paris: OECD.

Correa, C.M. (1989b), *Tecnologia y Desarrollo de la Informatica en el Contexto Norte-Sur*, Buenos Aires: Eudeba.

Correa, C.M. (1990), 'Software Industry: An Opportunity for Latin America?' (mimeo).

Costabile, H. (1982), 'Bases para uma Política Nacional de Software', in SEI *Boletim Informativo*, No. 6, Jan. -Feb.-March, Brasília.

Dados e Idéias (1987), Ano 2, No. 111, special issue '150 Maiores Empresas de Informática', São Paulo, Gazeta Mercantil S.A. Editora Jornalística.

Dantas, V. (1988), *Guerrilha Tecnólogica. A Verdadeira História da Política Nacional de Informática*, Rio de Janeiro: Livros Técnicos e Científicos Editora.

Deardoff, A.V. and R.M. Stern (1987), 'Current Issues in Trade Policy', in R.M. Stern (ed.), *US Trade Policies in a Changing World Economy*, Cambridge, MA: MIT Press.

Douidi, M.S. and M.S. Dajani (1983), *Economic Sanctions: Ideals and Experience*, London: Routledge & Kegan Paul.

Engel, M.H.C. (1986), 'Propriedade Industrial: Os Debates sobre a Proteção ao Software e sua Importância para a Transferência de Tecnologia' (mimeo).

Erber, F.S. (1989), 'Política de Informática e Política Industrial', Campinas (mimeo).

Evans, P.B. (1986), 'State, Capital, and the Transformation of Dependence: The Brazilian Computer Case', *World Development*, Vol. 14, No. 7, pp. 791-808.

Evans, P.B. (1989), 'Declining Hegemony and Assertive Industrialization: US-Brazil Conflicts in the Computer Industry', *International Organization*, Vol. 43, No. 2, Spring, pp. 207-38.

Evans, P.B. and P.B. Tigre (1989), 'Paths to Participation in High-Tech Industry: A Comparative Analysis of Computers in Brazil and Korea', *Asian Perspective*, Vol. 13, No. 1, Spring-Summer, pp. 5-35.

Farias, O.L.M. (1986), 'A Situação do Mercado de Software no Brasil', working paper, Rio de Janeiro.

FIESP (1983), *Contribuição à Definição de Uma Política de Automação na Indústria de Transformação*, São Paulo.

Fishlow, A. (1982), 'The United States and Brazil: the Case of the Missing Relationship', *Foreign Affairs*, Vol. 69, No. 4, Spring, pp. 904-23.

Folha de São Paulo (1988), 'Estados Unidos anunciam sanções de US$ 39 milhões contra o Brasil', 21 Oct., Economia, p. B-1.

Fregni, E. (1988), Política de Informática. É Preciso Privilegiar o Essencial, paper presented to the Seminar on Informática: Presente e Perspectivas, organised by APPD, Rio de Janeiro, 29 Oct.

Fundação Getulio Vargas (1990), *Conjuntura Econômica*, Vol. 44, No. 3, March.

Gaio, F.J. (1990), 'The Development of Computer Software Technological Capabilities in Developing Countries - A Case Study of Brazil', D.Phil. thesis, University of Sussex.

Gaio, F.J. (1992), 'Software Strategies for Developing Countries: Lessons from the International and Brazilian Experience', in Hubert Schmitz and Jose Cassiolato (eds.), *Hi-Tech for Industrial Development*, London and New York: Routledge.

Gaio, F.J. and L.M. Segre (1989), 'Uma Análise da Política de Software no Brasil', paper presented in the I Congresso Iberoamericano sobre Desarrollo de la Informatica (Situacion, Estrategias y Politicas), Quito, Ecuador, 13-15 Nov.

Galtung, J. (1967), 'On the Effects of International Economic Sanctions, with Examples from the Case of Rhodesia', *World Politics*, Vol. 19, April, pp. 378-416.

Graham, E.M. and P.R. Krugman (1990), 'Trade-Related Investment Measures', in Jeffrey J. Schott (ed.), *Completing the Uruguay Round. A Result-Oriented Approach to GATT Trade Negotiations*, Washington, DC: Institute for International Economics.

Griffith-Jones, S. (1989), 'A history of debt crisis management', in Stephany Griffith-Jones (ed.), *Third World Debt: Managing the Consequences*, London: IFR Publishing Ltd.

Grilli, E. (1990), 'Protectionism and the Developing Countries', in Enzo Grilli and Enrico Sassoon (eds.), *The New Protectionist Wave*, London: Macmillan.

Halliday, F. (1989), 'State and Society in International Relations: A Second Agenda', in Hugh C. Dyer and Leon Mangasarian (eds.), *The Study of International Relations. The State of the Art*, London: Macmillan.

Hatsopoulos, G.N., Krugman, P.R. and L.H. Summers (1990), 'US Competitiveness: Beyond the Trade Deficit', in Philip King (ed.), *International Economics and International Economic Policy: A Reader*, New York: McGraw-Hill.

Helena, S. (1980), 'A Indústria de Computadores. Evolução das Decisões Governamentais', *Revista de Administração Pública*, Vol. 40, No. 3, pp. 673-705.

Hewitt, T.R. (1988), 'Employment and Skills in the Electronics Industry: The Case of Brazil', D.Phil. Thesis, University of Sussex.

Hindley, B. (1990), 'Services', in Jeffrey J. Schott (ed.), *Completing the Uruguay Round. A Result-Oriented Approach to GATT Trade Negotiations*, Washington, DC: Institute for International Economics.

Hirschmann, A.O. (1945), *National Power and the Structure of Foreign Trade*, Berkeley, CA: University of California Press.

Hirst, M. org. (1985), *Brasil-Estados Unidos na Transição Democrática*, Rio de Janeiro: Paz e Terra.

Hufbauer, G.C. and J.J. Schott (1985), *Economic Sanctions Reconsidered: History and Current Policy*, Washington, DC: Institute for International Economics.

Jackson, J.H. (1988), 'Multilateral and Bilateral Negotiating Approaches for the Conduct of US Trade Policies', in Robert M. Stern (ed.), *US Trade Policies in a Changing World Economy*, Cambridge MA: MIT Press.

Jaikumar, R. (1986), 'Postindustrial Manufacturing', *Harvard Business Review*, Nov./Dec., pp. 69-76.

James, A. (1986), *Sovereign Statehood*, London: Allen & Unwin.

Johansen, L. (1987), 'The Bargaining Society and the Inefficiency of Bargaining', in F.R. Forsund (ed.), *Collected Works of Leif Johansen*, Vol. 2, Amsterdam: North Holland.

Jornal do Brasil (1985), 'Extremos Desnecessários', 10 Sept. 1985, 1 Caderno, p. 10.

Jornal do Brasil (1986a), Brazilian Foreign Minister interview, published 20 July 1986, quoted in *Veja*, 'Informática. Questões na mesa. EUA levantam dúvidas sobre reserva', 24 July 1986.

191

Jornal do Brasil (1986b), 'Sarney desmente Sodré. Reserva de mercado continua'. 1 Caderno, p. 10.

Jornal do Brasil (1986c), 'Lugar da Informática', 23 August 1986, 1 Caderno, p. 10.

Jornal da Tarde (1986), 'O que esteve por trás da reunião de Caracas', 10 Feb. 1986.

Kaempfer, W.H. and A.D. Lowenberg (1988), 'The Theory of International Economic Sanctions', *The American Economic Review*, Vol. 78, No. 4, Sept. pp. 786-93.

Kaplinsky, R. (1988a), *Industrial and Intellectual Property Rights in the Uruguay Round and Beyond: Policy Implications for Developing Countries*, Brighton, UK: Institute of Development Studies, University of Sussex, prepared for the Andean Pact.

Kaplinsky, R. (1988b), 'Industrial Restructuring in LDCs: The Role of Information Technology', Paper prepared for the Conference on Technology Policy in the Americas, Americas Program, Stanford University, 1-3 Dec.

Katz, R.L. (1981), 'Nationalism and Computer Technology Transfer: The Brazilian Case', M.Sc dissertation, Massachussets Institute of Technology.

Knorr, K. (1975), *The Power of Nations: The Political Economy of International Relations*, New York: Basic Books.

Kostecki, M.M. (1989), 'Electronics Trade Policies in the 1980s', *Journal of World Trade*, Vol. 23, No. 1, pp. 17-35.

Kramer, P. (1985), 'Diálogo de surdos: as relações Brasil-EUA', *Brasil Perspectivas Internacionais*, Rio de Janeiro, Pontifícia Universidade Católica do Rio de Janeiro, No. 5, Jan./fev., pp. 1-4.

Laird, S. and A. Yeats (1987), 'On the Potential Contribution of Trade Policy Initiatives for Alleviating the International Debt Crisis', *Journal of Economics and Business*, Vol. 39, No. 3, pp. 209-24.

Langer, E.D. (1989), 'Generations of Scientists and Engineers: Origins of the Computer Industry in Brazil', *Latin American Research Review*, Vol. XXIV, No. 2, pp. 95-111.

Lima, M.R.S. (1987), 'Informática e Retaliação', *Brasil Perspectivas Internacionais*, Rio de Janeiro: Pontifícia Universidade Católica do Rio de Janeiro, No. 16, out./dez., pp. 1-4.

Manso, E.V. (1985), *A Informática e os Direitos Intelectuais,* São Paulo: Editora Revista dos Tribunais.

Marshall, I. (1987), *Managing Free Vs. Fair Trade Policy during the Reagan Administration,* Santiago de Chile, Facultad Latinoamericana de Ciencias Sociales, Documentos de Trabajo n. 356.

Martinez, J. (1976), 'A inquietante expectativa de uma política de software', *Dados e Idéias,* Vol. 1, No. 6, pp. 16-19.

Maskus, K.E. (1990), 'Intellectual Property', in Jeffrey J. Schott (ed) *Completing the Uruguay Round. A Result-Oriented Approach to the GATT Trade Negotiations,* Washington, DC: Institute for International Economics.

McFarlane, G. (1982), *A Practical Introduction to Copyright:* London, McGraw-Hill Book Company (UK) Ltd.

McMillan, J. (1990), 'A Game-Theoretic View of International Trade Negotiations', in J. Whaley (ed) *Developing Countries and the Global Trading System,* Vol. 1, London: Macmillan.

MCT (1986), *Relatório dos Grupos de Trabalho de Recursos Humanos em Informática,* Brasilia, Ministério de Ciência e Tecnologia, Oct.

Meyer-Stamer, J. (1990), *From Import Substitution to International Competitiveness - Brazil's Informatics Industry at the Crossroads,* Berlin: German Development Institute.

Mineiro, P. (1987), 'A guerra da tecnologia', *Caderno do Terceiro Mundo,* No. 101, Aug.

Mitchell, C.R. (1989), *The Structure of International Conflict,* Houndsmills and London: Macmillan.

Moon, C.-I. (1990), 'The Future of the Newly Industrializing Countries: An "Uncertain Promise"?', in Dennis C. Pirages and Christine Sylvester (eds.), *Transformations in the Global Political Economy,* London: MacMillan.

Mowery, D.C. and N. Rosenberg (1989), *Technology and the Pursuit of Economic Growth,* Cambridge: Cambridge University Press.

Mussalem, J.S.M. (1987a), 'O que pensam os usuários sobre a regulamentação do software', *Gazeta Mercantil,* 21 July.

Mussalem, J.S.M. (1987b), 'Incentivar o software nacional e liberar o estrangeiro', *Gazeta Mercantil,* 17 Sept.

National Science Foundation (1987), *International Science and Technology Update*, Washington, DC.

Naya, S. (1990), 'Economic Performance: NIEs and Beyond', in Takao Fukuchi and Mitsuhiro Kagami (eds) *Perspectives on the Pacific Basin Economy: A Comparison of Asia and Latin America*, Tokyo: Institute of Developing Economies and the Asian Club Foundation.

Northedge, F.S. (1976), *The International Political System*, London: Faber & Faber.

Nossal, K.R. (1989), 'International Sanctions as International Punishment', *International Organization*, Vol. 43, No. 2, pp. 301-22.

OECD (1988), *The Internationalisation of Software and Computer Services*, Paris.

O Estado de São Paulo (1986), 'Evitar o Confronto', 16 Feb.

O Globo (1986), 'Negociação da informática com EUA acaba empatada. Flecha de Lima destaca cordialidade na reunião com Yeutter', 15 Dec. 1986, Economia, p. 13.

Paiva, S.M.C. (1989), 'Política Nacional de Informática: Intervenção do Estado, Resultados e Desafios', M.Sc. dissertation, Instituto de Economia Industrial, Universidade Federal do Rio de Janeiro.

Pearson, C. and Riedel, J. (1990), 'United States Trade Policy: From Multilateralism to Bilateralism?', in Enzo Grilli and Enrico Sassoon (eds.), *The New Protectionist Wave*, London: Macmillan.

Pereira dos Santos, M.J. (1987), 'A Proteção Adequada ao Software', *Revista de Direito Civil, Imobiliário, Agrário e Empresarial*, Ano 11, No. 40, abril/junho.

Perez, C. (1985), 'Microelectronics, Long Waves and World Structural Change: New Perspectives for Developing Countries', *World Development*, Vol. 13, No. 3, pp. 441-63.

Peritore, P.N. (1988), 'High-Tech Import Substitution: Brazil's Computer Policy and the Possibilities for Social Transformation', *Alternatives*, Vol. Xiii, No. 1, pp. 27-54, January.

Piragibe, C. (1985), *Indústria da Informática. Desenvolvimento Brasileiro e Mundial*, Rio de Janeiro, Editora Campus Ltda.

Bibliography

Piragibe, C. (1988), 'Electronics Industry in Brazil and the Role of the State: Some Aspects for a Comparative Analysis', in Clelia Piragibe (Coord), *Electronics Industry in Brazil. Current Status, Perspectives and Policy Options*, Brasilia: MCT/Center for Studies in Scientific and Technological Policy.

Piragibe, C.; Penna, M.V. and P.B. Tigre (1983), *Recursos Humanos na Indústria Brasileira de Equipamentos de Processamento de Dados*, Relatório de Pesquisa, Rio de Janeiro: IEI/UFRJ.

Ploman, E.W. and L.C. Hamilton (1980), *Copyright. Intellectual Property in the Information Age*, London: Routledge & Kegan Paul.

Pugel, T.A. (1987), 'Limits of Trade Policy Toward High Technology Industries: The Case of Semiconductors', in Ryuso Sato and Paul Wachtel (eds.), *Trade Friction and Economic Policy. Problems and Prospects for Japan and the United States*, New York: Cambridge University Press.

Putnam, R.D. (1988), 'Diplomacy and domestic politics: the logic of two-level games', *International Organization*, Vol. 42, No. 3, pp. 427-60.

Raiffa, H. (1982), *The Art and Science of Negotiation*, Cambridge, MA, Harvard University Press.

Ricupero, R. (1989), 'A disputa Brasil-Estados Unidos e o GATT', *Folha de São Paulo,* 26 Feb., p. A-3.

Rueschemeyer, D. and P.B. Evans (1985), 'The State and Economic Transformation: Toward an Analysis on the Conditions Underlying Effective Intervention', in Peter B. Evans, Dietrich Rueschemeyer and Theda Skocpol (eds.), *Bringing the State Back In,* Cambridge: Cambridge University Press.

Santarelli, D.E., Filler, M.S. and S.R. Comenetz (1985), *Comments on behalf of ABICOMP, Before the USTR, in the Matter of The Government of Brazil's Informatics Policy*, Washington, DC: Santarelli, Choate, Smith, Kraut & Carrocio, 11 Oct.

Sassoon, E. (1990), 'Protectionism and International Trade Negotiations During the 1980s', in Enzo Grilli and Enrico Sassoon (eds.), *The New Protectionist Wave*, London: Macmillan.

Schelling, T.C. (1960), *The Strategy of Conflict,* Cambridge, MA: Harvard University Press.

Schneider, H.-J. (1988), *Software Production: Organisation and Modalities*, Vienna: UNIDO.

SEI (1981), 'Relatório da Comissão Especial de Software e Serviços', Brasília.

SEI (1982), 'Transborder Data Flows and Brazil: the Role of Transnational Corporations, Impacts of Transborder Data Flows and Effects of National Policies', presented to the 8th session of the United Nations Commission on Transnational Corporations.

SEI (1984), 'Seminário Internacional sobre Tratamento Jurídico do Software', Brasília.

SEI (1986), 'Perfil da Administração Pública Federal', Brasília.

SEI (1987), 'Panorama do Setor de Informática', Brasília.

SEI (1988a), 'Relatório do Seminário de Software', Brasília.

SEI (1988b), 'Exame Sucinto dos Segmentos de Informática', Brasília.

SEI (1988c), 'Indicadores', Brasília.

SEI (1988d), 'Panorama do Setor Industrial de Informática', Brasília.

SEI (1989), 'Panorama do Setor Industrial de Informática', Brasília.

SEI (1991), 'Panorama do Setor Industrial de Informática', Brasília.

Serra, J. (1988), 'Conversão da dívida: realidade e alternativas', *Revista de Economia Política*, Vol. 8, No. 1, pp. 124-31.

Sistema Economico de America Latina - SELA (1988), *La Economia Mundial y el Desarrollo de America Latina y el Caribe*, Caracas: Editorial Nueva Sociedad.

Skocpol, T. (1985), 'Bringing the State Back In: Strategies of Analysis in Current Research', in Peter B. Evans, Dietrich Rueschemeyer and Theda Skocpol (eds.), *Bringing the State Back In*, Cambridge: Cambridge University Press.

Snyder, G.H. and P. Diesing (1977), *Conflict Among Nations. Bargaining, Decision Making, and System Structure in International Crises*, Princeton, NJ: Princeton University Press.

Sodre, R.A. (1986), 'Notas para a Reunião do CONIN do dia 22 de dezembro de 1986', Brasília: Brazilian Ministry of Foreign Relations (unpublished paper).

Srinivasan, T.N. (1987), 'The National Defense Argument for Government Intervention in Foreign Trade', in Robert M. Stern (ed.), *US Trade Policies in a Changing World Economy*, Cambridge, MA: MIT Press.

Strange, S. (1988), *States and Markets. An Introduction to International Political Economy*, London: Pinter Publishers.

Suzigan, W. (1989), 'Restruturação Industrial e Competitividade nos Países Avançados e nos NICs Asiáticos: Lições para o Brasil', in Wilson Suzigan *et al. Restruturação Industrial e Competitividade Internacional*, São Paulo, Fundação Sistema Estadual de Análise de Dados (SEADE).

Teece, D.J. (1987), 'Profiting from Technological Innovation: Implications for Integration, Collaboration and Public Policy', in David J. Teece, *The Competitive Challenge. Strategies for Industrial Innovation and Renewal*, Cambridge, MA: Ballinger Publishing Co.

Tigre, P.B. (1987), *Indústria Brasileira de Computadores. Perspectivas até os anos 90*, Rio de Janeiro: Editora Campus: INPES/IPEA.

Tigre, P.B. (1988), 'Business Strategies in the Brazilian Electronics Industry', in Clelia Piragibe (Coord), *Electronics Industry in Brazil. Current Status, Perspectives and Policy Options*, Brasilia: MCT/Center for Studies in Scientific and Technology Policy.

Tigre, P.B. (1989), 'Perseguindo o Alvo Móvel: Evolução dos Preços e Competitividade dos Equipamentos Eletrônicos Nacionais', Rio de Janeiro, unpublished report, Forum Informática.

Toni, A. (1989), *The Brazilian Electronic Computer Industry: Dependency and/or Development?*, Swansea, UK: Department of Development Studies, University College of Swansea.

UNCTAD (1989), *Impact of Technological Change on Patterns of International Trade*, Geneva.

UNCTC (1988), *Transnational Corporations in World Development. Trends and Prospects*, New York.

Urrutia, M. (1990), 'Trends in Latin American Development', in Takao Fukuchi and Mitsuhiro Kagami (eds.), *Perspectives on the Pacific Basin Economy: A Comparison of Asia and Latin America*, Tokyo: Institute of Developing Economies and the Asian Club Foundation.

US Commerce Department (1990), *The Competitive Status of the US Electronics Sector: From Materials to Systems*, Washington, DC: International Trade Administration.

US Congress, Congressional Budget Office (1987), *The GATT Negotiations and the US Trade Policy*, Washington, DC: US Government Printing Office.

US House of Representatives, Committee on Energy and Commerce (1988), 'Informatics Trade Problems with Brazil', Hearing before the Subcommittee on Commerce, Consumer Protection, and Competitiveness, 15 July 1987, Washington.

Wachtel, P. (1987), 'Introduction', in Ryuso Sato and Paul Wachtel (eds.), *Trade Friction and Economic Policy. Problems and Prospects for Japan and the US*, New York: Cambridge University Press.

Westman, J. (1985), 'Modern Dependency: A Crucial Case Study of Brazilian Government Policy in the Minicomputer Industry', *Studies in Comparative International Development*, Vol. 10, No. 2, pp. 25-47.

Wrobel, P.S. (1984), 'Política Nacional de Informática: o desafio está lançado', *Brasil Perspectivas Internacionais*, Rio de Janeiro, Pontifícia Universidade Católica do Rio de Janeiro, No. 4, nov./dez. pp. 1-4.

www.ingramcontent.com/pod-product-compliance
Ingram Content Group UK Ltd.
Pitfield, Milton Keynes, MK11 3LW, UK
UKHW041840280225
455677UK00010B/264